COLLAPSE OF A COUNTRY

Collapse of a Country

A Diplomat's Memoir of South Sudan

NICHOLAS COGHLAN

Foreword by Roméo Dallaire
and Shelly Whitman

McGill-Queen's University Press
Montreal & Kingston · London · Chicago

© McGill-Queen's University Press 2017

ISBN 978-0-7735-5126-8 (cloth)
ISBN 978-0-7735-5179-4 (ePDF)
ISBN 978-0-7735-5180-0 (ePUB)

Legal deposit third quarter 2017
Bibliothèque nationale du Québec

Printed in Canada on acid-free paper that is 100% ancient forest free
(100% post-consumer recycled), processed chlorine free

McGill-Queen's University Press acknowledges the support of the Canada
Council for the Arts for our publishing program. We also acknowledge the
financial support of the Government of Canada through the Canada Book
Fund for our publishing activities.

Disclaimer: The views of the author expressed herein do not necessarily
represent those of the Government of Canada. The names and immediate
circumstances of some individuals mentioned have been altered for the
sake of their personal security and/or privacy.

. Library and Archives Canada Cataloguing in Publication

Coghlan, Nicholas, 1954–, author
Collapse of a country: a diplomat's memoir of South Sudan/Nicholas
Coghlan; foreword by Roméo Dallaire and Shelly Whitman.

Includes bibliographical references and index.
Issued in print and electronic formats.
ISBN 978-0-7735-5126-8 (hardcover). – ISBN 978-0-7735-5179-4 (ePDF). –
ISBN 978-0-7735-5180-0 (ePUB)

1. South Sudan – Politics and government – 2011–. 2. South Sudan –
History – 21st century. 3. South Sudan – Social conditions. 4. Coghlan,
Nicholas, 1954–. 5. Diplomats – Canada – Biography. 6. Diplomatic
and consular service, Canadian – South Sudan. 7. South Sudan – Foreign
relations – Canada. 8. Canada – Foreign relations – South Sudan. I. Title.

DT159.947.C64A3 2017   962.905'1   C2017-902157-5
                                             C2017-902158-3

This book was typeset by Marquis Interscript in 10.5/13 Sabon.

For John, 1923–2016

Contents

Foreword   ix

Maps and Illustrations follow pages   xii, 82, 156

Prologue   xvii

1 Jihad and Crusade   3

2 A Garage by the Nile   23

3 I Never Thought It Would Be So Messy   38

4 The Murle War   52

5 Babies and Mothers   76

6 The Refuge-Seekers   83

7 These Are SPLM Ladies   95

8 The Knives Are Out   107

9 Juba Implodes   119

10 A Fight in Your Living Room   140

11 The Echo of Mille Collines   157

12 Communing with the Sky God   174

13 Maybe You Should Leave   190

14 Snakes Are Available   207

15 How Long Must We Suffer?   222

16 Riek Returns   239

Epilogue   245

Appendix A South Sudan: A Chronology   249

Appendix B Acronyms   253

Notes   261

Index   269

Foreword

ROMÉO DALLAIRE AND SHELLY WHITMAN

It was May 2015 in Kampala, Uganda, when we met Ambassador Nicholas Coghlan for the first time. We both remember feeling impressed that he would make his way from Juba to have discussions with us about how The Roméo Dallaire Child Soldiers Initiative might be able to make a positive impact in South Sudan. The ease of the discussions that ensued, combined with his genuine concern for millions of vulnerable people in South Sudan, particularly the children, gave us hope that maybe collectively we could find an entry point for new solutions.

Nick was a rare breed, demonstrating great humility while at the same time displaying immense intellectual understanding of the complex conflict in South Sudan. He is the ultimate example of a humanitarian at his core, yet seasoned with wisdom that has not deterred his desire to see a better world. It is without a doubt this that appealed to and impressed us both, as people who continually believe that all humans are human but recognize that this is not a belief shared by all of humanity.

Our visit to South Sudan in November 2015 would not have been possible without the assistance and support of Nick Coghlan. He demonstrated why the South Sudanese, as well as the NGOs and diplomatic corps, held him in such high regard. Walking through Pibor District on a day when temperatures reached upwards of 45 degrees Celsius, all of us in knee-high rubber boots, it was easy to forget that Nick was a diplomat. He carried himself as a man of the people, and it was clear he had conducted such missions more times than is possible to count. Local people waved to Nick as we trudged through the muddy terrain while he recounted the local politics and history. It was on this day that, together with Nick and UNICEF, we were able to negotiate the release of 300 children from the ranks of the Cobra Faction in Pibor district.

Reading this impressive account of Nick's time in South Sudan, it is challenging not to reminisce about Rwanda in 1994. All too often during our visit in November 2015 parallels were continually drawn between these two countries, and advice was sought in the midst of a very real and continual sense of impending disaster. Yet despite such comparisons, Nick did not lose hope. Instead he seemed even more determined to seek innovative solutions.

At the kind invitation of Nick and his wife Jenny, we attended a dinner at their residence over the course of that visit. It was clear that this was a couple that had endured the uncertainties and challenges of a conflict zone and reinforced each other's resolve. Both of them easily conversed about political dynamics and recounted stories about the people they had come to know in South Sudan with a great sense of hope.

In attendance that night was the United Nations special representative to the secretary-general for South Sudan, Ellen Margrethe Loj. Ellen began the evening by saying it was "General Dallaire's fault" that she had taken up this post in South Sudan. She had read *Shake Hands with the Devil*, and felt morally obligated to accept this position, as often too many good people fail to do, accepting her responsibility to make a difference in the face of evil. This encounter, and many others that materialized during this visit, provided a stark reminder that light can be shed in dark places no matter how dire the situation may seem.

Collapse of a Country: A Diplomat's Memoir of South Sudan is a book that must be read by anyone who wishes to understand the complexity of the birth of this new nation. It details the demands and moral dilemmas that can arise from undertaking an ambassadorial posting. Negotiating the political corridors of Ottawa, as well as the relationships with corporations and allies on the ground, is difficult during the best of times. Nick's personal account of how he managed his role as an ambassador during this time is a remarkable reflection of his passion and integrity.

Canadians often do not get to know those who represent us as a nation, selflessly committing their lives and those of their families to causes and people that may seem so remote from their own world. Ambassador Nick Coghlan was a beacon of light at a time when we were unclear what we were projecting to the rest of the world in terms of our participation in addressing some of the greatest humanitarian crises that existed. It is our sincere hope that many Canadians will read this book by one of those unsung heroes who exemplifies the essence of who we are as Canadians – a nation built on the premise that all human beings deserve to be treated with dignity with the opportunity to live in peace and harmony.

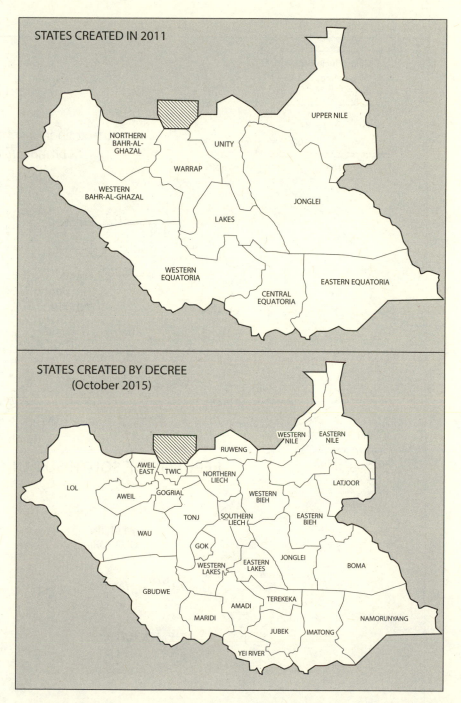

Above: South Sudan and its ten states at the time of independence (2011).
Below: South Sudan following the presidential decree creating twenty-eight states (October 2015)

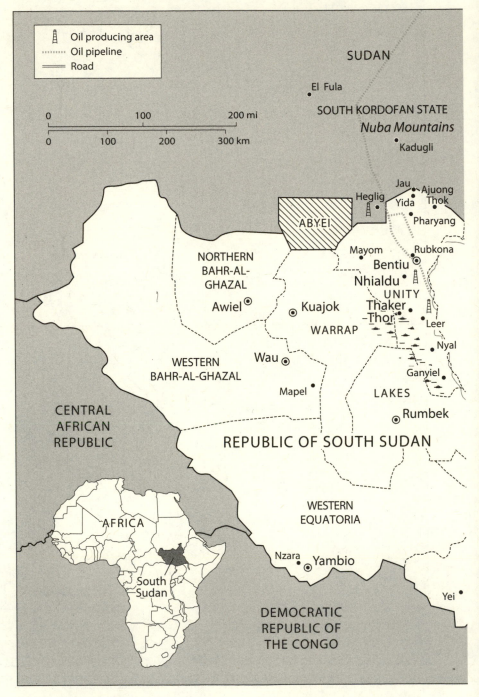

The Republic of South Sudan

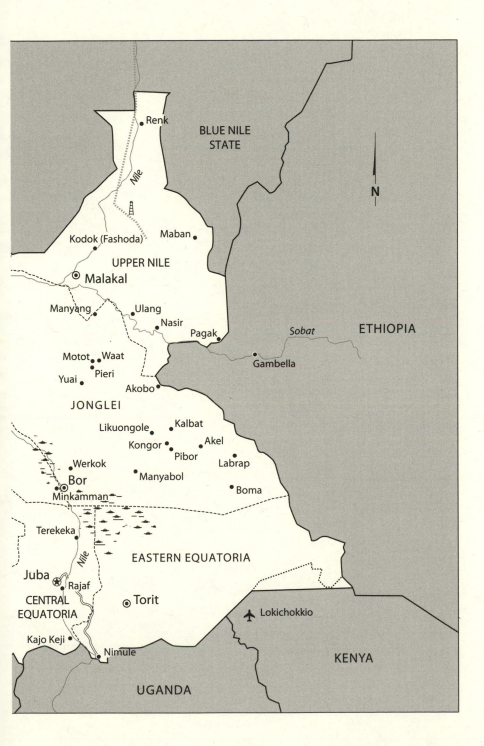

Prologue

Juba, South Sudan,
Monday, 16 December 2013

I woke at about three in the morning to thunder and lightning. Odd, I thought, as the storm passed and the rhythmic whirr of the ceiling fan took over again. The rainy season had ended a few weeks back. I drifted back to sleep.

Shortly after 6:00 a.m. it started to get light and I could hear a staccato crackling outside. I got up, rubbed my eyes, and pushed aside the net curtain. There was no sign of rain. I pulled on a pair of trousers, walked to the front door, and peered out. It was going to be another hot hazy day. John and Emmanuel, our two night guards, were standing across the paved courtyard by the main gate. John saw me and came over shouting.

"Mr Nicholas, please go back! Is problem, I think."

Jenny came out from the washroom and joined me at the door. "What's up?"

"I don't know. Sounds like shooting, maybe ..."

By now it wasn't just small-arms fire. There was the occasional heavier thump and you could feel the ground shake a little. Once the glasses and silver in our dining-room dresser tinkled. From the direction of the main road two hundred metres away, we heard a loud clanking noise over a heavy engine. I wondered where I'd heard that noise before, then remembered *Saving Private Ryan*. A tank.

I turned on the radio to Miraya, the English-language radio station run by the United Nations. There wasn't much hard news, just contradictory, repetitive reports of fighting overnight, some of it centered at Bilpam, the main barracks and headquarters of the Sudan People's Liberation Army (SPLA), about three kilometres from our home. The

SPLA spokesperson, Philip Aguer, was quoted over and over again as saying, "Everything is under control."

Jenny brought me my cellphone and I called the two other Canadian diplomatic staff in Juba, who shared a pair of apartments with their spouses at a new condominium complex a kilometre or so away. They were fine; they'd heard the shooting too, they'd even been out on the balcony to listen better. I told them to get back inside, not to leave the compound, and to call me if they needed assistance.

Wide awake now, I switched on my laptop, which was sitting on the dining-room table, rummaged around for the plug-in fob that allowed us access to the SIGNET communications system of the Department of Foreign Affairs in Ottawa, and sent off a very short e-mail to the late-night watch office, timed at 7:02 a.m.: "Heavy gunfire at military GHQ during the night in Juba; all Canadian staff ordered to remain at home pending clarification of the situation."

Jenny brought me a coffee. South Sudan, just two and half years old, was starting to fall apart.[1]

COLLAPSE OF A COUNTRY

I

Jihad and Crusade

Khartoum and Southern Sudan,
August 2000–2003

The second Sudanese civil war – "the Arab, Muslim North against the African, Christian, and Animist South" as the media shorthand had it – had already been going on for seventeen years when I arrived in Khartoum to open Canada's first permanent diplomatic presence in the Sudanese capital, in 2000. But a casual visitor wouldn't have known it.

The capital actually comprises three cities built at the h-shaped confluence of the Blue Nile and the White: Khartoum, Khartoum North, and Omdurman. They were almost free of petty crime and, although there were plenty of police around who would become agitated if you showed signs of wanting to take a photograph, there were rarely any soldiers to be seen. Only if you hung out for a few days would you start to notice that Khartoum's underclass – servants, road-sweepers, gardeners – were wearing European dress (none of those glamorous, dazzling white djellabiyas and turbans). Their faces were no blacker than those of the Sudanese aristocracy but they were more conventionally African-looking, many with puzzling horizontal scars running across their foreheads. They seemed to attend churches rather than mosques. What was particularly odd about them was that it wasn't clear where they lived. When the work day ended, they vanished.

The vast majority of this underclass, maybe two million people, lived in sprawling informal settlements of mud and sticks on the edge of town that were described by the government and aid agencies as "camps," although most of the structures had become permanent. Only high steel water towers, painted in black and white checkerboard fashion, served as landmarks when you tried to navigate your way around. There weren't many cars to be seen. Water was sold from pale blue oil drums towed on makeshift carts by tired donkeys. Many homes had enclosures, each with a goat and a few chickens, but the climate was too harsh and water too valuable to grow vegetables. Most people spoke a rough-and-ready version of Arabic, but an expert would tell you that they were also speaking Dinka, Shillook, Azande, and Nuer, among other languages.

These were refugees from the war in the South, or IDPs (internally displaced persons) in foreign-aid jargon. The government didn't offer them much beyond the land on which to build their shanties and attendance at any of the few government schools within reach. There was even a campus of Juba University in Khartoum, staffed by southerners whose former place of work was now a military camp.

Quite mysteriously, in the absence of mobile phones or other easy means of communication back then, the IDPs were able to remain in contact with their home communities, even though many had been away for fifteen years or more. By southern traditions, dowries in the form of cattle are payable on marriage. Bride and groom might both have grown up in Khartoum slums, but arrangements were somehow made for the necessary exchange of cows in distant Jonglei State. It was the same with land purchases. When at the end of our three-year posting in Khartoum we wanted to give Stella, our cleaning lady, a parting gift, she asked for money to help her to buy a plot of land in Juba, a place she had not seen in twenty years.

"But how will you do it? How will you pay the owner of the land?"

"It's easy. He has relatives here in Khartoum. I will give them the money, and they will tell him the land is now mine."

"Will the relatives give you a title to the land?"

"No, it's not necessary. Everybody knows each other: you cannot cheat."

There were also some southerners in government. The Nuer Dr Riek Gai, as of 2002, headed a body known as the Southern States Coordinating Council, a kind of shadow government in Khartoum for the regions that had been lost to the rebel Sudan People's Liberation Army; Dr Lam Akol, a Shillook from Upper Nile, was minister of transport; the Dinka Chol Deng was deputy minister of foreign affairs. A disproportionately large number of these exiles were Nuer. At various times they had been in rebellion against the central government, but had come in from the bush in 1997 to align themselves with Khartoum, some under the uneasy leadership of Nuer leader Riek Machar. Most would calmly tell you that they might return to fighting if the situation changed and were still supporters of self-determination for the South.

Two southern friends of ours were Alfred Taban and Nhial Bol. Alfred was a happy-go-lucky Equatorian who was the editor of the only English-language newspaper in Sudan, the *Khartoum Monitor*, and simultaneously a stringer for the BBC. Nhial was his junior colleague, a tall, looming Dinka who was a lot more vocal than Alfred. The *Monitor* was a very amateur broadsheet which routinely lifted entire stories from the internet without removing the hyperlinks or the ads. But it also ran historical pieces about the South and openly critical columns that took the fundamentalist regime in Khartoum to task on a wide range of issues, not just the conduct of the war. The *Monitor*'s circulation was small and the paper was perennially broke, but the Canadian Office helped by periodically buying full pages to run stories on development or human rights, while British colleagues slyly took out subscriptions on behalf of influential members of the governing National Congress Party.

The paper was frequently shut down and its offices were a favourite nightly stop for the censors. Alfred would agree to remove offending articles but then leave the spaces they had occupied artfully blank to make it obvious that the censors had struck. When they caught on and warned him against this, the paper ran uncaptioned variations on a single theme: cartoon characters with zippers for mouths.

I would quite often visit the cramped and airless office where the *Monitor* was produced. "Are you heading out of town?" I once asked Alfred, pointing to the suitcase by the door. "What? Oh, no. I just keep a case packed all the time. I never know when they will come and take me to prison."

Alfred wrote many of his best stories after periods in jail, where he was able to chat at leisure with other political prisoners of all persuasions, including the infamous Hassan al-Turabi, too radical even for President Omar al-Bashir. Sometimes I would hear pieces he had filed for the BBC World Service without even bothering to note that he was doing so on a phone inside a prison courtyard. He and Nhial were faithfully present at all events we hosted in our garden, where they could semi-legally partake of alcohol; they were scornful of the police who waited outside the property with sticks when we had large events, ready to beat anyone they suspected of imbibing.

Christian churches served as another unofficial rendezvous point for discreet agitation by southerners. All but the most far-out sects were grouped under the Sudan Council of Churches (SCC), which received a lot of external support and which ultimately played a significant role in the process that led to the Comprehensive Peace Agreement of 2005. Joy Kwaje, the traditionally built and always colourfully dressed Equatorian coordinator of the pioneering SCC women's program, was a genial counterpart and moderator to the perpetually angry Jeremiah Swaka, who could not wait for self-determination and took every opportunity to slam Western diplomats for not intervening more forcefully on the side of the rebels.

From Khartoum, the war seemed distant, only occasionally in the news. There were no front lines and, throughout the conflict, the government held on to the major southern towns of Juba, Malakal, and Wau. When you flew down to government-held towns from Khartoum, the aircraft would maintain an altitude of 10,000 feet until you were directly overhead, then descend in a nausea-inducing spiral, ostensibly to avoid anti-aircraft fire from rebel forces. Discouragingly, as you approached the runway it was common to see wrecked aircraft that had been pushed off into the undergrowth. At Juba, there were even a couple of downed MiGs, with their desert-brown camouflage, the victims of lucky (or exceptionally good?) shots by the SPLA from the far bank of the Nile.

In Wau, I would meet the governor in his run-down colonial-era office smelling of hornets' nests. In a darkly-curtained waiting area cooled by a languid and creaky ceiling fan, varnished wooden boards on the wall listed the names, in cracked gold paint, of district commissioners as far back as 1910. In a place of honour was mounted a rhino horn. The governor sat behind a large, bare, polished desk that looked as though it had seen very little use. As I sipped scalding tea from a small glass, engulfed in an excessively soft couch at the other end of the gloomy room, he would run through the list of complaints common to state governors everywhere in Sudan: funds were late for this, there were no funds for that, Khartoum was always promising but never delivering. What was surreal was that the governor talked about the enormous territory for which he was nominally responsible – Bahr-al-Ghazal – as if the government was actually in control of all of it, and not just Wau and its immediate environs.

For most of the 1990s you could, in theory, reach Wau by train from Khartoum. Once or twice a year, the government would load a train with food and military supplies for the Wau garrison. As it edged into Kordofan and towards areas not fully under government control, armed and mounted Arab outriders – Murrahaleen – would be recruited to fan out on either side of the tracks to provide a security buffer from attacks on the train by the SPLA. Their reward was a licence to pillage, rape, and enslave. By 2000, the rebels had blown up the track in so many places that the government gave up on the train. But the after-effects of the semi-annual swathe of death cut by the Wau train lingered on.

In 2002, I followed the train tracks in the white embassy Mitsubishi Pajero all the way from Khartoum to El Fula, the quiet and dusty capital of West Kordofan: a three-day ride, much of it at an uncomfortable thirty degrees from the horizontal as we drove awkwardly along the train embankment. In El Fula, at the beginning of the twenty-first century, the British charity Save the Children and UNICEF (the UN's agency for children) jointly maintained a slave-retrieval centre. Much was being made in the West, at the time, of the issue of slavery in Sudan. It seemed incredible that such a phenomenon still existed. The Switzerland-based Christian Solidarity International had been instrumental in raising the profile of the slave train, raising large sums of money, in the US in particular, for slave-redemption campaigns. Between 1995 and 2002 CSI claimed to have "bought" 64,000 slaves at an average price of fifty US dollars each.

At El Fula, there were indeed twenty or so former slaves, young people who had painstakingly been retrieved by Save and UNICEF from Arab families, but their owners had parted with them as a result of persuasion, not payment. The youths' real parents were being sought. Because most had been abducted when they were just infants, they spoke only Arabic and seemed understandably lost. Most had been employed as servants; one or two had been unofficially adopted. Had they been abused? Shrugs. It was true that they'd been forced into menial jobs and a few had not been allowed to receive schooling. But finding their true parents wasn't going to be easy, nor was it obvious that they would re-adapt to Dinka society.

For a number of years, the SPLA had found it expedient to publicize the slavery issue, which played very well with the pro-SPLA and anti-Sudan lobby in the US. In fact, the SPLA supremo, John Garang, was designated by CSI to represent it at the UN's Commission on Human Rights in Geneva in 1999. But lately, a number of investigative journalists had cast doubt on CSI's work. There was evidence that Westerners had been repeatedly duped, on a massive scale, into redeeming fake slaves (to the benefit of the rebels and other middle-men), and that the practice of redemption was itself feeding the slav-ery business. An SPLA general, Aleu Ayieny Aleu, was among many top SPLA officials subsequently to confess that "it was a hoax."[1] Aleu testified that a relative, SPLA captain Akec Tong Aleu, had been "forced several times to pretend as an Arab" and pretend to sell chil-dren, on camera, to CSI.

Bentiu and the adjoining town of Rubkona, in what is now called Unity State but was then still known by southerners as Western Upper Nile, also remained in government hands throughout the war, but less securely. Bentiu always had a nucleus of Arab traders, but this was the land of the Bul clan of the Nuer people, the second-largest ethnic group in Southern Sudan after the Dinkas. The area was stra-tegic, in that the Sudanese oil industry began to take off here in the late 1990s with the help of a blue-chip Western company, Canada's Talisman Energy (formerly BP Canada). Talisman had developed a stake that had originally been acquired by Chevron, then passed on to two successive juniors (State and Arakis).

From 1997 to 2003, the dominant military force here was a Bul Nuer militia known as the South Sudan Unity Movement (SSUM), under the command of a fearsome warlord called Paulino Matiep. Paulino was loyal to the Khartoum government and opposed to both the SPLA and, periodically, his one-time ally and fellow Nuer Riek Machar (notwithstanding the fact that Riek was also aligned with Khartoum).[2] In fact, Paulino wasn't really loyal to anyone but him-self, and to some extent this applied to his generals as well. It was safe enough to fly into the airstrip at Heglig, which adjoined the main oil-pumping station and which was defended by regular government troops. But anywhere else – including Bentiu – it was wise to check a few hours before departure as to the mood on the ground.

I once met Paulino Matiep's most capable general, Peter Gadet, when he was government-aligned, and later – although I did not know it when emerging from the aircraft – when he had defected and was generally sympathetic to the SPLA. He clearly wanted to make an impression. On my second visit, and after I had introduced myself, he said bluntly: "My ambition is to kill a Canadian." He gestured in the general direction of the Heglig oil installations, below the horizon, where at any one time there would be twenty or so Canadian oil-workers.

I considered this for a moment, looking at his heavily armed body-guards lolling in the shade of a nearby tree, AK-47s across their knees, picking their teeth, before asking, "So why haven't you attacked Heglig yet?"

"Hmmm. Good question." He paused for a long moment. "You see these guys?" he asked, gestured at the young men under the tree. "Heglig is well-defended. I know that better than anyone. But it's just a pile of aluminum and steel, with some oil tanks. Why would I want to attack it? There's nothing in it for my men: no cattle, no women, no revenge. And some of us would probably get killed."

I found Paulino himself in a straw-roofed *tukul* just outside Bentiu. He sat uniformed in a heavy armchair in the near darkness in the center of the mud-floored hut with half a dozen armed men grouped symmetrically behind him. He wore a beret and fashionable sun-glasses in which, as I entered, I could see myself and the low doorway reflected. He didn't say a word when I introduced myself, nor did he interrupt me with any questions. I had a brief to raise with him the alleged use of child soldiers by his militias. I'd suspected my instructions from HQ were naïve; now I had no doubt. There was a long pause after I said my piece, then he half-turned to say a few words in Nuer to one of the aides behind him and I was ushered off to meet the civilian authorities in Bentiu proper.

The Canadians at Heglig, the heart of the oil operation, were housed in a complex of prefabricated Canadian cabins – complete with English and French notices – which they shared with their Chinese, Malaysian, and Sudanese partners in an uncomfortable four-way oil production consortium. Most had little knowledge about or interest in the complex conflict that consumed the neigh-bourhood. Part of my responsibility, as Canada's sole diplomatic rep-resentative in Sudan, was to warn them that their lives could be in danger, but most did not take my warning seriously. A few frankly admitted they were making so much money that they tried not to think of the ethical consequences of directly fuelling a civil war.

It was the job of Talisman's security advisors to have a better han-dle on things. This they did. Usually they were able to tell me what Peter Gadet or his fellow-general, Tito Biel, had been up to recently, where Paulino Matiep was, and who was currently aligned with whom. The situation shifted month to month, sometimes from week to week, and gave the lie to those simplistic analyses of the war I'd read before coming to Sudan. The security advisors – both confusingly named Mark – were also, counter-intuitively, responsible for the Canadian oil company's Corporate Social Responsibility (CSR) programs. This made more sense than first appeared, because if you wanted to win over the local population in support of your commercial activities, you needed a sophisticated understanding of the competition. And given that Talisman was keen for the government of Canada to take a less sour approach to its presence in Sudan, the two Marks were diligent in flying me around the concession to various locations where they were involved in Good Works.

My first such expedition was to Mayom, the home of the Bul Nuer towards the western edge of the concession. The landscape was utterly flat, everything bright green: it was October, late in the rainy season. Most of the town consisted of circular, straw-roofed *tukuls*, but there were a few long, shoebox-style concrete government buildings adjoining a large open space the size of several football fields. Here were three or four thousand civilians, mainly women and children, seated in lines and awaiting relief handouts from Talisman's national staff.

We stopped to talk through an interpreter. Many people had walked for days. One family lost two children en route, drowned in a swamp; another spent a night hiding from wild animals inside a large, thorny acacia bush. A woman showed me the tightly woven straw cradle in which she had ferried her baby, Moses-like, through the swamps. The women knew they were running from fighting but couldn't say whose side the fighters were on. One of the few men nodded when I asked, "Peter Gadet?" but no one was familiar with any of the many acronyms that applied to the different militia groups.

We flew by helicopter to another town, Pharyang, in the east and not far from Heglig itself. Here Talisman had erected a large open-sided hangar, with pre-fabricated containers serving as a clinic around the perimeter. They'd trained national staff to provide primary healthcare services; the place was quite well-attended. To the disappointment of the Marks, none of the international non-governmental organizations (NGOs) operating in the area would have anything to do with them; in fact, they were positively hostile. The Canadians should expect that, I thought, but it must have been tough on the national staff, who just thought they were doing a job that needed doing.

———————

Over in the northeast of Southern Sudan, on the east bank of the Nile, was Malakal. Like Wau, it was technically under siege, but years would go by between serious rebel attacks. As you came in low across the river to land on the east-west-aligned runway, you could see a tank parked in the long grass pointing straight across the river; in early 2003 it looked as though it had not moved for months and was no longer manned.

At this time, President Bashir felt comfortable enough to hold the country's principal Independence Day celebrations in Malakal. To this end, the runway was paved and the terminal building was equipped with modernistic clear plastic tables and chairs. The entire domestic fleet of Sudan Airways – three or four rather tired Boeing 737s, their yellow and blue markings streaked with oil stains – was taken out of service to fly the diplomatic corps and hundreds of dignitaries down from Khartoum for the day. The climax was a large rally at the soccer field that culminated with one wave after another of the Sudanese equivalent of three cheers, with ceremonial walking sticks brandished aloft.

I came for a final visit to Malakal in July 2003, just before leaving Sudan. My aim was to ride a barge north on the Nile to Kosti, and en route see the site of the Fashoda Incident, the famous face-off between Britain and France that marked the apogee of the British Empire. For seven enervating days, the barge was leaving "*bukra*" – a term that old Sudan-hands like to say means, "*Mañana*, but without the sense of urgency." I spent much of the time at the bustling waterfront, where flat-sided river boats came and went day and night: always to and from the North, never to the rebel-dominated South. There were men who made a living from shredding automobile tires and selling the long rubber slivers as shoelaces or ties for packages; small boys scurried around, carefully sweeping up individual grains of sorghum that had spilled from sacks brought upstream from Renk. You could buy great sheaves of yellowing straw for your roof, harvested from the marshes across the river, and bundles of bamboo poles to be used as beams or for walls; there was fresh fish from the Sobat River, a tributary that joined the Nile just above Malakal; even a small crocodile for sale, its mouth firmly lashed.

I was there on a Friday. Most of the men of the town came out in newly laundered and dazzlingly white djellabiyas, with small white skullcaps, and made their way to the massive square-towered mosque in the centre of town.

When we finally set off, the captain insisted on giving me his cabin, high up on the bridge of the powerfully enginned blue and white "pusher," a kind of tug that propelled a massive, flat-topped metal barge in front of it. I also had the use of the only chair on board, a purple plastic lawn chair with a broken back. There was a small city on the barge: a men's hairdresser, a makeshift bread-oven, a teacher running through his English ABCs in front of an easel. Goats roamed free and had occasionally to be restrained from eating timber travelling as cargo. On either side of the roof the military manned a mortar pointing outwards, but no one seemed to seriously expect any kind of rebel attack. Much of the territory we would be traversing was the ancient Shillook Kingdom and the Shillooks were not actively aligned with the SPLA then.

We passed the site of Fashoda late one hot afternoon. It was no more than a low promontory, a bend in the river with a small white-washed monument briefly visible. Two or three hundred metres back was a treeline with a few *tukuls* dimly visible: the town of Kodok. The smoke from their fires drifted and hung lower over the still and darkening waters of the Nile. I heard the deep grunt of a hippo as our wake disturbed him in his wallow.

Juba used to be known as Gondokoro. Its location was strategic, this being the narrowest part of the Nile before the rapids at Rajaf – ten kilometres upstream – were reached and the river thus became unnavigable. For many years, Gondokoro was the furthest outpost established by Europeans before "Darkest Africa" was reached. Here Arab traders coming south from Sudan and Egypt would pick up their cargoes of slaves and ivory before returning north. Here one Victorian explorer after another gave up the unequal struggle up the Nile, retreated, and set out to look for its source by overland approaches through East Africa. And it was at Gondokoro that on 15 February 1863, Speke and Grant, descending the Nile after the discovery of what they thought must be its source in East Africa, met Samuel Baker and his indomitable wife journeying up the river. Thus they solved the last great remaining geographical mystery.

Juba had been the centre from which the British administered Southern Sudan through the later years of the colony, and it saw a brief burst of new building in the period between Sudan's two civil wars (1972–83). But since the second phase of the war had begun, it had become largely a garrison town. Khartoum made the fullest possible use of its tarmac airstrip (the only such facility in the South) to keep Juba well-stocked and defended, and the SPLA, notwithstanding its control of much of the hinterland, was unable to take the town.

Most people remember where they were on the day of 9/11. I was in Juba.

Late afternoon after a day-long seminar at the principal UN compound, we'd driven in the UN's white Land Cruiser – one of only a dozen or so non-military vehicles in town – to the Comboni sisters' compound. Here, it was well-known, you could get the best (the only…) homemade ice cream in all Southern Sudan, made by real Italians. The sisters all seemed to be at least seventy years old, and few spoke much English: Italian was still their lingua franca. They received us with the kind of hospitality that Italian grandmothers display in sentimental black-and-white movies from the fifties.

In a quiet moment, one of them turned on the TV. They'd only had it a few months and we were proudly told it was one of only three sets in Juba. Intent on my pistachio ice cream, I watched it out of the corner of my eye. The sisters had not turned the volume on, I saw what looked like a moderately competent disaster movie. After a few minutes, someone asked for the volume to be turned up.

The full horror started to sink in. The nuns seemed curiously uncomprehending. I thought I'd better turn on my Thuraya satellite phone. As the office in Khartoum was a one-Canadian show, I wasn't really supposed to leave it: unofficially, I'd given the entry code to the front door to my office manager, as HQ in Ottawa had surely guessed. "You'd better get back," my wife Jenny said unnecessarily. "They're saying it's Osama bin Laden. Didn't he use to live here?"

It wasn't permitted to fly directly from government-controlled parts of Sudan to areas under rebel control except if you were the International Committee of the Red Cross (ICRC), and even then, you ran the risk of being shot at by nervous troops on either side. Relief aircraft chartered by the United Nations, under a carefully negotiated agreement known as Operation Lifeline Sudan (OLS), could take off from either Sudan or northern Kenya and drop food into rebel-held areas, but only if departing from Kenya were they allowed by Khartoum to land in those areas. Much of the time and energy of diplomats in the Sudanese capital was expended in assisting the United Nations to have the agreement respected: all too often flights were denied clearance, ostensibly because they would be endangered by insecurity in the area in question but really to deprive rebel-controlled populations of humanitarian relief.

Diplomats based in Khartoum were supposed to ask permission before going to rebel-held areas but, working on the assumption that such a request would likely be denied or just not answered, no one ever asked. The routine was to take the Kenya Airways flight from Khartoum to Nairobi where, depending on precisely which area you wanted to visit, you sought a permit from either the Sudan Relief and Rehabilitation Agency (for SPLA-controlled areas) or the confusingly similar Relief Association of Southern Sudan for the less extensive areas under the influence of forces loyal to Riek Machar. (Although for a long period Riek was aligned with the government in Khartoum, the fiction of separateness was maintained right up until the moment he defected back to the SPLA and RASS merged with the SRRA.)

After a couple of days, permit in hand, you boarded a light aircraft at Nairobi's smaller airport, Wilson, for the flight north again, to the small border town of Lokichokkio, called simply Loki by the cognoscenti. Your ten or twelve fellow passengers were often an interesting lot. I travelled a couple of times with Republican congressman Frank Wolf, a strong supporter of Christian Solidarity International, who once had a valise full of dollars with him for slave redemption. Often there would be missionaries, another diplomat or two, UN staff, and members of the large group of non-governmental organizations that sheltered under the umbrella of Operation Lifeline Sudan.

Loki, the UN base adjoining the airfield, was a small walled city whose blue steel gates closed every night with a loud clang. Turkana County was a lawless place at the best of times, and tribal conflicts that had nothing to do with the war in Southern Sudan often spilled into the town. Although in these years Loki represented one of the largest communities of aid and development workers in the world, there was an odd myopia about what was going on in its immediate neighbourhood. Intra-Turkana feuds that killed dozens every month, and local droughts leading to great hardship, were not considered to be of any interest.

There was a large cafeteria inside the UN compound, a bar called Murphy's, and TVs strategically positioned under trees that brought you CNN and the BBC. Staff lived in relatively comfortable straw-roofed *tukuls* that bore the names of senior UN administrators that had worked at Loki over the years. I was often allocated to "Thomas Ekvall," who had moved on and become UNICEF's director in Khartoum.

Outside the base were other private camps, some of them with swimming pools, where you would find people who worked for organizations known euphemistically as "Non-OLS." These were NGOS that scorned the constraints and principles that participating in the UN's OLS implied (for example, a commitment not to carry combatants or weapons) and prided themselves as being freer spirits and truer humanitarians than their OLS counterparts.

Some of these outfits were indeed highly principled. Some were not. All profited cynically by shadowing UN aircraft on their daily runs dropping food into Southern Sudan before peeling away from their unwitting escorts to unauthorized locations. The non-OLS pilots would sit at one end of the bar in the Loki camps, the OLS crews at the other, the former loudly telling tall stories of dodging MiGs over the Nuba Mountains so as to shame their more law-abiding counterparts. Many of the pilots were Canadian, partly because the favoured aircraft in this part of the world were rugged Canadian-built Twin Otters and Buffaloes.

There was an almost tangible sense at Loki that you were at the base camp of a crusade. Norwegian People's Aid, a large non-OLS organization, was known – not so much in criticism as with admiration – as Norwegian People's Army. No one saw any irony in condemning Sudan's fanatical government for pursuing a *jihad*, a holy war in the South, while the noticeboards at Loki were plastered with "Wanted: Evangelists" ads. Even in the company of UN and OLS partners, it wasn't always wise to mention that you were based in Khartoum, which was seen as the seat of all evil. I was asked, scornfully, "How can you sleep at night?" On one occasion, the people at the table I was sharing at the canteen ostentatiously got up as a group and went to sit outside as soon as they learned where I came from.

Not everyone was a fellow traveller. On my first visit to Loki, I was invited by the UN's World Food Program to observe an airdrop from one of the fleet of white C-130 aircraft semi-permanently based at Loki for this purpose. It was an exciting adrenaline trip, a canny tactic on WFP's part to persuade donor countries like Canada to keep giving. The calm discipline of the flight crew as, two hours in, they pinged their GPS over the drop zone on the preliminary reconnaissance run; the tense countdown as they came in for the first live run, at 150 metres above the ground; the upward lurch; a thump, then a moment of weightlessness before we levelled off and a laconic message came from the dispatcher at the rear door, "Three pallets away; on target."

I was quite moved when we banked around. There I could see the white sacks of sorghum scattered in a tight circle on the red-earth drop zone. What could be simpler, what could be more heartwarming than this: the delivery from the air of sacks of desperately needed food into the arms of the starving?

When we pulled away from the second drop, the pilot tapped me on the shoulder. He pointed down with a stabbing motion. It was no use trying to speak; the roar of the Herc's four turboprop engines as we gained altitude again was deafening. But down there in the drop zone, I could see armed uniformed men ushering away the women and children who had been waiting patiently and piling up the sacks for their own use. I turned back to the pilot, who just shrugged lightly and studied his instruments.

The diversion of food aid – not just by the SPLA, but also by the Sudan Armed Forces in areas under its control – was widely acknowledged in aid circles, and was seen as the cost of doing business. But there was great reluctance on the part of humanitarian organizations to discuss or publicize it, lest donors reduce their financial support. Some of this concern was well-founded – who would pay the immediate price if the airdrops were suspended? – but some was self-serving: WFP, MSF, and a hundred others are worthy organizations, but they also represent careers for thousands of people, and careers have to be justified.

Yambio, deep in the woods of Equatoria close to the Congolese border, was in the hands of the SPLA throughout the war and, although slit trenches had been dug in various locations as bomb shelters, it was said that the only aerial danger was falling mangoes. Nonetheless, the welcome on my first visit was not a warm one. "So you're from the country whose oil company is killing our people up in the oil fields?" was the rhetorical question from the leader of a small posse of uniformed SPLA, as the little white Cessna Caravan on which I had arrived lifted off on its way back to Juba.

Later I met with General Samuel Abu John, the de facto military governor. I was reminded of my encounter with Paulino Matiep. Abu John was treated with awed reverence by his entourage, his every grimace or grunt eliciting some fawning reaction.

I'd explored around town during the afternoon and seen electricity wires hanging loose from their posts; the roads were deeply rutted and impassable to any motorized vehicle; the only functioning school consisted of a group of children sitting in the shade of a tree, listening to their teacher run through the alphabet. The very few services on offer – a primary health-care centre, bore holes, and hand pumps – were courtesy of foreign organizations and the UN. So, hoping to start a discussion on the developmental needs of Yambio, I asked Abu John, "What do you need from us Western countries, here in Yambio?"

"Stingers."

"What?"

"Stinger missiles; to shoot down the Sudanese Antonovs. That's what we want you to send us."

The old warrior listened with apparent patience. It could have been boredom: the night was dark. I explained why the Canadian International Development Agency was not in a position to supply lethal weapons to his rebel army. At one point, he interrupted brusquely, "Why not? You're a Christian country, aren't you? Why won't you support us?"

I went on at length about how a government like Canada's becomes "rich" – as Abu John evidently perceived it to be – and I ended up by asking why an assembly-line worker in Windsor, Ontario, would wish to see a part of his hard-earned wages diverted to help the SPLA fight a war in a country he had likely never heard of. Abu John listened, thoughtfully I believed. So, I pushed my luck. "You've been in control here for twenty years. But there's no electricity, no proper school, you can't use the roads …"

"We've been fighting a war," he broke in. "That's been our priority. We want the Arabs out."

"What will be your priority when the war ends? What will you do for Yambio?"

"What will we do? Well, that will be up to you. You'll bring the schools and all those other things."

In the end, he sent me off to talk to Commander Mary, the county commissioner (the only female of this rank in the whole SPLA, a matter of some pride to her). The people's daily needs were obviously considered to be women's work. Mary was a lot more constructive. She walked with me to show me the women of the town digging some new communal latrines and, when we went back to her bare office – dirty yellow walls, a faded colour poster of John Garang, a thick coat of dust on the desk, that characteristic smell of hornets – she pulled out a sheaf of papers covered with handwritten names and numbers. She was starting a rudimentary tax system, she said, but it was hard going. "So many people just have no money. And as you know we have no currency of our own: we use Kenyan money, Ugandan money, Sudanese pounds."

Before I left, Abu John summoned me to see him again. He'd evidently not been displeased to have someone be contrary with him. Sipping beer, he reminisced about his long years as a fighter. He'd undergone military training in Khartoum and, bizarrely, he claimed that Saddam Hussein had been a classmate. "This explains why Sudan backed Iraq's invasion of Kuwait in 1991," he said.

I let that ride. I was more interested in what motivated the average SPLA foot-soldier, how the commanders built morale, what they said to them before a battle. The old man was silent for a long time. I prompted him: "Is it Dr John's dream? The New Sudan?"

The New Sudan was John Garang's oft-voiced ideal of a unitary, democratic, and secular Sudan. It was one that was appealing in the Western world at the time, if only because it maintained the principle that the colonial-era borders of Africa should remain sacrosanct. "The New Sudan? No, it's certainly not that ... That's Dr John speaking, that's for you *Khawajas*..." (the Arabic term for white people).

He paused for so long that I thought he would not answer. Then he spoke. "What do we fight for? Well, I fight for an independent South Sudan. I want nothing to do with the Arabs, none of us do. But the men..." and he gestured into the dark. "The men, I think that maybe some of them fight for that too. But not so many."

Mapel, far to the northwest of Yambio and almost within sight of government-controlled Wau, was much more bomb-prone: before being shown my *tukul*, I was assigned my own trench (distinctly uninviting, with five centimetres of dirty water and a dead rat in it). The staff of Tearfund, whose therapeutic feeding centre Canada was supporting, knew exactly how to distinguish between the engine sounds of Sudanese Antonov bombers and the UN's Hercules aircraft.

The village was not much more than a few dozen straw-roofed huts spread over a large area in the hot, red-earthed scrubland. It was well over three hours' flying time from Lokichokkio, which meant that Tearfund's modest operation was at the very far end of a long and very expensive logistical chain: everything from toilet paper to bottled water came in by Cessna Caravan. The three expatriate women who ran the show (the staff of aid-focused NGOs are disproportionately women) were young, earnest, and very Christian. Theirs was not a comfortable life, and they were not earning much money, if any. On Sunday morning, there was a good crowd of children, some with their parents, for an informal and ecumenical service; English hymnals and prayer books were distributed from a large pile kept in an otherwise locked store room.

After the service, I helped prepare lunch. There were a few children hanging around at the wicker fence.

"Shall I invite them over?" I asked.

"Well no, that won't be necessary" was the brisk, Irish-accented response. "We only give them lunch if they come to church, you see."

Back in Khartoum, as 2002 became 2003, the talk was of a peace process. The United States, the UK, Norway, and Kenya were all playing active roles as round after round of consultations took place in various locations in Kenya. Canada played only a minor part, nominating successive peace envoys (Lois Wilson, then Mobina Jaffer). The highly controversial presence of Talisman (cast by the SPLM/A as enabling to Khartoum) was something of a millstone round Ottawa's neck and, notwithstanding my own appointment in 2000 to the one-person office in Khartoum, we had not the diplomatic depth to sustain long-term peace support. In July 2002, a preliminary accord was signed at Machakos. It set out the broad principles of a settlement, but it would take a further two and half years before the Comprehensive Peace Agreement was finally signed on 9 January 2005 at Naivasha.[3]

Even as the war wound down, Khartoum would seek to manipulate the delivery of foodstuffs and medicines to favour the population under its control and deprive those under SPLA influence. Obstruction was usually of the passive-aggressive kind. When a new overall head of the UN – Mike Sackett, an Australian – arrived in 2002, he pressed hard for greater cooperation. In response, the Foreign Ministry simply never made the necessary arrangements for him to present his diplomatic credentials, which in turn gave government officials an excuse not to meet him. He had to leave, frustrated, after six months.

Sackett was succeeded by the UK's Mukesh Kapila. He became frustrated in a different way.

As the talks in Kenya gained momentum, they became virtually the only topic of discussion. At meeting after meeting, the US, the UK, and others hammered home the point that we must not lose sight of the vital objective for all of us: a deal to bring the civil war to an end. It was not difficult to be convinced. The human and material cost of twenty years of war – maybe 2.5 million dead – had been catastrophic, and peace looked to be within reach. An embryonic peace arrangement in the Nuba Mountains of South Kordofan was held up as an inspiring example. In this single, ethnically homogenous region, the rebel SPLM and the Khartoum government had come to the table and agreed to a ceasefire mechanism by which under the supervision of a modest and ad-hoc international force supervised by a Norwegian general, both military establishments worked together to keep the peace. Then the UN and aid agencies came in behind with a concerted program of mine clearance, rehabilitation of bore holes and other infrastructure, and humanitarian assistance.

But there were niggling questions surrounding the peace talks in Kenya. In the first place, Nuba (along with another area of rebellion in Blue Nile State) was not considered historically to be part of the South, as administered in colonial days. It looked very much as though the mainstream SPLM/A would, in the end, sacrifice these two territories to Khartoum's control in return for a clear offer of self-determination for the "true" South. And then there was the matter of another disputed territory – Abyei – whose status the British had left unclear when they left in 1956. Its permanent residents were Dinka, and therefore "southerners," but for half the year the Dinka were outnumbered by nomads (Misseriya) who were Arab, Muslim, and clearly northerners. Abyei similarly was put aside for later.

Most niggling of all was rising tension in the far west of Sudan. In 2002, Jenny and I had been hiking in the mountains of Jebel Marra, in Darfur. It was spectacularly beautiful, but in the villages surrounding the massif the tension was palpable. Pastoralists and nomads were clashing with sedentary farmers on an ever more frequent basis and there was a sense of both sides being manipulated and armed, one by elements discontented with Khartoum's decades of neglect, the other by fiercely repressive forces in the government itself. As 2003 advanced, scarcely a week passed without news of some massacre perpetrated by nomads or a revenge attack by farmers, with civilians, as always, caught in the middle.

Mukesh flagged this disturbing tendency as one deserving a lot more of our attention. He warned that the Khartoum government was taking advantage of our obsession with the North-South process to literally get away with murder in the west. A short time later he would quit, in anger at the world's indifference to the horrors of Darfur. There is no question that, as diplomats, we should have listened more to Mukesh, not only on ethical and humanitarian grounds, but on geo-political grounds as well. The Darfur conflict was likely to destabilize Chad and the Central African Republic, and it was naïve to imagine that a newly autonomous – or independent – government in Southern Sudan would not instinctively find at least some common cause with the Darfur rebels.

Darfur and the fate of the South came to be intertwined, inasmuch as by "giving away" the principle of self-determination for the South – and later, by letting the South leave, unopposed – Khartoum came to feel that it had done the West a huge favour. So huge that it deserved not only to have sanctions lifted by the US, but to have the West not interfere over Darfur. When, on the one hand, sanctions were not lifted and on the other the pressure increased over Darfur, whatever small amount of goodwill there may have been in Sudan towards South Sudan soon evaporated.

In acknowledgement of some of the pitfalls that might follow a peace accord with the South, the United Nations Development Program (UNDP) commissioned a set of investigations entitled Planning for Peace. A number of scenarios were looked at, several of them problematic. An autonomous Southern Sudan would, for example, inherit most of the country's oil resources, but would be captive to the pipeline that ran only north, through Sudan proper; the massive, heterogeneous SPLA would need to be largely disarmed and its forces redirected into productive employment; the rebel mindset of liberation at the expense of discussion and dissent would need to be replaced with modern democratic thinking, anti-Khartoum motivation with a more positive vision. Above all, the South/South tensions that had always existed but had only occasionally been visible to outsiders – as when warlord Riek Machar defected to Khartoum with his Nuer cohorts – would need to be addressed and healed.

There was one large white ring binder for each big issue identified, and they started piling up on the shelves of the UNDP office. The ambassadors of Western countries periodically expressed polite interest in this kind of thinking, but not for long. They were always brought back into line. "We must not lose sight of the ball …" the US chargé d'affaires would intone to approving nods. "We'll worry about the rest of those problems later."

A Garage by the Nile

Juba, South Sudan, 2012

A lot happened after I left Khartoum in 2003.

The peace deal – the Comprehensive Peace Agreement, or CPA – was signed and came into effect in 2005. It provided for an interim period of six years, so that the signatories (the SPLM and the Khartoum government) could make unity attractive by empowering southerners politically and through development in their grossly under-serviced region. At the end of this period, there would be a referendum in the South asking whether Sudan should remain as one country or the South should become independent.

Canada, meanwhile, maintained its office in Khartoum, by now independently of the British Embassy. Its status was upgraded from the nebulous term "office" to "embassy," but no resident ambassador was appointed, a reflection of the desire in Ottawa to keep the reviled Khartoum government and its ICC-indicted president at arm's length. The title chargé d'affaires was now used instead of head of office. There was a general sigh of relief in the Canadian capital when Talisman – whose presence had initially provoked the opening of the office – sold its interest to an Indian company. But for a while, the attention of my successors was consumed by Canada's substantial support to UN peacekeeping operations in Darfur and to related regional peacemaking efforts. When the contribution to the African Union/United Nations Mission in Darfur (UNAMID) declined – on account of diminished interest in peacekeeping by a new government in Canada and of frustrating obstacles being placed in the mission's way by the Khartoum government – the embassy's role turned to political monitoring and to keeping an eye on our substantial humanitarian assistance program.

I stayed in touch from a distance. One cynical friend commented by e-mail, "You'll see; the best incentive for unity will be three years of independence."

When the six years were up in the second week of January 2011, the referendum was duly held. Some were surprised that Sudan allowed this to happen. But nobody was surprised by the result: 98.83 per cent in favour of independence. There was meant to be a simultaneous referendum to determine the fate of Abyei but this was postponed *sine die*, as there was no agreement over voter eligibility and the precise demarcation of the district. A "popular consultation" for the regions of Blue Nile and South Kordofan (Nuba Mountains) was also put off. A month before the South's independence was formally declared in July 2011, locally based army units loyal to Khartoum attacked elements affiliated to the SPLM/A, thus launching a mini-war in the Two Areas that continues to this day.

Notwithstanding these ill omens, Sudan was the first country to recognize the newly independent South Sudan, which became the 193rd member of the United Nations on 9 July 2011.

Canada was number twenty-five in recognizing the country: not speedy, but not especially slow either.

A small coterie of Sudanophiles within Foreign Affairs at the Lester B. Pearson Building in Ottawa was keen that we now establish a substantial presence in Juba, in recognition of the enormous humanitarian and developmental challenges we knew the new country would face, the large South Sudanese diaspora in Canada, and the historical involvement of Canadians in the creation of South Sudan. For several years since 2005, we had one, sometimes two officers from the Canadian International Development Agency (CIDA) attached to the innovative six-nation Joint Donor Office in Juba. This presence was now augmented by the posting of two additional CIDA officers, of an officer from the Stabilization and Reconstruction Taskforce (START) within Foreign Affairs, and, ultimately, of a political/administrative officer, also from Foreign Affairs.

This diplomatic consolidation was undertaken virtually by stealth. The creation of new embassies by the Canadian government is a slow and cumbersome one at the best of times. But there was a perception by bureaucrats in the years leading up to 2011 (for the result of the referendum had been widely forecast: we knew embassies would be opening) that Prime Minister Harper's administration would not go for a new embassy in a place that had slipped from the political radar, that offered few opportunities for bilateral trade or investment (in the short term at least), and that was likely to place even more demands on an international aid budget that successive governments had been cutting for years. This was also a time of austerity in the public sector, and the accoutrements of international diplomacy are tempting targets for cost-cutters.

Accordingly, no physical office appeared on the books, but the premises occupied by the Foreign Affairs political officer had a modicum of space that could be used as a working location by all the staff at no extra cost. Also, to avoid raising eyebrows on the top floor of the Pearson Building, the political officer was to be called head of office, not ambassador, just as I was when I opened in Khartoum. The Canadian ambassador to South Sudan was to be the same individual who was high commissioner to Kenya, Uganda, and Rwanda, and ambassador to Somalia – resident in Nairobi, Kenya.

This arrangement caused polite mystification in friendly foreign ministries, among the large diaspora in Canada and, no doubt, at the Southern Sudan liaison office that had opened in Ottawa pending the referendum. While it was understood that we wished to maintain a low diplomatic profile in Khartoum on account of political misgivings, surely this did not apply in Juba, where we were spending up to one hundred million Canadian dollars a year on development and humanitarian assistance?

The question was a fair one. We looked inept, inattentive, possibly cheap. But in the end, the substance of the office's work was more important than its title. Although the arrangement would give me many headaches, I could not fault the officials who had decided on the stealth route; had a more conventional process been attempted, there would likely have been no Canadian presence in Juba at all.

So, the Canadian office in Juba, by the time I returned to the greater Sudan a year after the South's independence, was the converted garage of the residential villa in which Jenny and I lived. It was in a neighbourhood called Thongping, reached by dirt road.

In addition to our exiguous working premises, the bureaucratic fuzziness surrounding the Canadian presence had other frustrating consequences on the ground. It meant we were not authorized to recruit locally engaged national staff (LES), who would likely have been able to undertake many routine tasks much more effectively and cheaply than I could. We had no receptionist to screen visitors. The mission finances, modest as they were, had to run through my own bank account; although the funds were small, the fact that three currencies were involved (the Canadian dollar, the non-convertible South Sudanese pound, and the widely used US dollar) made keeping track of things difficult and necessitated long explanatory conversations with the often- perplexed auditing staff at the Canadian High Commission (i.e., embassy) in Kenya. We were not connected to the government-wide communications system except in an ad hoc manner. Allowing us secure communications systems was out of the question, in spite of our increasing need, over the years, to speak frankly to HQ regarding the challenges of security and of dealing with the government in Juba. Although the high commission in Nairobi was officially responsible for providing support, their distance from the scene and their lack of familiarity with the extreme conditions in Juba meant that this never worked as well as intended.

There were three other staff: Catherine, Caroline, and Nancy. The ladies were all single. This wasn't by order. My predecessor had come with his wife but she had concluded after a few days that, without a compelling job that could keep you busy seven days a week, life here would be very unattractive, and returned to Ottawa.

Life in the garage resembled a reality TV show. Under the circumstances – this was possibly the least developed Canadian diplomatic mission in the world, in the world's least developed country – humour, resilience, and informality were of much greater value than the classic diplomatic requirements of formality, tact, and seriousness. We each sat against one wall, our laptops perched on rickety locally bought tables. Any conversation between two people necessarily included the other two, but there would occasionally be desperate bursts of confidences between three when one of the group crossed the room to use the washroom; this was awkwardly housed behind a door that didn't lock, and whose top half was glass, inadequately curtained. If you really needed to talk to someone privately, you could always send an e-mail. But these took an unpredictable amount of time to arrive and would sometimes lead to unexpected bouts of giggling as, an hour after despatch, the recipient would look over his or her screen and meet the eyes of the sender.

Early conversations quickly dispelled any delusions of grandeur about my title. Nancy (emerging from the washroom): "Nick, we're out of toilet paper."

Catherine, as the aircon wound down and four laptops beeped one after the other: "Nick. That'll be the generator. I think you need to look at it."

Caroline (also emerging from the washroom, an hour later): "Nick, it's not flushing. And we're still out of paper."

Mostly, people got on well considering their close quarters. Catherine and Caroline lived in adjoining duplexes fifteen minutes' drive away and shared a vehicle coming in. You could tell when Catherine had overslept by the rather determined and tight-lipped way Caroline would sweep in through the door, Catherine looking embarrassed in her wake; you had the feeling they hadn't spoken too much on the drive in. Nancy would arch her eyebrows quietly and catch my eye over the iPad where she was catching up on the overnight news on CBC.

There were no fixed telephone lines in South Sudan, so calls came in on people's cellphones. You could immediately tell if one of the ladies was talking to an expat or a South Sudanese, because the English of most nationals was idiosyncratic and demanded a similar response: "You are where? You are footing to office? OK, you come now. I mean Now Now." Telephone etiquette was rare, and callers invariably assumed you could identify them by their voices. But even when they said their names, there were still problems. "You are Deng? Deng who? Sorry, many Dengs in South Sudan. Which Deng?"

For contact with Ottawa, we had a speakerphone "spider," which allowed communication using voice over internet protocols (VOIP). This meant that each and every conversation was public. Often they were conference calls, but by putting the device on "mute," you could safely get on with some undemanding work or hold an offline conversation as long as you were attentive to expectant pauses from the other side of the world. During windstorms, common between April and November, waving branches would interrupt the wi-fi signal from the antenna on top of the compound's water tower, and all communication would cease. Because the conference calls were invariably scheduled after work hours, it was occasionally tempting to invent tempests.

There was a very active, even racy singles' scene in in Juba, characterized by Sunday-afternoon pool parties, expat brunches at any one of two or three favoured hangouts (especially Le Bistro), tennis at the single Juba court, yoga at two rival sessions on the weekends. Catherine – blonde, in her late thirties, and often dressed in adventurous confections of her own making – made the most of it. Caroline was the same age but more sanguine about things. "The place is full of MBAS," she sighed one quiet Monday morning. "Married but available." Indeed, Juba was full of apparently unattached expats. The literally thousands of civilians with the UN were all unaccompanied, as were most of those with the international non-governmental organisations. It was an easy-come, easy-go kind of place. Most people were being very well paid and there only for nine months or a year, and few were interested in serious relationships. "And if they're not actually married," Caroline went on sourly, "you can guarantee they have a lot of baggage."

Among the male diplomatic corps, Faheem – the suave first secretary at the Egyptian Embassy who resembled a young Omar Sharif – had a certain notoriety. He could often be spotted sipping strong black coffee at Le Bistro, engaged in earnest conversation with any of the young female aid workers who seemed to arrive weekly by the planeload. Catherine was dismissive of his charms. But she appealed to me on one occasion when, after an academic lecture, he sidled up to her and asked if she would like to try some Turkish Delight at his apartment. "Pretend you're my father!" she hissed, pulling me into the conversation.

Nancy, a little older, had a different problem. A neighbour, one Mr Singh, kept sending her importuning e-mails and text messages. But these ceased when, after a worrying night of drunken goings-on and gunfire outside her gate, it was decided to move her to an apartment hotel for the rest of her posting. When she said goodbye to one of the guards, he remonstrated with her, "But Madam, it was just a pistol!"

There was no respite from Mr Singh, who two years later tracked Nancy down by e-mail in Ulaan Bator.

———————

To uninitiated friends in Canada, I would explain that humanitarian aid is designed to keep desperate people alive from one day to the next, whereas development assistance is meant to take the country towards a state where people can look after themselves. As the old cliché has it, "humanitarian" is giving a man a fish, "development" is teaching him how to fish. Overseeing complementary Canadian programs in these areas meant attending a bewildering number of meetings with United Nations agencies known by their acronyms. These were not always intuitive; UNFPA, for example, is the United Nations Population Fund. There were meetings too with representatives of other Western countries (here known as "the donors"), with officials from government offices that were in receipt of assistance, and so on. The aim was to ensure coordination in international aid, to see that it reflected what was both wanted and needed, and to keep an eye on how well our money was being spent.

My specific contribution was to try to figure out the political scene and provide an analytical framework for what we were doing. This meant following the news closely, keeping up on the political gossip, reaching a certain version of the truth by triangulation, and reporting home to Ottawa. This could be challenging. Hard, reliable news was a very rare commodity in South Sudan; rumours were often fantastic and alarmist, and the two most popular electronic sources – Sudan Tribune and Radio Tamazuj – were not always professionally researched. But every so often, one of the most colourful of the rumours would be verified, and no political officer in the field wants to be trumped with truly important news by his desk officer at HQ.

We did not do the one thing that most South Sudanese wanted us to: issue visas. But we did offer what most Canadians think embassies should: consular services; that is to say, assistance to Canadians in South Sudan. Nearly all the Canadians we saw, with the exception of a few working for the United Nations or NGOs, were of South Sudanese extraction. They had fled to Canada as refugees during the war years and returned to try their luck at home. Extrapolating from self-reporting of individuals to Statistics Canada during the most recent census, it was thought that there were some 15,000 South Sudanese in Canada, largely in Alberta.[1] Based on the duration of the validity of a Canadian passport, and on the number of inquiries we received each week, I calculated in turn that (even more approximately) a thousand or so were back in South Sudan.

Most routinely, I would accept payment for applications for new passports for these dual nationals, shipping off the forms for processing at the Canadian High Commission in Nairobi, and delivering the passports when they arrived back from Canada after three or four weeks. Often, I would spend an hour commiserating when people dropped by on Monday mornings to the dedicated consular container adjoining the garage. There were many cases of men who had come back to South Sudan (leaving their wives and families in Canada) to look for work, but had found none and were now penniless – and hoping for a flight to Canada. There was little we could do except put them in touch with their Canadian family to see if they could assist. Such contacts could be surprisingly interesting. As the months went by, I listened to dozens of family odysseys, to dreams, and tragedies. Everyone who had gone to Canada had done so in a state of destitution. Often, they had lost the rest of their family to war. They'd made epic treks to neighbouring countries and spent years in refugee camps in Ethiopia or Kenya until they secured that critical interview with a Canadian immigration officer and the treasured ticket west.

In a material sense, many had not done well in Canada. Lacking education, they had taken menial or labouring jobs. A relatively high number had ended up at the meat-packing plant at Brooks, Alberta, a town which had become a home away from home for the South Sudanese because of a succession of churches that had sponsored them. But they had learned English, had sent their children – all of them, not just the boys – to school, and, in the case of those I saw in Juba, had developed an admirable desire to come back and help build the new South Sudan.

The tragedy was not always what had happened to them years ago in Southern Sudan. It was the reception they were given upon their return. A few secured plum jobs in the Foreign Ministry; there was at least one minister and several members of parliament. But the majority ran into an unexpected degree of resentment. "Where were you when we were fighting and dying?" they'd be asked. "Living the high life, I suppose. Well, you'll just have to get in line." So it was that precisely when this new country needed literate, educated, and idealistic people to kick-start it, all the key positions went to that class of persons who were the least qualified of all: the war veterans who knew a lot about fighting, nothing about democracy, and nothing about government.

It was on one of those Monday mornings when I was leafing through an expired passport in our little white container that I first heard about the Cuban Jubans.

———————

The war that began in 1983 was focused initially in the Jonglei region, east of Bor and the River Nile. The fledgling SPLA took heavy losses; the civilian population even heavier. There came a moment when rebel leader John Garang, foreseeing that this was going to be a long struggle, gave explicit orders that orphaned boys should, whenever possible, make their way to the refugee camps that had quickly sprung up in Ethiopia and Kenya, to wait until they would be able to contribute to the cause.

There has been a lot of revisionism here. First, it is overlooked that Garang's principal aim was for those who left to return and fight as soon as they were big enough to hold a gun, which could be as early as the age of thirteen or fourteen. Further, while girls were not explicitly discouraged from running to the camps (or indeed from joining up to fight), cultural norms required that most stay home to care for infants, the old, and the infirm; as in every war, women and girls thus paid a disproportionately high price in this conflict.

The Red Army was the name given to the legions of young boys the SPLA began to train in the refugee camps, marshalled by Red Army Inspectors. Sometimes it was only a year or two before they were recalled home. All too often they were used as the first line of attack, cannon fodder for Sudanese tanks and machine guns. The Red Army, I learned from former recruit Peter Biar, took casualty rates as high as 90 per cent. The surviving members of this band of brothers, aged between twenty-five and forty-five, may be as high as 10,000 globally; the central stripe in the flag of South Sudan honours them. Over the years, a large number kept in contact with each other, held reunions, recalled the old battle songs (not your average elementary school reunion), and, early in 2013, came together in Juba to form the Red Army Foundation, a self-help group.

I went to the event at the run-down Nyakuron Cultural Center. It was an oddly moving combination of pride and nostalgia, sadness and idealism. While the RAF's just-elected chairman, Deng Bol Aruai Bol, looked on from his wheelchair on one side of the stage, Biar – the foundation's founder – grandiloquently recalled the early days. "We were unique among the battalions of the SPLA: we were the Red Army. We were tragedy and magnificence, we were desperation and glory. We were pushed to the very edge of doom. It was the best of times; it was the worst of times."

Many speakers – you could tell by their accents, their dreadlocks, their cool shades – had spent time in North America or Australia. But when it came to joining in the army's lilting anthem, entitled simply "1987," they sang along in Juba Arabic with tears in their eyes. Old generals took turns telling stories of how the Red Army had saved the day, time after time. Some of it was unabashed, even war-mongering nostalgia. One lumbering lieutenant-general in a sack of a suit recalled how they had destroyed a Sudanese convoy attempting to relieve Akobo. "We had given up; you saved us." But there were references to today's difficult times as well. "Many things are going wrong today. I am happy that the Red Army is back."

The history of the Red Army pointed to the odd combination of idealism and extreme disregard for human life that characterized the SPLA in the war years, and whose legacy we still lived with. These men in their thirties and forties represented the hope of this new country, its future leaders. But they had been trained to be killers when they were as young as ten. They saw those massacred who in other contexts would have been their playmates. It would take more than a generation for South Sudan to get over this situation. Just waiting for the old generals to die wouldn't be enough.

Not all the boys who went to Ethiopia and Kenya were drafted. A lucky few, deemed unfit for military service, were labelled "Seeds of the Nation." This is where the Canadian angle came in. With the support of Ethiopia's Marxist dictator Mengistu Haile Mariam, these brightest and best were sent to Cuba's Isle of Youth, where they received good schooling, many in medicine. But when word filtered back to the Ethiopian camps and to Cuba of the terrible losses their brothers were taking, many began to get cold feet about returning. They looked for other options. And with the simultaneous collapse of the Soviet Union and of Mengistu's regime in 1991, staying on in Cuba became moot. For Fidel, the boys were a financial burden he could no longer bear, but the new government in Ethiopia had no interest in having them back. A significant number – now fluent Spanish speakers – moved to Canada as twice-over refugees.

"We all remained in close contact," one of the Canadians told me when he came in with his passport. "It was like an old boys' club. We'd speak Cuban Spanish together and reminisce about the old days, about Ethiopia, about our childhood."

"So you were able to practise medicine in Canada?" I asked.

"No," he replied ruefully. "Few of us were fully qualified, we were still too young. And in any case, Cuban qualifications wouldn't have been recognized … It was really hard. We did all sorts of work, anything we could get."

"And then?"

"Then we started to understand that independence was really coming. We wanted to help, we were so excited, we wanted to go back, to do something … But what could we do?"

In 2006, a group approached the University of Calgary and Samaritan's Purse Canada – a faith-based organization affiliated with Franklin Graham's US-based Samaritan's Purse – to seek help to return as doctors. "So we did nine months' upgrading in Calgary, then a residency in Kenya … *y aquí estamos*! They call us the 'Cuban Jubans.' We often meet up at the Havana Club. The owner's a Canadian too; it's where they have the best salsa in South Sudan."

A few weeks later, I flew out with a little group of the Cuban Jubans to Akobo, in the far east of Jonglei on the border with Ethiopia. We were going to inaugurate a facility built by Samaritan's Purse with Canadian support and were taking along the state minister of health. One of the doctors was bringing his Kenyan-born wife to see his hometown for the first time (and to meet the in-laws). Another was to meet his prospective bride – also for the first time – after many arduous negotiations between Canada and Jonglei over the number of cows to be paid. He had a photo of her on an iPad that he proudly but nervously passed around. The mood on Samaritan's Purse's tiny aircraft veered from nervous jocularity to dead silence.

Akobo is a small town set amid swamps. It is more beautiful than it may sound, the length of a shady dead-straight avenue of plane trees planted in colonial days. The hospital was constructed by Presbyterian missionaries in the seventies and some of the outer buildings were crumbling, but as South Sudanese medical facilities go this was a good one, in green, spacious grounds. Through Samaritan's Purse, and to support the doctors' return, Canada had equipped a lab for blood testing and other diagnostics. An innovation had been the adaptation of microscopes to run on batteries and LED lights, as mains power was erratic to non-existent in most of South Sudan. Particularly valuable was a rugged and portable battery-powered ultrasound machine that allowed staff to make advanced diagnoses in remote districts accessible only by boat for much of the year.

Most patients we met were children suffering from malaria. There was also an intriguing seventy- or eighty-year-old lady who had fallen out of a tree and broken her arm, and the wrenching case of a two-year-old with severe malnutrition. Carlos, the young Congolese in charge, told us it was the fifth time the little boy had been brought in; this time they would try to keep him here for at least two months. His father was an alcoholic; the family social outcasts.

That trip ended happily. As we waited on the aircraft, worried that we might not get back to Juba in time for dark, the young groom-to-be came sprinting up. "Well?" we asked, ignoring his apologies. "Was she how you expected? And the parents?" The answer, as he gasped for breath, was a simple thumbs-up and a broad smile.

Ajak Abraham was another of the Cuban Jubans. He wrote out his story for me:

I was born on 15 March, 1972 in Malakal, South Sudan (although it was then known as Sudan). I belonged to a big family: my father married 4 wives and had 17 children. 4 of us followed his footsteps to become medical professionals: 2 docs and 2 nurses.

The second civil war broke out on 16 May 1983; it was not that easy. The government of Gaffer Mohammed Numeri was killing innocent people all over the South and especially in Bor, where the rebellion against his regime began. You cannot imagine how many lives were lost during those years of civil war. If you said any bad word against Numeri you would disappear overnight. I felt that if I could reach Ethiopia I would get a gun and return to fight against the dictatorship of Numeri. I did military training but Dr. John Garang did not allow me to come and fight. Because he said that we have another war to fight: to get educated, to go to school and return to help in the construction of our country when it became free.

For many years we waited to return to South Sudan but the war continued. I arrived in Luanda, Angola on 28 June 1986 and I spent 3 days there. Then, I arrived in Cuba on 1 July 1986.

However, Fidel Castro refused to send us back anymore to Africa because many of graduates from Cuba were being sent to the front line to fight; some of them were killed. That was why we went as refugees to Canada, until our country became free and we could return back home for the reconstruction of our nation.

I knew that Canada was a beautiful country but I did not know anything about snow: it was a big shock to me. At first it was difficult because I did not know how to speak English.

I like Canada because it is a country of opportunity and a peaceful nation, schools are there available to everyone who wants to learn. The only thing I dislike from Canada is the snow. I used to have contact with friends and relatives from South Sudan when I was there in Canada.

When the Comprehensive Peace Agreement was signed in Sudan in 2005, I was very excited and began thinking about going back home to help my people. I decided to come back because I knew that I would reunite with my family and to help my people. As you know our country has been experiencing a lot of difficulties, not only medically but in different areas.

When I finally came home, I was very disappointed to see the suffering of my people. Roads were very bad, buildings destroyed, no infrastructure at all. Now I am hoping to go for postgraduate education so I can help my people with new expertise.

But I do miss Canada.

Weekends, Jenny and I would sometimes walk along the garbage-strewn dirt road from the office, past a few bleating goats or ducks waddling around in pungent waste water, to the newly constructed Juba Regency Hotel, where there was a pool. One day I did a double-take when I looked up from my book and there, sitting calmly by the edge of the water scratching himself, was a large grey vervet monkey. The Ethiopian pool superintendent (nearly all the hotels were Ethiopian-run) smiled to us as he walked past with some fresh towels. "He used to live here," he explained with a shrug. "He keeps coming back; he does not know what has happened."

On Sundays, we'd join up with Catherine and a few friends and pack our inflatable kayaks in the back of a couple of Land Cruisers and head down to the river. The current was sufficiently fast – and the temperature so high – that paddling upstream was very hard work, so we had to make complicated logistical arrangements to be picked up several kilometres downstream from where we had put in. A favourite starting point was the Rajaf police academy, about ten kilometres upriver from Juba on the west bank of the Nile. One of the odder legacies of war was that, years after its end, officials remained extremely self-important and instinctively suspicious of foreigners doing anything without written permission. Perhaps they were unconsciously copying the Sudanese way: to leave the Sudanese capital, even to visit archeological sites, you needed a permit. But after we'd been to Rajaf five or six times, the police usually lounging around in the shade by the water's edge would just wave us onwards.

Barely ten minutes downstream from Rajaf, you'd find yourself racing towards the narrow bottom of the V that was the Rajaf Rapids. This one-kilometre-long stretch of white water was the obstacle that led the Victorian explorers of Upper Egypt finally to abandon their river-bound search for the source of the Nile, and look instead for its headwaters by coming in through East Africa. In a barely river-worthy toy canoe without lifejackets, these rapids could be quite intimidating, more so towards the end of the dry season. Then the river was low, and jagged black rocks jutted up through the brownish-white foam. Sometimes the standing breakers would swamp us, making the little grey rubber kayak impossible to steer, and we'd end up broadside before tumbling into the warm water. It could be quite a long swim to the reedy banks, where we'd bail the boat out and start again.

But below Rajaf the water was flat. We'd edge over into narrow side-branches of the river that seemed to be in a different place every time we came, and drift silently down. Bright yellow weaver-birds would flit through the branches to their ball-shaped woven nests; tall herons would eye us silently. When the sun climbed too high and there was no wind, we'd take turns flopping over the side to cool off. In season, we'd edge under the overhanging branches of huge mango trees and, holding on as the current tried to sweep us downstream, fill the kayak with twenty or thirty fresh mangoes. As we approached the banks, small naked children would rush down and wave, calling out, all in one breath, "How are you I am fine!"

After a couple of hours, the large rectangular block of a hotel that was being built at the Juba end of the Nile bridge would come into sight. We'd start to see pale blue water-tankers backed down to the river's edge, their big hoses loading fresh water for the city. There would be dozens of women doing their laundry, children splashing around energetically in the shallows, and tall and very black men pondering us speculatively as they soaped themselves. The river seemed to accelerate as we approached the bridge, and we'd line up to run through one of the five or six apertures formed by its visibly shaking pilings. You didn't want to get pinned sideways to the bridge supports.

Shooting out again from the shadows, on our left we'd pass a favourite place for expats to have their Sunday lunch: Da Vinci Restaurant. Then we'd be running past the port area, where great flat grey-painted steel barges and their three-storey pushers had nosed into the bank. Usually we'd be spotted by a couple of suspicious soldiers who would stand up and start shouting at us, but the current soon carried us past. We'd pull into the left bank at Mango Club, just in front of a huge, upended and semi-sunken rusty barge that, so the story had it, had been sunk by speculative shelling by the SPLA during the war.

Some days, instead of Rajaf, we'd put in at Mango and head downstream from Juba. There the river was wider, the banks less populated. Once, after we'd been picked up at the riverbank following a leisurely three-hour paddle north, we had to stop on the narrow and rutted dirt road that was taking us back to Juba. We found ourselves among herders of the Mundari people who were encamped a little way from the river's edge with thousands of cows. The cattle were uniformly pale, dun-coloured, with absolutely enormous curving horns up to a metre long; from above, the herd looked like a huge bed of thorns, gently undulating. Here and there, dung fires gave off thick grey and white smoke that hung low over the animals and made the yellow sun of this windless morning look orange. Ethereally tall and thin young men, naked and with spears in hand, moved gracefully about.

It was startling and frightening when one of the herders came out to the roadside. He was smeared from forehead to toe in grey ash – to keep the insects away – and had a ghost-like appearance. His short frizzy hair was a bleached yellowy-blonde, an effect of the cow urine that served as another form of insect repellent. If we hadn't been sitting in an air-conditioned Japanese vehicle, the scene could have been from a thousand years ago.

3

I Never Thought It Would Be So Messy

Juba, 2012

It didn't take long to get around the capital, located on generally flat land on the east bank of the Nile. At its centre was a network of twelve or fifteen kilometres of tarmac roads, with Airport Road leading up a gentle hill to a pair of city blocks that contained most government ministries as well as the National Legislature. This had been built as a regional assembly in the seventies. Close by was the presidential palace, still known by its old military name of J-1; it was invisible from outside its walls and guarded by a pair of ceremonial sentries in dark blue uniforms with gold epaulettes.

Around the city at some distance were two or three very distinctive granite outcrops, but it was often hazy and these were difficult to see, so it was quite easy to lose your bearings – there being no street signs, and little agreement as to what the main streets should be called. At night, the darkness was extreme, and it was not a good idea to lose your bearings. Negotiating our way home from a party at 9:00 one evening, we took a wrong turn into the back entrance for parliament. We were immediately surrounded by heavily armed soldiers who banged their weapons on the embassy Land Cruiser, alternately shouting obscenities and the word "Spy!"

Most of the roads were of deeply rutted brown or red earth, strewn with garbage that gave off an odour from which you could never really escape. Goats, ducks, and chickens were hazards to be avoided; occasionally you would encounter a few cows lumbering stolidly along, their heads swaying under enormous sets of horns. There was a tall, completely naked man striding up and down Airport Road at all hours, head down and muttering to himself; nobody appeared to pay him any attention. In the rainy season, some of the roads turned into longitudinal lakes and it was easy to get bogged down.

It rarely took more than ten or fifteen minutes to get anywhere, but the roads were so poor and unpredictable that I left the job to our office drivers, Mandrea and Abanja (and later David). The principal hazard was *boda bodas*, the local name given to motorbike taxis that would weave in and out of the traffic and cut you off with studied insouciance; none of their riders wore helmets and accidents were frequent. The rest of the traffic was made up of expensive Toyota V-8s with tinted windows belonging to senior government officials, white Land Cruisers with the logos of the UN or 180 or more international non-governmental organizations, and diplomatic vehicles distinguished by red and white number plates with a different code for each country.

When we had visitors, they often asked us what they should see in Juba. This left us scratching our heads. In the older part of town, if you carried on straight from the airport instead of turning right to the ministries, there were a number of low stone buildings used largely as warehouses that dated from maybe 1910, as did a nearby mosque with a high, square tower. John Garang was buried in a fenced-off area next to a grandstand that was used for public events, but you couldn't visit the grave; in fact, you were likely to be shot if you got too close. In the middle of one roundabout, informally known as Time Square on account of a no-longer-working digital clock on a black pylon, there was an inconspicuous grey marble monument that listed the principal explorers that had come this way, but you had to be quick to make out the names of Charles Gordon and Emin Pasha as you careered around. Probably the best thing to do was just to sit and look at the Nile, from a table at Da Vinci, under the shade of a mango tree.

One of the rituals of diplomatic life, shortly after your arrival at post, is to pay calls on your counterparts at friendly "likeminded" missions. This helps you find out what the consensus view about your host country is, and also ensures that you make your way onto other embassies' guest lists for receptions and meetings.

In every capital, the constellation of missions is different, both in size and in the way in which the embassies relate to each other. In Juba, there were twenty-eight foreign embassies in 2012, with the "donors" making up one club, the Africans another. Then there were the Chinese, who had major oil interests on both sides of the new Sudan/South Sudan border and were big players too, but by no means an easy fit with the donors; they usually abstained when it came to criticism of the new country at the UN in New York. Japan, often considered a member of the Western club, had a large development program but was an outlier vis-à-vis the rest in that – like China – it was reluctant to engage in anything that might look like criticism of the host country. But to their credit, both Japan and China were major contributors of troops to the UN's peacekeeping operation; they far outdid the West (including Canada: our contribution was around ten mid-level officers, compared to Japan's 400-strong contingent). Among the G-8 countries, only Russia had no presence. Russia had no stake to speak of in South Sudan but could be unhelpful in New York; it usually voted according to the climate of its relations at the time with the US, and not on the issues at hand.

Within the Western grouping was a self-selected subset known as the "troika": the US, the UK, and Norway. These three countries worked together supporting the long negotiations that had culminated in the 2005 Comprehensive Peace Agreement and had generally continued to function as a unit ever since. The troika, by design or by default, had given the new government in South Sudan the impression that they spoke on behalf of the entire Western diplomatic community. This created resentment among lesser but still significant donors such as Canada and the Netherlands, and some awkwardness for the ambassador of the European Union, in that one of its members (the UK) claimed a relationship with the host government that was closer than (but not as financially significant as) that of the EU as a whole.

The troika had special weight between 2011 and 2014, because the special representative of the secretary-general (SRSG) of the United Nations for South Sudan – the czar of the UN's largest peacekeeping, and later humanitarian, operation in the world – was the Norwegian Hilde Johnson, and the Norwegian ambassador had privileged access to her that by rights should have been enjoyed equally by all member states.

———

While the US was, as usual, the biggest mission in town, I decided to start my rounds with the British who – given their extensive historical knowledge of the greater Sudan and (compared to the US) their more hands-off approach to self-determination for the South – seemed to me best qualified to be both neutral and knowledgeable.

Indeed, it was the British who had, for the purpose of internal administrative convenience, drawn the line that now determined South Sudan's northern border.

"Ah yes, the maps…" said Ambassador Alastair McPhail, soon after we had sat down in his spartan office in the grey two-storey prefabricated building that served as the British Embassy, on a compound shared with several other European countries. "You know, the South Sudanese believe that we have hidden away in London the map that will justify their claims to all those pieces of land still in Sudan that they believe should be theirs … It's cobblers, of course."

McPhail, a plain-speaking and rather dour Scotsman, had been on this file for at least a decade and was closely involved in the negotiations leading up to the peace agreement. He was proud of his title as the dean of the Western diplomatic corps in Juba. "I have to say that the UK is still basking in the afterglow of the huge enthusiasm generated by the presence of Foreign Secretary Hague on Independence Day; what they liked above all was that he announced the immediate opening of our embassy, complete with ambassador in place. That was me, although I was possibly the only ambassador in the world living in a tent."

The ambassador was not at pains to hide that the United States was the UK's preferred partner in South Sudan's difficult transition from war to peace, from utter deprivation to economic promise. He was dismissive of occasional pronouncements by government officials tending to minimize the US's contribution. "They could have no better friend than Washington." He was worried by some signs of xenophobia, occasionally reminiscent of the Eritrean experience, and was also concerned that all too often, notably in the drafting of a bill regulating the activities of non-governmental organizations (NGOs), Juba was aping Khartoum, but with no sense of irony.

The ambassador was a lot less enthusiastic regarding the third partner in the troika: Norway. He left no doubt that he had little time for SRSG Hilde Johnson (formerly Norway's international development minister), an animosity that he confessed went back years, and was short with her book on the peace process. Reviewing the first eighteen months of the existence of the Republic of South Sudan, McPhail described the government's performance as "underwhelming" (practise that in a slow Scots brogue). He was disappointed (but not surprised) that neither party had yet got over the acrimony of their divorce. Juba continued to take the Western donors for granted (as did the SPLA in war time). "We are all doing a lot ... but often we get a lot of nonsense in return," he declared.

Over to the Norwegians, and Ambassador Hanne-Marie Kaarstadt. Norway had always been good at carving out foreign policy niches for itself – Sri Lanka, the Middle East, Colombia – and sticking with them year after year, regardless of political change at home. Results were often slow in coming – if at all – but one effect of this approach was that, in a few locations around the world, Norway punched way above its weight. Over the decades, Oslo had stuck not just with certain issues and countries but – in the case of Southern Sudan – had also stood by its major non-governmental agencies (Norwegian People's Aid, Norwegian Church Aid) in the form of dependable and substantial funding. A spin-off from this close, sustained focus was the cadre of Norwegian experts who moved effortlessly from government to non-governmental organizations, to the UN and back again. Hilde Johnson (previously on the board of NCA, and a government minister) was such an individual.

In Juba at this time, the niche for Norway wasn't just its long history and its developmental investment; it was oil. After an ill-advised foray by South Sudanese troops across the border to the oil-pumping station at Heglig, in January 2012 Juba had shut down its wells rather than pay Khartoum what it considered to be extortionate fees for use of the sole export pipeline, which ran north through Sudanese territory. At a stroke, it deprived itself of 98 per cent of its revenue. Much diplomatic capital on many sides had since been expended bringing the two countries to a tentative agreement signed in Addis Ababa in September 2012. "The turning on again of the taps," the ambassador suggested, "this is the point of agreement that has the best chance of success, because both countries stand to gain so much. But the key will be to keep cooperation at a very technical level. We have to keep it all rational."

It was hoped that getting the money to flow on both sides would build trust and set an example for other more politically contentious areas of cooperation. The critical area would be metering. "The thing is," Hanne-Marie went on with a smile, "the oil fed into the pipeline by a multitude of feeders has to match the output in Port Sudan, which in turn has to match the quantity of oil put onto the market."

It was widely thought that the sudden dismissal some time ago of the top China National Petroleum Company (CNPC) executive in South Sudan was linked to the discovery of a pipeline that bypassed the existing metering system, sparing CNPC from paying its full share of transit and other dues to both governments. Norway had offered itself as the third-party supervisor of metering arrangements. "But don't forget," the ambassador said, "oil will probably only be a short-term resource here. The projections show maybe eight or ten years more of good production, no more. They all have production peaking in 2014–15; the happiest story has non-oil revenues rising to meet declining oil income, with the two crossing in 2019. But I think that is pretty optimistic."

Oil was only one of many bones of contention between the two Sudans. The ambassador singled out the ongoing conflict in the Nuba Mountains as the most intractable issue. "It's become a matter of desperation, one of cultural survival. This is why the SPLA/ North is making increasingly reckless attacks, including on Kadugli, killing civilians … and meanwhile Sudan is going all-out for a military solution, confident that the international community – having pushed hard on both South Sudan and Darfur – has no appetite to intervene."

Internal political machinations were currently giving much grist to the Juba rumour mill: "It seems to me that that political alliances within the SPLM/A are far from settled," the ambassador said. There was, to begin with, that longstanding tension between those who were in the bush, those who were in comfortable exile in Kenya, Uganda, or the West (including Canada), and those who were in Khartoum. Then there was resentment and mutual suspicion concerning the myriad militias that were pulled into the SPLM/A's big tent at the time of the Comprehensive Peace Agreement and following. There was a large segment of the military who were bitter over the April 2012 pull-back from Heglig, another segment aggrieved over wage cuts and late payment, a further group that was upset over how demobilization was being managed. And then there were the perennial ethnic tensions that put paid to the original Addis Agreement after the first civil war. "But with all of this going on, President Kiir has been invisible; he has communicated no vision. With the oil now coming back on line, he needs more than ever to be seen and heard – expectations need managing."

My own expectations (or at least hopes) that the ambassador would be disposed to have the troika relax its exclusivity went nowhere. She thought the troika was already being too lax in allowing the EU and the UN to join its discussions with government. I could see why she was being so defensive. Tiny Norway, whose financial commitment to South Sudan was substantial but by no means in the very top tier, had unique access that it did not wish to dilute in the name of diplomatic collegiality.

My Dutch colleague commented philosophically, "It would be a bit like Britain or France voting to expand the UN Security Council. I think you have a saying in North America that covers it: turkeys don't vote for Christmas."

US ambassador Susan Page had been involved with Sudan for over a decade, like her old friend Alastair McPhail at the UK mission, and all her assignments with the foreign service had been in Africa. Her surprisingly cramped office was in a labyrinthine building adjoining the EU compound that needed some renovation and had been the headquarters of USAID in Southern Sudan for many years.

This ambassador was also disappointed but not greatly surprised by the travails of the South Sudan administration since independence. "It seems that the government – or at least President Kiir – lacks vision; nobody knows what he wants to do with the country, where he wants to take it. He is showing signs of paranoia, making his foreign trips shorter. He's right to be afraid," she suggested. The threat was not necessarily from Vice-President Riek Machar – "it is not conceivable that a Nuer could garner sufficient support to rule South Sudan" – but from other Dinka personalities, some of them highly placed. Particularly disappointing, in the US's estimation, had been the lack of governmental follow-up to loud and repeated pledges to crack down on corruption and make the country's rulers more accountable to their people. "At the very least they could have confiscated a few flashy cars ... but nothing has been done."

A major obstacle to the progress of this new state which was beyond the government's control, Page mused, was the absence of a culture of entrepreneurship. This had led to an influx of Ugandans, Kenyans, and many others, who had taken over markets and small businesses. As and when Arab traders were allowed to move into the South again, this shortcoming would become even more apparent (and could further aggravate nascent xenophobia). "The issue is a cultural one," she said. "It will take more than a generation for things to change. Dinkas are proud, not prepared for service ... it is beneath their dignity."

I raised an issue that had come up at an earlier meeting with Mireille Girard, the country representative of the UN's High Commission for Refugees (UNHCR): the current location of the principal refugee camp that accepted persons fleeing war in the Nuba Mountains. Yida was perilously close to the border and vulnerable to attack from Sudan, and its proximity encouraged the SPLA/N to use it both for R&R and for recruiting. Page sat up in her chair: "Those refugees should be left where they are! It would be shameful to try to persuade them to move elsewhere by bribing them with education and agricultural support!"

This position was held only by the US. The explanation for it was years of commitment by successive US administrations to the cause of the Nubans, and to American NGOs, especially Franklin Graham's faith-based Samaritan's Purse, working in Nuba against the objections of the Khartoum administration. Moving the camp further away from the border would make their job more difficult. I'd learn more about this in the course of a number of visits to Yida.

Pretty much everywhere in the world, the US is accused of secretly – or not-so-secretly – plotting to secure access to oil. The conspiracy theorists believed that South Sudan was no exception. "Well, Exxon is certainly planning a joint venture with Total for Jonglei State, but as you can guess, the security situation there means things aren't going anywhere ... As for the active oil fields, what with the goings-on of the past eighteen months and the prospects for things staying sticky for a while yet, I can't imagine anyone's too interested in replacing the Chinese on the border."

And the troika? Ambassador Page responded cautiously, "I hear you." But she would never do anything about it.

———

In Khartoum a decade earlier, I'd seen a lot of Nhial Bol, the tall and then very thin Dinka who, along with his boss, the much bulkier Alfred Taban (from Equatoria), kept the English-language press going amid great difficulties. Disciple and master subsequently had a falling out, but both had moved to Juba with the signature of the Comprehensive Peace Agreement. Bol's *Citizen* – with a pair of warthogs eyeing each other as the dots on the *Citizen's* i's – controlled most of the market, with Alfred's *Juba Monitor* appearing only sporadically.

The *Citizen* had a print run of about 8,000, sold for two Sudanese pounds (then worth fifty cents US), and reached most of South Sudan sooner or later. Newsprint was imported from Uganda (twenty-five to thirty tons represented a three-month supply) and the paper was printed on an outdated press in a large corrugated-iron shed off Airport Road, quite close to the Canadian office. Running to sixteen pages, this was not a world-class paper: many stories were printed verbatim from internet sources (complete with hyperlinks, as in Khartoum) and the grammar and punctuation of the locally produced articles were sometimes idiosyncratic. But at least there were no gaping white spaces such as I used to find in the *Khartoum Monitor* after the censors had descended and no need for cheeky but captionless cartoons of zippered mouths. A regular column featuring often obscene one-line jokes attracted no attention whatsoever.

The paper did take on controversial themes. Over a period of ten days in October 2012, it ran criticism of ostensibly racist and anti-Sudanese comments made by the speaker of Israel's Knesset, a lively discussion on the death penalty, and a worthy if very wordy multi-part series on "Why Corruption Is a Bad Thing."

Nhial Bol was as tall as ever, but had bulked up and scarcely fit in the tatty armchair in his dark office, where the power was off. "So, what are your red lines?" I asked him.

"Well, they vary. Right now, it's anything said by or about Lam Akol, and corruption in government."

Lam Akol, a Shillook politician whom I'd known in Khartoum where he had been a minister, was still in self-imposed exile in the capital of Sudan and was widely whispered to be plotting subversion. And on the corruption front, the story on the street was a letter supposedly written by the president to seventy members of the elite asking them to return US$4 billion embezzled from government accounts. The US Embassy was rumoured to have a list of the addressees. Surprise, surprise: none were thought to have responded with a cheque.

Nhial was periodically summoned for friendly warnings on both these questions.

"So, would you call this censorship?"

"No, I don't take it that way. When I have news, I'm prepared to publish ... and I don't think they'll necessarily throw me in jail again."

Very occasionally, visitors would turn hostile, even aggressive.

"So, how do you deal with that?"

"Very simple," he answered with a light smile. "I tell them that if they go for me, my people will come after them and kill them all. They usually go away then."

I'd see quite a lot of Nhial subsequently; as in Khartoum, he was not shy in responding to invitations to diplomatic gatherings. "Yes, there is a tendency towards dictatorship in South Sudan," he'd admit. "But you know what? This will never be a dictatorship like Eritrea's. To be a dictator you have to be efficient and you have to have a vision. Neither apply in our case." What there was, in lieu of focus, he would go on, was a "violent, authoritarian instinct." Nhial recalled a ludicrous situation in which media representatives were violently ejected from covering a completely non-controversial ceremony at John Garang's mausoleum. "Paranoia is the rule. No one in government has any concept at all of media liaison and the idea of embedding reporters with the military is a completely alien one. Did you know the entire South Sudan delegation to the recent peace talks in Addis was forbidden to speak to South Sudanese media and no South Sudanese media were allowed anywhere near them?" he asked.

Fourteen months from independence, Nhial thought the main failure of the government was its failure to provide any meaningful services. "There's no focus ... They don't know what they want and they don't know what to do ... So much international assistance is being wasted." More positively, he felt that the interethnic feuding many had thought would take place after the war was not (yet) materializing. Much of the violence seen in rural South Sudan, he said, was the result of a lack of access to justice, although cattle disputes quickly took on a tribal colouring if not immediately halted.

Citizen TV would be Nhial's next venture. He showed me two carpet-lined studios, pointed to a dusty pile of electronic equipment that he had picked up in a fire sale a few years earlier, and said that he'd already secured agreement from Zain Telecommunications to broadcast using their telephone towers. "And I've got this great scheme that will allow us to beam our signal down-Nile from Juba as far as Bor, from a floating barge. As long as we get it in exactly the right position, we can avoid any hills ... What do you think?"

Eleven years after seeing her in Khartoum as a leading light of the Sudan Council of Churches, I caught up with Joy Kwaje, MP, in her quiet office off echoing hallways on the top floor of the National

Legislature. Always colourfully dressed in the traditional Equatorian way, including a large turban, she served several of the post-CPA years as an MP, then was appointed chair of the South Sudan Human Rights Commission, and was back in parliament as chair of the Parliamentary Committee of Information, Telecom and Culture, and representing a Juba constituency. She was quieter these days, more pensive; not just older, but also sobered by the responsibilities and compromises of prominent public office; her tenure at the Human Rights Commission had not been a comfortable one.

Her committee had three media-related bills on its agenda: the Broadcasting Corporation Bill, the Media Authority Bill, and the Access to Information Bill. Right through 2015, the so-called "Media Bills" would remain controversial. Periodically there would be rumours that they had been passed into acts, but then there would be counter-claims that no one had actually seen a signed version of any of them. Alfred Taban seriously suggested at one point that the three bills had been lost and/or were languishing in a locked drawer "to which no one has the key."

"The most difficult is the Media Authority Bill," Joy Kwaje told me, after we had quietly reminisced for a while in the dark (there was no power in parliament either). "It was first tabled in 2007, withdrawn following widespread complaints, and re-tabled in July 2012. Its stated intent is to safeguard the independence of the media. But this is completely undercut by provisions that allow the government to name all members of the supervising authority." Her committee was looking at regional experiences, including those of Tanzania, Ghana, and Kenya. Tanzania was also being looked at as a possible model for the Access to Information Bill.

She considered her cultural responsibilities to be important. Top of the agenda in late 2012 was an ambitious project to construct a national museum, possibly with support from UNESCO and the British Council. "Yes, I know there are enormous financial pressures on the government," she conceded. "But, you know, we really need to do everything we can to create a sense of nationhood … before it's too late. Every country needs a national museum, somewhere that people can learn about their own country."

Joy admitted, hesitantly, that South Sudan remained a de facto one-party state: "It is really important, in this context, that civil society and the media be empowered to speak out and hold the government's feet to the fire. Unfortunately, the Sudan Council of Churches is in" – she grasped for an appropriate euphemism – "some disarray, a transition phase." She trailed off and looked at me with a weak, tired smile. "You know, Nicholas, when we were in opposition it was so easy. It's a lot more difficult now than I ever thought it would be."

Jeremiah Swaka, Joy Kwaje's perpetually angry sidekick at the Sudan Council of Churches in Khartoum, had also prospered. He was now undersecretary at the Ministry of Justice. After making an appointment, I went round to see him in his office. He was a little greyer but otherwise unchanged. "Yes, yes, Nicholas, sit down," and he waved me impatiently into an armchair.

Over the next hour and a quarter, one person after another came in. Jeremiah would break off in mid-sentence, grab whatever file was timidly proffered to him, berate the official at the top of his voice, and send him packing again to redo, rewrite, resubmit. The interruptions grew longer and longer, and his temper rose each time. After a time, I quietly got up. He didn't even see me go.

I didn't bother him again. His job was an important one. The Ministry of Justice oversaw the drafting of every single piece of legislation that was passed to the legislature, and undertook the rewrites as required. But he had a reputation now of being arbitrary, rude, and difficult, and his ministry allowed the passage of bills that sometimes were as bad as those against which he had railed so virulently and loudly in Khartoum. Like Joy Kwaje, Jeremiah Swaka was finding the transition from opposition to government a challenging one.

Time had not treated Alfred Taban, Nhial Bol's former boss at the *Khartoum Monitor* and now editor of the *Juba Monitor*, so well. Repeatedly imprisoned and beaten by the Sudanese authorities, he had subsequently suffered two strokes. Mentally he was still fine, very much the voice of reason and moderation and widely respected by his peers as the dean of the South Sudan journalistic fraternity. But he was frail and slow on his feet, his voice a little slurred, and he had neither the ethnicity nor the character that would have allowed him to threaten any would-be persecutors.

When we first caught up in 2012, Alfred was having real problems keeping his paper in business. On account of their falling out (or so I deduced...), Nhial would not allow him access to the *Citizen*'s printing press, then the only one in Juba. So text for the *Juba Monitor* was set on computers in Juba and sent by e-mail to Khartoum, where the paper was printed; it was then dispatched on the morning Marsland flight (when there was one ... services could be suspended for weeks on end) back to Juba, for onward distribution.

To my unspoken question, Alfred chuckled and replied, "You know, we can be as critical as we like of Sudan, as long as no copies of the paper are allowed to leak from the press into Khartoum." He confirmed many of the observations made to me by Nhial Bol, in that there was no direct censorship in South Sudan and very few – if any – taboo subjects. Corruption was a sensitive theme but after running a story on the subject, the most Alfred might expect was a call or a visit from an official. "It is nothing like what I used to go through in Khartoum," he said.

The problem was more the unpredictability and sheer amateurishness of security officials. Much later, in the wake of the December 2013 crisis, Alfred would have his entire print run seized, "Because we ran a photo of Riek Machar on page 1, Salva Kiir on page 3." Another time, production was halted because of an article that suggested that the internal conflict in South Sudan was ethnic in nature, by then a commonplace observation. We talked about corruption and some of the names circulating at the time. "Pagan Amum?" (Then SPLM secretary-general and top government negotiator.) "He's salted away millions. The finance minister, Kosti Manibe? Well, he has a well-deserved reputation for probity and tight-fistedness ... did you know that he's restricted the right to sign customs exemptions to only two named individuals?"

I was pleased to hear this about Kosti, our landlord. Although we often talked about nothing more than maintaining the trees in the yard, it was some comfort to be told that Alfred, at least, did not think I was in league with a person seen as an out-and-out crook. "But you know what happens?" Alfred went on, in reference to Kosti Manibe. "This drastically cuts down on vast amounts of imports coming in tax-free. So, instead, more and more favour-seekers go directly to the president. He drinks heavily most nights. So, if you want a favour you wait until he is far gone and then present your written request for signature."

On account of his honesty, Alfred suggested, Kosti was quite likely to be fired; he was simply too great an obstacle to the movement's patronage machine. And that is indeed what happened. The president's support base, he continued, had over the past year or so withered to his fellow Bahr-al-Ghazal Dinkas, notably the then governor of Northern Bahr-al-Ghazal State, Paul Malong, and the governor of Western Bahr-al-Ghazal, Rizik Zachariah Hassan, whom Salva Kiir vigorously (and intemperately) supported on the occasion of recent violent uprisings in Wau, publicly stating, "I too would have shot those demonstrators."

Contrary to longstanding popular wisdom, Alfred thought the country could now accept a Nuer president, i.e. then vice-president Riek Machar. But would Riek actively manoeuvre to seek the top office? Probably not (this with some prescience): "He will wait until things implode, then move in." Alfred pointed out that, in an effort to marginalize his rivals from the Bor Dinka within SPLA power structures, Salva Kiir had effectively empowered many Nuers. While the Bor Dinka were still disproportionately represented on the military general staff, the then chief of the general staff, James Hoth, was Nuer, as were a significant majority of the lower ranks of the SPLA.

Like many South Sudanese who had returned either from Khartoum or from the broader diaspora, Alfred complained that all except those who "were in the bush" were treated as second class when it came to political preferment. With some bitterness, he added, "As if we did not suffer in Khartoum as well." He reflected on the last time we had met. "All that time, I was sure that one day we would gain independence. I never doubted it. But I never thought it would be so messy."

4

The Murle War

Pibor, Jonglei State, 2012–2015

Juba International Airport in 2012 had a strong claim to be the worst international airport in the world. By the time I left, in 2016, its credentials were even stronger: for nearly a year it had been possibly the only capital city's airport to close every weekend for runway repairs.

Incoming aircraft usually took the precaution of executing a preliminary circle well before landing, to scan the vicinity thoroughly. The airport had no radar, and electricity cuts often meant the tower lacked radio communication as well, so it was a good idea to perform your own air traffic control. As you landed, you could make out the wreckage of a downed MiG in the long grass on one side, and the dusty remains of a Trans Arabian 707 pulled off to the other. The pilot parked wherever he could, so you might have to walk up to a kilometre in blazing hot sunshine to reach the ramshackle, one-storey terminal.

The arrivals hall was the size of a classroom, with no air conditioning or fans, and it never seemed to be cleaned. Here you might have to wait up to an hour to have your passport stamped by a usually surly official or, having waited patiently for forty minutes, you would be inexplicably directed to another line with no one in attendance. A glass partition separated this room from an adjoining one where another man in a uniform would wordlessly demand your just-stamped passport again, idly examine every page for what seemed like minutes, and, if you were lucky, wave you on.

Bags were delivered through an irregular hole bashed in the wall of the second room. They were then passed through a single scanner (if the electricity was on) to pile up on the filthy floor at one end of the scanner's short conveyor belt. By this point, there could be seventy or eighty sweating passengers crammed into the room, each craning to see if their bag was one of those accumulating. If yours was one of them, you needed to force your way through the scrum, seize the bag, heave it up onto the adjoining waist-high wooden counter, and try to catch the eye of the solitary policeman whose role it was to open, search, and mark every incoming case with a chalk hieroglyphic. Non-diplomatic passengers would have their clothes rifled through and a few random items – usually ladies' underwear – pulled out onto the counter with momentary interest before the officer moved onto the next bag, forgetting the all-important chalk mark. By waving my red diplomatic passport, I was usually able to escape this humiliation.

Next came more pushing through the crowd to a narrow doorway where a final policeman asked to see the chalk mark and your baggage tag. Then out into the blazing sun, the dirt-paved carpark, and the touts shouting "Taxi" at you.

Departing was even more of an ordeal. Most traffic left early in the morning, and there could be five or six hundred people trying to force their way into the similarly sized departure hall. The inevitable bad-tempered policeman on a stool controlled the first entry point. There was no point in showing up prudently early, as he would not let you in until you were visibly panicking about missing your flight. Once inside, you needed to identify which of the rickety wooden tables around two sides of the gloomy, unlit classroom was yours; they varied each time, with the UN and the commercial companies vying daily for the prime spots.

It was always necessary to force your way through with your elbows, using your bag as a battering ram, so crowded was the room. Once you knew the drill, your first objective was the single scale concealed behind a pillar. Here the bag was weighed, the figure in kilos scribbled on your ticket by a small boy. Even by 8:00 in the morning you were irritated and sweating profusely; so was everybody else. Check-in at the counter relied on laptops the harassed staff had brought with them; however, the power would often be out, so that everything had to be done manually. With boarding pass in hand, you heaved your bag to the outgoing scanner and – with trepidation – watched it disappear through another hole in a wall.

Passport control occupied the third side of the classroom. It never took less than half an hour to get through, as the four fingermark-smeared windows were always under-staffed. Woe betide you if the visa of the person ahead of you was not in order; the officer would disappear for fifteen minutes and a wail of despair would go up.

Running at ninety degrees to this lineup and confusingly bisecting it was another slow-moving single file to get into the departure room where, once again, every bag would be searched. Here the red diplomatic passport was of no use. Once inside and hotter than ever, you would usually find that the fifty or sixty metal chairs were occupied and people were standing on all sides and in the aisles. You might spot a pair of empty seats in the middle but once you forced your way through to them, you would find that a foul-smelling liquid was dripping from the ceiling and had inundated the rubbish-strewn floor. In one corner the TV was on, usually tuned to Al Jazeera broadcasting in Arabic. As for the washroom: a single stall for men and another for women had been built out into the room; the men's door did not close, and both sides smelled as if they had never been cleaned.

Many of the office's diplomatic visitors to Juba would later thank us for what they said was the single best piece of advice they had been given: "When leaving South Sudan, take all measures to ensure that you do not need to use the airport washrooms." Over the course of four years, I made many exits from JIA, but it never got any better.

———————

A frequent destination over my first year or so was Jonglei State.

The state – which took up most of the territory of South Sudan that lies between the River Nile and the Ethiopian border – was the largest of the country's ten, the most undeveloped, and one of the most ethnically complicated. The state capital, Bor, birthplace of the war in 1983, was a Dinka stronghold, but the Nuer occupied northern and eastern swathes and the smaller Murle tribe was centered on remote Pibor County. Only Bor was more or less accessible by road all year round. Once the rains began in April and May, most of the rest of the settlements of Jonglei became islands in a swamp for eight or nine months.

If you talked to anyone in Juba about the Murle, there would often be a grimace of distaste. "The Murle? The most primitive people you can imagine. They are all syphilitic, that's why they abduct Nuer and Dinka children."

The epidemiologists would argue over the prevalence or otherwise of syphilis,[1] but much of the stigmatization of the Murle was due to the fact that they had been sympathetic to Khartoum during the war (or rather, unsympathetic to the SPLA) and during periods when the SPLA occupied Pibor in the civil war, the military in turn did nothing to endear themselves to the Murle. In the post-war years Pibor was ignored, and antagonism between the Murle and their neighbours grew deeper, manifested in unusually bloody bouts of cattle-raiding and abductions. It was very difficult to find objective commentary, but most people with whom I spoke considered that blame for this fell primarily on the Murle.

The Murle term for non-Murle, I learned from NGOs working with cattle-camp youth, was *moden*, which also meant "enemy."[2] Unlike the Dinka and Nuer, whose hierarchies were based on seniority with chiefs and elders in the lead, the Murle were predominantly stratified into age sets,[3] each one of which named itself. Age-set loyalty was so strong that in the case of one set coming into conflict with another – which was frequent – age loyalties were stronger than blood ties. Thus, a young man might kill his brother rather than betray his set, and might compete for women with his own father.

As in the case of the Dinka and Nuer – but more so, for very few Murle were urbanized – social and cultural life revolved around cattle. Jon Arensen, the pre-eminent expert on the Murle (whose son Mike was now following his lead in South Sudan), describes how they acquire their individual names:

> All Murle boys receive a secret name when they become a man. A father gives his son a large ox with beautiful colors and spreading horns. The boy then makes a riddle based on the color of this name-ox. He then goes to an old man who remembers the Toposa language. The riddle is shortened to a couple of Toposa words and this becomes the boy's manhood name for the rest of his life. He will tell his friends his new name, but the meaning remains a secret.[4]

Cows – these days up to eighty or ninety – are the essential element of a Murle dowry, which is divided among the bride's relatives; the Murle speak of relatives as "people who have cattle between them" (*atenoc*).

In 2010, David Yau Yau, a tall young Murle of the Bothonya age set and a former student of theology, ran for parliament in Pibor county against the preferred candidate of the SPLM. He lost badly. Allegedly with some support from a dissident ex-SPLA general

– George Athor – he launched a desultory insurrection in and around Pibor, sustained by the weapons Athor was able to obtain for him from the Khartoum government. This insurrection came to an end in mid-2011. But when in 2012 the SPLA began a brutal campaign of civilian disarmament in Pibor (subsequently documented in detail by Amnesty International[5] and Human Rights Watch[6]) and Athor was killed in mysterious circumstances, Yau Yau went back to the bush and revolted again. This time, with Murle bitterness against the Dinka-dominated SPLA deeper than ever, he was able to recruit a much larger cohort. Indeed, so aggressive had the disarmament campaign been that hundreds of children voluntarily joined his ranks.

In March 2013, after a long build-up including the shipping of tanks across the Nile by the SPLA, the first major armed clash occurred. The SPLA, with my old friend from Unity, Nuer general Peter Gadet, in command, claimed to have killed seven rebels and captured armaments in the first confrontation. There was speculation that the Ethiopian military had been recruited to ensure that Yau Yau did not escape. The government forces also cemented an alliance with the traditional enemy of the Murle to the north, the Lou Nuer. The most influential of the Nuer prophets, a colourful leopard-skin-clad figure with sea-shells in his hair who went by the name of Dak Kueth, held a meeting in Waat with 500 Lou warriors. After sacrificing cattle and examining their entrails, he instructed them to wait for the SPLA to finish their operations first, but to move to the borders with Pibor "in preparation."

The UN, in light of these developments, warned diplomats in Juba, "We are heading for a bloody offensive." The UN Mission in South Sudan had a modest 148 troops in this, the hottest spot in the country; a tiny number compared with, for example, the 15,000 that MONUSCO simultaneously had stationed in the Democratic Republic of Congo's hotspot, around Goma. Better than nothing, you would think. But the Indian battalion in question would not do foot patrols. Its commander required a generous forty litres of fresh water per man per day; this kept one Mi-8 helicopter ferrying water every daylight hour. The cynics in Juba considered them useless.

On 23 March, I received word through NGO friends that the Lou Nuer had begun mobilizing in Waat, Pieri (Nyirol County), and Yuai (Uror County). "They are sorting out their weapons," my contact said, "mostly in Pieri under the eye of Dak Kueth, and preparing to move towards the border of Pibor." A couple of days later, Catherine and I teamed up to take an UNMISS helicopter out to Pibor. It was an hour to Bor, another hour and a half east to Pibor, the clattering in the empty hold making all conversation impossible. Below us, what was remarkable was the emptiness: pancake-flat savannah with scarcely a tree, only the very occasional and very lonely *tukul*, on a slight elevation, breaking the monotony. Occasionally there would be a flash of silver sunlight, reflected from below, to remind you that much of what looked like an easily walkable plain was in fact swamp.

The airstrip at Pibor was a litter-strewn field of rutted mud. It was still hard-baked at this, the end of the dry season, but in the Wet it would be a heavy, black morass that clung to boots in great clumps. We were met by Vijay, the genial Indian UN air ops liaison-officer, and shown a residential container in which to dump our bags, and we headed off to explore.

"Town" was a small group of three or four one-storey concrete buildings in a compound overlooking a river that was all but dry that day, and a few hundred straw-roofed and mud-walled *tukuls*. I was struck, as I often would be in South Sudan, at how temporary, how tenuous this settlement seemed. But I remembered that Pibor had been something of a regional centre in colonial times. A brass plaque in the small colonial-era Christian chapel that sits within the presidential grounds in Khartoum recalls the death of a young man killed in a flying accident at Pibor in the 1920s.

The market was a fifteen-minute walk away: a street 150 metres long, with twenty or thirty shops on each side, made mainly from corrugated iron sheets and plastic sheeting. Only about half of the shops were open. A lorry was loading goods: it was emptying the shop, not replenishing it. There were dozens of well-armed men milling about, a few of whom were visibly inebriated.

Figuring out what each uniform meant in South Sudan was an arcane science, especially when jackets and pants were mismatched, flip-flops often replaced boots, and more pride was taken in designer shades and tassels in the gun barrel than in military dress. But there had recently been an influx of the tan-uniformed, loosely organized auxiliary police, and there were also many usually rare military police about, with bright red shoulder flashes. These were a response to public grievances against the Pibor garrison of the SPLA for ill-discipline and drunkenness. Absolutely everyone was flouting the commissioner's repeated requests that firearms not be brought into the market. We were in and out of the market several times over the next two days; we never saw a single UNMISS soldier on patrol.

Over at the county offices, Joshua Konyi, the bulky Murle county commissioner (the senior civilian authority) was in relaxed mode, lolling in a plastic chair under a tree in the compound. Camped just outside his fence were thirty or forty soldiers; medium-calibre machine guns lay strewn around on the ground. More than your average personal-protection squad, I thought. "Kuburin's men," Konyi said with a nod.

This was a group of rebels who, with their commander James Kuburin, had defected from Yau Yau to the SPLA several months earlier. But their arrival in Pibor, and Kuburin's desire for a haircut, led to a tragic misunderstanding. The commander had his hair trimmed in the market, had no money to pay, words were exchanged, and a grenade was tossed. Within half an hour, half a dozen people were killed and nearly 200 *tukul*s were burned by the SPLA. Kuburin himself, we learned from the commissioner, was fighting alongside SPLA frontline troops against Yau Yau. But his men did not feel comfortable living in the main SPLA garrison and were huddled up against the commissioner's offices.

Konyi was much more interested in discussing the campaign against Yau Yau than any impending Nuer attack. "Johnson Biliu – the SPLA commander – expects to reach Yau Yau's heartland at Akel in a day or two … Peter Gadet's in Boma, covering any escape attempt: I think we will get him." He added casually that Yau Yau had received air-dropped supplies from a Sudanese Antonov on 17 February, six weeks earlier, at Akel. This allegation was by no means far-fetched. Over the past several months, the UN had observed Antonovs flying low in the area. Although the peacekeepers did not offend diplomatic sensitivities by suggesting their nationality, there was only one place they could have come from.

The commissioner laughed when I alluded to the eventual "capture" of Yau Yau; taking him alive was not on the cards. But Konyi wasn't just a Murle patsy for the SPLA. He recognized that the criticisms made by Human Rights Watch, Amnesty, and the UN[7] of the army's botched disarmament campaign early in 2012 had been justified: SPLA brutality had boosted Yau Yau's popularity and ranks. It was the SPLA and not Yau Yau, he said, which had recently taken to placing skulls on roads where they knew international aid organizations and the UN would be transiting. "They see the international community as meddlers, blocking pursuit of Yau Yau." Asked to contemplate the end state of the campaign, Konyi admitted: "Fighting alone is not a solution … we need development; improved communications; services; education; jobs for youth. Above all: water."

An odd-seeming request in a swamp. But Jonglei wasn't a swamp all year. When it dried up, the cattle had to move, and it was the migration of cows that triggered conflict as much as anything else.

We stayed at the UNMISS base, a collection of air-conditioned containers within a low mud berm where there was in places some razor wire, but you could step over it in others. The Indian colonel in charge of INDBATT 2, Giri, was very hospitable. We were served a fine hot curry with poppadoms on a table with a crisp red cloth and silverware; a number of the officers, with trim moustaches and Indian/British accents, joined us. The atmosphere was quaintly colonial and the men clearly enjoyed having Catherine at their table; there probably wasn't another English-speaking woman within a 150-kilometre radius.

Giri was young but well-informed, articulate, and well-briefed on his prime responsibility: the protection of civilians. He explained the various outreach activities his men had been taking vis-a-vis the civilian population of Pibor and outlined his worst-case plan. This had him dividing his contingent into four fifty-man groups to secure the safe passage of up to 5,000 civilians into the compound, with strategic use of their three white armoured personnel carriers plus other vehicles. He was illuminating about the recent shooting of a junior Indian officer. "It was a wake-up call to our men … At first, they could not understand why anyone would want to shoot at them, when they had come to bring peace … now they are angry." He went on: "For most of my men, this is the first time they've ever left India, and it'll likely be the last. You see, they are just country boys. They have no idea."

As a result of the shooting, he added, the contingent would now take a more aggressive stance: it would immediately return fire when fired upon, and would not hesitate to use warning shots should lives appear to be at risk. The principal intelligence asset available to UNMISS in Jonglei, the colonel went on, was the sole Mi-8 helicopter – Rwandan – that was equipped with infrared sensing that allowed it to detect significant human mobilization. More conventional surveillance was no longer possible with helicopters required to fly so high (following the loss of a UN helicopter in late 2012 when the SPLA mistakenly shot it down) that they could see nothing.

After dinner, with permission from the colonel, the officers retired to watch Bollywood movies or cricket games on their flat-screens. I rummaged through a pile of month-old newspapers and magazines from India in my spartan, brightly lit container. In the morning, I guiltily used someone else's daily ration of fresh water on a shower, and over breakfast we watched skinny boys from the Punjab doing push-ups and synchronized exercises under the stern direction of a blue-turbaned Sikh major.

The SPLA's optimism about capturing or killing Yau Yau at Akel was misplaced. When we showed up later that morning to have the commissioner escort us across the river to meet with General Johnson, we learned the general was "very busy." This was no euphemism. Only minutes earlier, the commissioner had learned that the army had come under fire at two locations along the route of their advance towards Akel: Kalbat, and the Kongkong River (about twelve kilometres apart).

By the time we flew out by helicopter an hour or so later, you could see a large column of black smoke rising into the hot air twenty kilometres east of the Pibor airstrip. These were destroyed SPLA transports or "technicals" (heavy machine guns mounted on four-by-fours). Later we learned that Yau Yau had successfully ambushed Gadet – not in Boma after all, notwithstanding Commissioner Konyi's assurance – and that he had had to be pulled out of a burning vehicle. He was lucky to have escaped.

On the way back to Juba, we needed to change aircraft in Bor. While we were waiting, an articulate and pleasant-seeming young Dinka who was also waiting, who had just taught us a card game and explained how many cows he had paid (eighty) for the new wife he had yet to see, began spontaneously to talk about the Murle. "They will never be changed … they are just like that. They will never live in harmony with anyone. Really, there is only one solution."

"And what's that?"

"Well," he hesitated and giggled nervously, "some would call it genocide."

––––––––––––

Barely three weeks later, on 9 April 2013, a United Nations convoy en route from Pibor to Bor, accompanied by an INDBATT platoon (thirty-five men, commanded by one of the officers we had dined with), was attacked with rocket-propelled grenades and machine guns at 8:30 in the morning. There was a heavy exchange of fire for about thirty minutes; firing subsided after a further half hour. A captain who had suffered three head wounds managed to call his HQ in Pibor for assistance but succumbed to his wounds; the lieutenant-colonel also died. Among the civilians who died were four Kenyan borehole contractors. All the vehicles in the convoy were seriously damaged. The attackers numbered about 200. By the time responders reached the scene, many of the bodies had been stripped of their boots and other items of clothing.

I attended the ramp ceremony for the dead peacekeepers at Juba airport. In forty-degree heat, several hundred civilian UN staffers gathered to say their farewells, along with two hundred uniformed UN peacekeepers. Hilde Johnson gave an emotional address, breaking down in tears as she listed the children and spouses of the deceased; she expressed the gratitude of the UN towards India. The government of South Sudan was represented by the deputy minister of foreign affairs, a disappointingly junior personage given the nature of the occasion. Other speakers were circumspect in attributing blame for the attack, but the government official was categorical: "This was David Yau Yau: he will be eliminated, along with his followers." He was also quite plain in laying a large part of the blame on "another government" (Sudan's).

It was never really clear who had organized the attack. The UN, as stipulated in the wake of events such as this, commissioned its own board of inquiry. The results were not made public. This led to widespread speculation that the Indian peacekeepers were inadequately prepared for the ambush – in fact, that their weapons were not loaded. It was also suggested that they had allowed many of their arms to fall into the hands of the attackers. The government suggested formally to diplomatic missions that Yau Yau be indicted by the International Criminal Court.

I was soon back in Bor again. I stayed at the South Sudan Hotel, owned by a successful businessman called Ayii Duang Ayii. Mr Ayii charged US$200 for a modest-sized room that, like all hotel rooms in the country, was so heavily curtained as to be always gloomy. I had paid fifty dollars extra for the privilege of air conditioning, which did not work. When – on check-out – I accordingly suggested I should only be billed $150, I was met with very firm insistence that I had asked for the $200 option so that is what I must pay. Not for the first time, I said to myself that the South Sudanese should always leave the commercial hospitality business to Kenyans and Ethiopians (as they usually do).

Over at the State House, overlooking the wide Nile, Governor Kuol Manyang received me in his office, under the ubiquitous twin photos of a balding John Garang and the Stetson-hatted Salva Kiir. He had been an SPLA commander in Jonglei in the war years, ex-confidant of John Garang and close ally of the president. It was he who had formally seconded the proposal that Kiir succeed Garang on the latter's death in a helicopter accident in August 2005, days after Garang had become the first vice-president of Sudan. Kuol's seconding of Kiir was important, because it signified the approval of the Bor Dinka (a sub-grouping shared by Garang and Kuol) for a Bahr-al-Ghazal Dinka taking over the top job. The war had begun in Bor, a large proportion of the general staff were Bor Dinka ... so this was by no means a given.

Kuol was a Big Man, physically, and not normally eloquent. But today he was in an unusually expansive, even affable mood. With some gentle prodding, he recalled his childhood in the fifties. "I was a very bad student ... You see, it was such a long walk to school and there were so many things to do on the way ... But then I was sent away to school: that is what changed my life." His year of forty-one boys was engineered by the British educational authorities in such a way that the students constituted a cross-section of Southern Sudan: "You know, the friendships I made then – with Dinka, with Nuer, with Shillook, they are still strong; I talk to my old school friends all the time ... We need to start those boarding schools again: this is one way to make this one nation."

He recalled his role in the creation of the Red Army, recounting how, as a sector commander, he had ordered hundreds of children out of Jonglei and to the sanctuaries of Kenya and Ethiopia from 1987 onwards. He glossed over the recruitment of many of the same children as child soldiers, insisting instead, "All of those boys who ended up in Canada, the USA, and Australia ... it was the best investment we ever made."

The long-term answer to Jonglei's difficulties, Kuol predictably stated, was development. More specifically, he wanted to see a crash program of road-building to link Jonglei with the rest of South Sudan and internationally. A priority should be a road that linked Bor to the Murle heartland; the current road was only open three months of the year on account of flooding and, even then, was very difficult to transit. Next, the development of water holes and reservoirs would encourage settlement and discourage migration-related conflict:

> We need to reduce our dependence on cattle ... during the war, you know, I ordered that no dowry was to exceed seven cows: three for each of the bride's parents, one for the wedding cere-mony. This rule held. Anyone who broke it, you see, I had them shot. But also people saw that all this got in the way of the war effort ... I know we can't shoot people now. But somehow, we have to get people who now depend on cattle, into sedentary stock-raising and into other economically productive areas.

Turning to the topic of the day, he said that he thought David Yau Yau was holed up near Labrap, north of Jebel Boma. But the SPLA, having eventually taken control of those rustic drop zones in the swamps of Akel, were no longer pursuing him actively. Kuol Manyang did not say as much, but it seemed that following the attacks the day Catherine and I had left Pibor, the army had taken a beating and had, for the time being, lost its appetite for pursuit. Frequent reports of desertion reached me through Western defence attachés. No attempts were being made to negotiate with Yau Yau, according to Kuol, but although the military campaign against the rebel leader had stalled, no one was in a mood to take prisoners either.

The peace commissioner gloomily intervened with a heavy hint. "It will not end well ... the only way Yau Yau might now surrender is if he is offered international guarantees for his own safety." Waxing philosophical, Kuol added that in his experience, "Peace talks have limited use ... if people followed the logic that peace talks imply, there would be no conflict in the first place." Signalling dismissal, he concluded by asking rhetorically, "Are people religious because they love God, or they fear the punishment of hell? At school, I listened because I was hit if I did not."

By July 2013, Pibor was completely cut off by the rains. The restive, unpaid SPLA garrison had gone on a rampage, resulting in the deaths of several civilians, but had then settled into a more deter-mined routine of digging trenches and erecting earthwork defences in the expectation of an assault by David Yau Yau from the east. The allegation that UNMISS had been assisting in these preparations reinforced popular perception in Pibor that the UN had sided with the SPLA. The Indians insisted that they had been helping only with drainage around the SPLA garrison and with clearing vegetation to lessen the risk of misdirected SPLA fire hitting its own men, but the perception lingered.

Estimates of how many civilians remained in town varied from a paltry 150 – the maximum number that had occasionally sought refuge in the UN's lightly fortified compound – to 550; this down from the peacetime figure of 10,000, and 5,000 when Catherine and I had visited in March. County Commissioner Konyi had drawn up a list of 115 civilians for evacuation, and the UN was to begin this. Although David Yau Yau and his surprisingly sophisticated publicity (complete with a website) claimed to have Pibor encircled, all firing over the past few days had been outgoing, by nervous SPLA. In broader Pibor County, Yau Yau was now able to come and go at will.

In this tense situation, the White Army finally swung into action out in the swamps north of Pibor to take on Yau Yau's Murle rebels. This semi-mythical militia of Lou Nuer youths, widely (but possibly erroneously) thought to be named for the ash they daubed on their naked bodies to deter mosquitoes, had a long history, with its roots in colonial days.[8] They appeared and disappeared almost magically whenever the Nuer homeland was under attack or went on the offensive. The White Army had most recently formed in in June – July of 2011, and again over the Christmas / New Year period of 2012–13, both times to attack the Murle homeland. On or around 5 July 2013, 10,000 Lou Nuer began to mobilize, converging – war flags flying – from dozens of points in northern Jonglei on Nyandit, southwest of Akobo.

UN and SPLA reconnaissance detected nothing until a virtually chance encounter. Called upon by the SPLA to assist with the medevac of two hundred wounded personnel, thirty-six Nepali peacekeepers landed by helicopter near Manyabol. They witnessed a column of 6,000 Lou Nuer running slowly to the northwest, shedding their wounded as they went. A three-minute video taken on a smartphone briefly went viral; it was an amazing spectacle that reminded me of the old movie *Zulu*. The UN did everything it could to suppress the video, in which the Nepalis can be heard excitedly asking each other if they're getting good footage. It appeared to occur to nobody that it was their role to inhibit, if not prevent, organized armed attacks of the kind that was under way. A friend who worked for an aid organization sniffed, "It was like they were tornado chasers."

Piecing reports together post-facto, it looked as though the Nuer had gone in search of David Yau Yau, at the time thought to be holed up at Manyading. But Yau Yau was able to inflict heavy casualties with the use of mortars. All this time, the Nuer-commanded SPLA in Pibor stayed in their barracks. There were some suggestions that there had been collusion between the SPLA and the White Army, even that ammunition had been passed over.

What was happening in Jonglei was now known as "The Crisis," and was attracting international and diplomatic concern. Under the leadership of the colourful and aristocratic European Union ambassador Sven Kuhn von Burgsdorff, diplomats chartered a helicopter from UNMISS and, in missions spaced two weeks apart in August 2013, flew first to Murle territory (Pibor) to argue for moderation, and then to the de facto Lou Nuer capital of Akobo to the same end.

UNMISS by now had two companies in Pibor, totalling 240 men; one was Indian, the other Nepali, but the commanders were Indian. They had five tracked light tanks; patrolling within the town was very limited (in fairness, there was no longer much civilian population to protect) while outside the town perimeter, flooded conditions would prohibit any movement for at least four more months. The market was closed, but one or two small traders had set up shop in improvised locations near the SPLA garrison.

Lieutenant-Colonel Ranawat, the new Indian commander, reported to us that a nucleus of internally displaced persons (exclusively women and children) came and went in and out of Pibor from their refuges in the bush almost every day. "Most of the Murle wounded in the last Lou attack are still out there," he said. "We are not in a classic IDP situation; the Murle are scattered everywhere in small groups of ten or twenty, wherever there is high ground."

Under his tree in the courtyard in front of his office, we again found our old friend County Commissioner Joshua Konyi. He had a piece of paper at hand and read out to us: "328 Murle killed; 170,000 cattle looted; twenty-two women and children abducted; eleven wounded ..." Why so few reported Murle wounded? Konyi shrugged and went on, through an interpreter, "The Lou Nuer fight and march in columns, their wounded are concentrated; we Murle fight guerrilla-style, so casualties are surely very widely spread, most likely in inaccessible locations."

Konyi kept returning to the matter of the cows. I had the impression that they were a lot more important to him than the lives of his fellow tribesmen. A few days earlier he'd spoken by satellite phone with David Yau Yau, who was at Manyading, five or six kilometres from Likuongole. "I don't accept the amnesty offered by President Kiir," Yau Yau had said. "Amnesty is for criminals; I am not a criminal; I am a rebel. I'll talk to the [government's church-led] High Level Peace Committee, but I want the UN to guarantee my security ... I'm not going to talk peace just with you."

What might Yau Yau want? Konyi smiled. "His own comprehensive peace agreement. He wants Pibor to be carved out as a separate state within South Sudan, with its own Murle-led and staffed military. It just won't happen."

Gathered outside the county commissioner's offices were well over a thousand internally displaced Murles, all women and children, the adults clutching their World Food Program–issued ration cards. I talked to three or four.

"I walked five days to come here," said one.

I asked where the men were. The answers were evasive. "Are they looking for their cows?" I pressed.

"Yes, of course. The cows. This is our life."

―――――――――

The Wet had well and truly arrived. Two weeks later Akobo, like Pibor, was a morass of black mud, and UN peacekeepers graciously allowed us to ride atop their white armoured personnel carriers to our first meeting, a formal encounter with the local SPLA commander. Heavily armed SPLA soldiers, ribbons of ammunition over their shoulders, lounged around barefoot. The commander was well-prepared, and melodramatic. "Jonglei," he started after a long pause to gain our attention, "is a triangle of death. Every young man has a finger on a trigger. In this part of South Sudan, persuasion and negotiation will only get you so far; the gun has always talked loudest. This is what the Murle and the Lou Nuer understand and respect."

In contrast to Pibor, where the SPLA were hated and feared, in Akobo they were respected and looked up to. This was all about history and ethnicity. The SPLA these days was Nuer-majority and, while the S P L A had split during the war and one faction took Akobo over to Khartoum's side for some years, Murle-dominated Pibor was always fiercely opposed to all factions of the S P L A. When we met with a group of young men, they all denied having raided the Murle. On the other hand, they admitted, "We can never disobey our elders."

More interesting and articulate was a group of elderly women. They had all lost husbands or sons in the fight with the Murle, and complained that they could no longer leave the town limits. "The Murle men are all around ... we cannot sleep anymore; they will attack in the fields, or if we are fishing ... so we have lost all our crops as well as our cattle." Many families were surviving only on wild foods; the women showed us some of the plants they had gathered in the swamps. When pressed, they said it was the men on both sides who were the problem but they did criticize the Murle women as well. "They love their cows too much; they rejoice every time their men bring more cows home from their raids." They maintained that they tried to dissuade their own men from participating in endless revenge attacks, but one lady wryly said it all: "They are Nuer men; this is what they do."

The Akobo county commissioner was also frank. "We have become addicted to war. The Murle culture is to steal cows by guerrilla stratagems while the Nuer culture is to take our revenge through mass attacks." But after decades of this cycle, who was to say what was provocation and what was response?

Fighting dragged on, and the civilian population was pushed into ever-more remote locations: islands in the swamp, with no external access. In October 2013 I made a one-day visit to Kongor, in the heart of territory controlled by David Yau Yau, close to near-deserted Likuongole. Helicopter access was secured by the UN on a daily basis by means of a paper trail through the S P L A High Command, and a satellite-telephone chain that led to Yau Yau, who maintained two civilian-liaison officers at Kongor for this purpose. But even with such guarantees, the Russian and Ukrainian Mi-8 pilots working for the UN's World Food Program steered a prudent, zigzag course around the military encampments of the two forces (both of whom had anti-aircraft capabilities) as we shadowed another Mi-8 bringing in three tons of sorghum, cooking oil, and nutritional supplements to this island in a swamp.

Kongor from the air was a strange sight, alive with colour, smoke, and movement as we clattered in after two hours flying low over the featureless green plains. The island was dominated by a huge white WFP Rubb Hall tent. Once we settled on the ground and took our earmuffs off as the rotors wound down, I could hear a lively babble. There were crowds everywhere, the women all colourfully dressed, some bare-breasted, many with the odd frame-like contraptions of beadwork on their heads and bone pieces in their lips that are typical of the Murle.

Over a period of two weeks, 12,000 people had been allocated one month's rations by the UN. The numbers were imprecise not on account of any lack of rigour in the registration process but because many were unable to reach Kongor. Adults were able to swim across a deep and wide river but several small children had drowned as their parents tried to ferry them over in cooking pots, on their shoulders, or aboard crude rafts made out of tarpaulins stuffed with dry grass. Mothers were given rations on the basis of their estimated family size.

There were almost no men around, just a handful of chiefs with ostrich-feather fly whisks. World Food Program staffers, careful to guard their neutrality, wouldn't say where they thought the rest of the men might be, but I assumed that many were in the ranks of David Yau Yau. The main role of the chiefs seemed to be to select women to assist in food distribution while they looked on from the shade. Women were unloading the helicopters, carrying on their heads fifty-kilogram sacks of sorghum, piles of plastic cooking-oil containers, cases of Plumpy (high nutrition formula); they were also doing all of the cooking and gathering of firewood while caring for hordes of small children.

As is typical in such feeding stations, there was an elaborate series of fences and tables, a maze through which new arrivals were processed and registered. Long lines of women waited patiently, many nursing infants. At a signal the whole line would advance, each holding to the dress of the woman in front, like kindergarten children on a school outing. Every adult was given two ration cards of slightly different format with a unique number; as they were registered, one forefinger was inked, and when they received their ration the little finger was similarly inked, this to forestall double-dipping of relief supplies. The indigo ink (part of a $2 million Canadian contribution to the relief effort in Pibor) was deliberately of a different colour to that being used in similar operations in Gumuruk, Labrap, Pibor, and Dorein, also in Yau Yau territory.

I talked with the chiefs. "Yes, we are grateful for the food, and the medicine," they allowed. "But we also need medicine for our cows." "And rubber boots," added one. "You can see how muddy it is here. But we only need them for us chiefs."

The chiefs were sympathetic to Yau Yau, whom they alternately called David or the General, saying they trusted him. There was also trust in Catholic bishop Paridi Taban, who was attempting to mediate a peace process. "But we will not go back to our homes until David tells us to." They admitted they feared the SPLA (who had several hundred men in Likuongole) even more than their arch-enemies, the Lou Nuer; they believed that they had sufficient intelligence capabilities and strategies to deal with the Nuer, but not the SPLA.

Médecins Sans Frontières was running a surge medical clinic in Kongor. They had been there five days and expected to remain ten more, treating up to 200 cases per day; the prevalence of malaria was unexpectedly high. Two other NGOs, Save the Children and Non-Violent Peace Force, had instituted a rough-and-ready program to ensure that there were no children without adults caring for them, checked registration records for possible abductees (which were then cross-referenced into a national system), and organized "child-friendly" spaces with some play activities. Given the long-standing isolation of Jonglei and the recent years of conflict, they thought that it was unlikely that any of the women or anyone under eighteen in the camp had ever received any formal education.

In May 2014, and contrary to what County Commissioner Konyi had predicted, the stubborn David Yau Yau eventually got his way. With Bishop Paridi mediating, a peace agreement was signed by which he would "reintegrate" his so-called Cobra Faction (also known as the South Sudan Democratic Movement/Army) into the regular SPLA, and Pibor County would be granted a special status, autonomous from Jonglei State, and become the Greater Pibor Administrative Area (GPAA). Yau Yau, whom we had once been invited to indict and send to the International Criminal Court, would be its chief administrator (with the title "Honourable") and the GPAA would be allocated, as start-up funding, the astounding figure of 680 million South Sudanese pounds. This was over two hundred

million US dollars, far more than the annual government allocation
to any given state.

The resolution of the Jonglei Crisis had followed a well-worn pattern. A Big Man becomes dissatisfied with the status quo and finds
himself unable to get his way by peaceful means. He takes to the bush
and assembles an armed militia. He creates mayhem. In the end, he
accepts an offer of cash and promotion and comes back in. Until next
time. The practice often brought peace in the short term, but over the
medium to long term, it encouraged and rewarded rebellion.

It also meant moral and ethical dilemmas for donor countries. A
particularly poignant one was posed when, in the process of reinte-
grating his forces into the regular SPLA, Yau Yau began the systematic
release of hundreds of child soldiers from his ranks. As this process
went on, at one location after another, "soldiers" and camp followers
under eighteen years of age were winnowed out and processed by
the government's Demobilization, Disarmament, and Rehabilitation
(DDR) Commission, before being passed to UNICEF and a clutch of
local and international partners. When I next visited the Pibor region,
in April 2015, UNICEF told me four batches had been released,
as follows:

- Gumuruk – 27 January – 249 released
- Pibor – 10 February – 301 released
- Vertet – 6 March – 108 released
- Likuongole – 21 March – 654 released

Still to come were releases in Pochalla and Boma of an estimated
600 more children, producing a total of around 1,800.

Officials from UNICEF and the DDR Commission would proceed
to each location well before the target release-date. They observed the
process by which the former rebels were assembled, brought to
parade, and then separated out. After being disarmed and exchanging
a uniform for ordinary clothes, each child was interviewed individu-
ally and in private by DDR officials, who inquired as to where they
came from, who their parents were, and under which commander
they had served. This information was cross-checked with the commanders and with other children in the units. Although some cases of
attempted fraud had been detected, Fatuma, UNICEF's senior child-
protection officer (who had overseen child demobilization efforts in

Sierra Leone and Liberia as well), was confident that 95 per cent of the children were bona fide.

DDR officials then passed the children on to UNICEF, who housed them in hurriedly built interim care centres. These were nothing more than fenced compounds of straw huts, but they offered room and board, education, and recreational activities such as art and sports. The first priority was to join up the children with their families. This could take time, as sometimes one or both parents had left (or had died), or they were from smaller outlying settlements. At Gumuruk, 115 of the 249 children released had been reunited. When they moved in with their families, the families received a three-month sustenance package, plus a modest cash allowance.

At Likuongole, three age groups of children had been assembled to meet with me: under eleven years old, eleven to fourteen, and fourteen to eighteen. In the case of the younger group, children from the village were also invited in to help normalize the atmosphere; most of the soldiers were from the other two age groups. The mood was a happy one. An informal art exhibit had been set up in one of the tents. All the groups sang for me, and I quizzed them about polar bears, hockey, and snow. With none of the children having ever seen or felt ice, this was difficult, but there was real interest when I picked up a stick and demonstrated the rudiments of hockey.

Then, with a translator, I met privately with three boys and two girls. There were only three girls in this group but UNICEF thought there might be more in the ranks than had immediately surfaced. "No, we joined because we wanted to," was the unanimous but counter-intuitive answer to my first question. Nearly all had joined David Yau Yau in 2012, when the SPLA had gone on its violent rampage in Pibor County, under the guise of a forced disarmament exercise. Children were beaten and/or held underwater to oblige them to say where their parents were keeping weapons. Many followed their fathers and elder brothers into the bush where the charismatic Yau Yau then assembled them into a surprisingly effective guerrilla force (numbering, I learned from UN security analysts, 15,000 to 20,000 in total – much larger than I had thought).

Many of the boys had served as bodyguards. Fatuma explained why. "The commanders do not trust each other, often with reason. But young boys are intensely loyal. They will literally die for their commander, whom they see as a father." Not all had or knew how to use weapons. The younger children were employed as runners, cooks, or firewood cutters. The two girls I spoke with – one of whom, thirteen years old, appeared to be disturbed – had served as water carriers. Although UNICEF's initial examination showed no signs of sexual abuse, Fatuma told me that evidence of this can take weeks to emerge. The older boys were given military ranks; one fifteen-year-old told me he had been a lieutenant, and indicated his "pips" with his fingers.

The three boys, one fingering his silver crucifix, had been in direct combat. All had lost friends in battle. They recounted how they had assembled at the Akel swamp at night for weapons to be air-dropped from Khartoum.

"And what do you want to do now?"

There was no hesitation, no sense that they had been prompted. "We want to go to school. We know we must have an education."

Of the three, one wanted to go to university, the second to be a *wali* (chief), the third to play football professionally.

I had no intention of seeking out David Yau Yau. But it was difficult to refuse when, back in Pibor with the rain teeming down, a messenger arrived at UNICEF's tented camp to invite me to meet the Honourable. Even seated behind the shiny wooden desk in his office, Yau Yau was an imposing figure of a man with a beetling forehead. He was fluent in English. On his in-tray sat a New Testament; as a young man, he had studied theology. I felt slightly queasy. This was a warlord. But I thought we needed to make the most of his "humanity" in releasing the children, for who knew when he might head back into the bush. So, I swallowed hard and praised his foresightedness in releasing the underage soldiers, suggesting that he was setting a positive example for the rest of South Sudan. In response, he delivered some quite well-thought-out remarks. Some of these were of the shopping-list variety, but I could not fault his putting education and health at the top of his requirements for the Greater Pibor Administrative Area. This was literally the most underdeveloped county in what was possibly the most underdeveloped country in the world; the situation could hardly have been more dire.

Likuongole, where I'd seen the children who had just been released, was a case in point. There was one three-room primary school, with one trained teacher and four volunteer teachers ... and now 1,300 children to be educated. The SPLA were still encamped at the school in Pibor itself; they slept and cooked in classrooms and had filled one room with weapons from the Cobra Faction.

Yau Yau admitted he was frustrated that the 680 million SSP allocated to his new regime in the previous year's national budget had not yet been delivered, but I knew there was no money in Juba. All the Big Man's "ministers" had been working gratis for nine months. I didn't think he was helping his case by insisting on recreating in benighted Pibor all the structures of a fully fledged South Sudanese state; what had been *payams* were promoted to counties (seven in total), *bomas* were now *payams*; persons who would have had the civil service rank of director were deemed to be ministers. Because Pibor had been set up as a Murle homeland in counterpoise to the surrounding Nuer and Dinka, Yau Yau wanted all logistics and all discussions to be with Juba, not with the much closer Jonglei capital of Bor (where the acting governor was now Nuer). All this was extremely inefficient.

A lot (including the fate of the child soldiers) was going to depend on what the international community would do for Pibor. Should we overcome our squeamishness and help him out, if only for the sake of the children? As I left his office, I caught the eye of the uniformed and armed fourteen-year-old guarding his door. I hesitated, wondering whether to say anything or not, but I kept quiet and headed out into the teeming rain.

In November 2015, Canadian general (retired) Roméo Dallaire, famously the commander of UN forces at the time of the Rwanda genocide of 1994, visited South Sudan at the invitation of UNICEF to bring profile to the issue of child soldiers and advocate for the SPLA to renounce their use. Over the past few years, Dallaire had espoused this as a personal crusade.

Aboard an Mi-8 chartered by UNHAS, we juddered to Pibor to see how things had gone over the past six months. It happened to be 11 November – Remembrance Day in Canada – and as Dallaire, with his earmuffs on, sat peering out of the round portholes of the helicopter at the swampy grassland a thousand feet below us, it was hard not to imagine he was thinking of Rwanda. "Child soldiers, you know, are a warning sign, a precursor of genocide …" he'd warned at a small reception we'd held for him the night before.

In a rudimentary new classroom, one of a pair built by UNICEF, we sat with a group of forty boys. It was encouraging to learn that six months after the releases none had dropped out of school. One boy solemnly read a document that expressed their gratitude for having been extracted and their wish, above all, to remain in school. The English was too good to be true, but when are schoolboys' presentations to visiting VIPS ever truly spontaneous?

The boys relaxed a little in conversation. Dr Shelly Whitman, one of Dallaire's staff, spent some time showing them a specially designed deck of playing cards featuring the roles typically played by child soldiers: bodyguards, frontline soldiers, water carriers, cooks, and messengers. The children opened up a lot more, laughing as they pointed to a card and then to boys who had played that particular role.

We trudged through the inescapable thick black mud to meet with the deputy chief administrator (the Big Man, Yau Yau, was away in Juba) and a raft of local officials. These included two generals, one in the uniform of the regular SPLA, the other in that of Yau Yau's own group, the Cobra Faction. There was uneasy laughter as it was explained that the Cobra men had now been integrated into the mainstream army; it was obvious that the Cobra commander was not about to give up his uniform, let alone recognize his SPLA colleague as his superior.

The Cobra general largely kept his own counsel; he looked battle-worn and had almost no teeth. But when Dallaire started to play his most effective cards – picking up the general's exact rank from his shoulder-boards and relating his own personal history, including the facts that he was the son of a soldier and his children were also soldiers, the old warrior started to ease up. Almost without warning, as the meeting was closing, he made a clear commitment to round up the last of the child soldiers in the area – "Yes, there are still some more in the bush" – and deliver them into the hands of UNICEF. "But," he added, appealing to Ettie Higgins, the senior UNICEF staffer with us, "you must treat the boys like cows. You put your cows in a corral so that they cannot roam free. So, you must put these boys in a school; this you must promise."

Back in Juba, Dallaire met with Kuol Manyang, now defence minister. I'd warned him that it might be best not to challenge the minister outright for the public position of the government was that there were no child soldiers in the army, and indeed he played it diplomatically. Half an hour into the meeting, as if having an after-thought, Kuol summoned Paul Malong, his chief of staff, into the room. "It was interesting," Dallaire said to me afterwards. "You could immediately tell who was the controlling one in the room: I could tell by their body language, when I pushed across the table a copy of our child-soldier manual ... Kuol deferred nervously to Malong."

Next day, Malong assembled a group of more than twenty officers of the general staff and Dallaire's team spent nearly three hours dis-cussing with them the pros and (with more emphasis) the cons of using child soldiers. Shameless flattery played its part. "I told them that if they really wanted to be seen internationally as a professional army, and one day send peacekeepers on UN missions, then they must renounce the use of any boys under eighteen. They really seemed to get this."

At the end of the visit I invited Dallaire to a small dinner with Ellen Loej, who had replaced Hilde Johnson as the special representative of the secretary-general, the top UN job in South Sudan. Loej had told me earlier how interested she would be to meet Dallaire. "You know, I was reading *Shake Hands with the Devil*[9] when they made me an offer to come to South Sudan," she said. "I wanted to think that the UN had learned its lesson from Rwanda, so I took it on."

Admitting that he had nothing but scorn for the SRSG with whom he had served in Rwanda, Dallaire quizzed Loej intensely on the situ-ation in South Sudan. The SRSG responded with a frankness and a degree of self-flagellation that I had never seen her display in public. It was a lively, intense discussion lasting two hours, until the curfew was knocking, and it left both of them looking pensive.

Dallaire later confessed in a worried tone, "You know, there is a smell here in South Sudan ... I just can't get away from it. It reminds me of Rwanda, before hell broke loose."

5

Babies and Mothers

Jonglei, Bahr-al-Ghazal, Western and Central Equatoria, 2012–2015

Canadian prime minister Stephen Harper, towards the end of his ten years in office, had the reputation of being cold and calculating. But he had one abiding passion that seemed to indicate a much warmer personality, a truly caring person. At the annual summit of the G-8 held in 2010 at Muskoka in Canada, Harper announced a major governmental commitment to the health of young mothers and infants in the developing world – a field known to development junkies as MNCH (Maternal and Neo-Natal Child Health). Over the next few years this became his signature legacy,[1] an outstanding push forwards in an era that otherwise saw Canada's international aid programs steadily decline both in size and in ambition.

South Sudan suffered from one of the highest infant and maternal mortality rates in the world.[2] It was said that a young woman was more likely to die in childbirth than finish primary school (although this was as damning an indictment of educational opportunity in the country as of its health record). Accordingly, South Sudan was a major beneficiary of the Muskoka initiative: through the World Health Organization (WHO), Canada supported the construction of eight maternity wards, while through the United Nations Population Fund (UNFPA), we launched a program to train midwives and nurses. At the time of my own arrival in South Sudan, I was told by the governmental chief of nursing training that there was a grand total of eleven professionally trained midwives in the country. We had much to do.

One of the privileges of being the head of a diplomatic mission – however vague my title might be – was that occasionally I got to inaugurate things, even though I was rarely the one who had worked to bring the project to fruition. In October 2012, only a couple of months after I'd arrived, Caroline and I took a rather bumpy early-morning flight on one of UNHAS's light aircraft to Bor, one hour to the north of Juba, to inaugurate the first of the eight maternity wards.

The usual large crowd had been assembled under canopies in the courtyard of the hospital. Caroline was slated to be one of the warm-up speakers but, as the speaker before her started to wind down and I looked over to where she had been sitting, I was dismayed to see her bolting away. Three or four evidently concerned spectators followed her.

There was a minute or two of confusion, then federal health minister Dr Michael Milli Hussein gestured to me to stand in for Caroline. It was more than an hour before things wound down. By now Caroline was back in her seat. "It was all incredibly embarrassing," she said. "You remember the flight was a bit rough. I really wasn't feeling well, in fact I thought I was going to be sick, so that's why I left ... I found a bed to lie down on, but ... oh, it was so awful!"

"What do you mean?"

"Well, everybody gathered around. There was Jehan, the state health minister. She put her hand on my stomach and ... started praying!"

I dined out on the story for weeks (it was of course a complete misunderstanding; Caroline was only a little travel-sick), but my turn came when, on a subsequent visit to the hospital, I asked to pay a quick visit to the washroom.

"Oh, you must use our brand-new toilet," said the ever-helpful Jehan.

I pulled the steel door behind me, did what I needed to do, then tried to open the door again. And tried, and tried. It was seriously jammed. There was a single window high up on the rear wall, but it looked too small to climb out of and there was no way to reach it. After about ten minutes, I heard voices in the corridor: "But where is the ambassador? I hope he is not lost."

I summoned up my courage, banged on the steel door and shouted, "I cannot get out. I am stuck!"

There was a significant silence. Then footsteps rapidly approached. Much rattling of the door, then cries around the hospital corridors. "The ambassador! He is stuck in the toilet! He cannot get out! We must help him. Deng, go find a hammer, or a crowbar, that will do."

The next facility to be inaugurated, in September 2013, was at Yambio, in Western Equatoria, the leafy, verdant town in the jungle where years before I had met the old warlord Abu John and Commander Mary. We stayed, as before, at the former district commissioner's house, now a UN guesthouse. At lunch with government officials the next day, I told the man sitting next to me, the state minister of information, about my earlier visit. "Oh yes," he said, not showing the slightest surprise. "Mary is my mother."

Federal minister Dr Michael, who had been with us in Bor, had now been replaced by Dr Riek Gai, another old acquaintance who – the last time I had seen him, in 2003 – had been chairman of the Southern States Coordinating Council in Khartoum. Dr Gai was the keynote speaker when we made our way to the hospital where the foundation stone for the new ward was to be laid. "Canada was with us throughout the struggle … and they are with us now," he began, to widespread clapping. Less predictably, daringly even, he went on to praise the governor, Joseph Bakasoro, who had stood in the 2010 elections as an independent, against the approved SPLM candidate … and won. "You were not afraid to take on the SPLM machine. South Sudan needs more people of your independence and energy. I know the SPLM will be broad-minded enough to welcome challenges."

After his speech, I was presented with a large straw hat with tufts sticking up from the crown. The purple dye later bled all over my forehead, making it look as though I had been in a bad fistfight. I became afraid to take it off. Then there was the customary cultural show. This was a set of songs and dances by the hospital staff in traditional Azande garb. After a couple of minutes there was some giggling from the back, and the MC started to become agitated, suggesting with a throat-cutting gesture that enough was enough.

"What's going on?" I whispered to my new friend, the minister of information.

He smirked, hesitated, then replied, "They're singing that they haven't been paid for weeks. I don't think the minister is very happy."

For my part, when it was time for me to speak, I stressed that the ward would only be as useful as its staff, from doctors to midwives and nurses, and even to cleaners and cooks. And, at the minister's discreet suggestion, I dwelt on ethics, since South Sudan was struggling to impart medical ethics to its practitioners. Even the idea that strikes should not be allowed to lead to the death of patients seemed to be quite alien to this community. I also took the opportunity to warn parents not to allow their children to marry too young. Fourteen- and fifteen-year-olds were not ready to have children, I said, and if they did both they and their offspring would be at risk.

After the ceremonial laying of the foundation stone, we toured the hospital. MSF/Spain was running things, with a total staff of over 200. I was impressed, but in talking to Equatoria State officials I could see they were uneasy at the state's continuing dependence on the international NGO community. This unease was even more visible when, in the afternoon, we travelled to Nzara where a dormant government clinic adjoined a more lively, well-attended one run by the Comboni sisters.

In another telling incident at Nzara, the minister informed the county commissioner that it was his plan to send one doctor from Juba for each of the state's ten counties.

"Minister, I've heard these promises before," was the blunt reply.

"Well, you wait and see. If you'll provide the housing, I'll send you the doctors."

In September 2013, shortly after our visit to Yambio, Minister Gai managed to persuade the president – who did not often venture from Juba – to take advantage of an already-planned visit to Wau and call at the general hospital to launch another construction project, our third maternity ward.

I flew in the day before. Wau had not changed that much in twelve years. It was still the site of the only traffic lights in South Sudan, and those lights were still not working. I was warned to be very early. It seemed most unlikely to me that the president would be on time, but I obliged by getting a ride from my hotel to the hospital in pre-dawn darkness, with the visit scheduled for 9:00 a.m. – or might it even be 8:30? No one was sure. The hospital complex, most of it dating from the 1920s and '30s, was swarming with ladies sweeping up leaves, the presidential band setting up, and frightening technicals hurtling about at random. The plaque was found to have a spelling mistake and a second was rapidly ordered. Amazingly, it arrived in time.

With the staff of 250 doctors, nurses, and midwives assembled in lines, and sundry dignitaries (including half the cabinet, and Interior Minister Aleu in a fluorescent blue nylon suit) also gathered, the president, all in black, arrived on time. The Canadian head of the World

Health Organization in South Sudan, Dr Abdi, summoned up his nerve and approached Salva Kiir's car as he stepped out. "Mr President," he said diffidently, and he pointed with one hand at his trademark black Stetson, holding in his other hand a white baseball cap adorned with a Canadian flag and the WHO logo. The president was not in the least fazed. He immediately took off the Stetson, gave it to an aide, and wore the cap for the rest of the visit.

We stood around the plaque in the blazing sun, solemnly studying the plans of the yet-to-be-built ward, and I was given ten minutes to talk to the president. After a brief diversion into some old history – my last two visits to this part of the country, thirteen years earlier – I outlined Canadian health programming. I made the point that infrastructure is important but more important would be the people that the government placed in these facilities. With a wink from the minister of health, I exhorted the government not to stint on staff, and emphasized that improving South Sudan's child and mother mortality statistics would take both vision and patience. The president lived up to his reputation as "the strong and silent type" by saying nothing, though he did appear interested and appreciative.

Talking to the crowd in Arabic, he (I think) expressed his gratitude to Canada as an "old and long-time friend of South Sudan." Turning to the health minister with a jocular chopping gesture, he said he would be back to open the finished building in four months' time "… and if it is not ready … you will pay the price!" Martin Lomuro, the minister for cabinet affairs, confided to me that he had been advising the president to get out into the field more frequently. "He needs to put his finger on the pulse … His advisers protect him; they tell him nothing."

––––––––––––

It was satisfying to see robust physical infrastructure going up in a country where 95 per cent of the edifices were straw and mud. Minister Gai frankly confessed to me that the opening of new installations earned him great credit with the president. But a much greater challenge was the creation of a cadre of trained staff, so we invested not just in buildings but also in training midwives. Two of the most fulfilling days of my tenure in South Sudan were graduation ceremonies at the Kajo Keji School of Midwifery and Nursing.

Kajo Keji is a small, bucolic town in low hills to the south of Juba, in Central Equatoria State hard on the border with Uganda. The road

there was really bad and subject to attacks by bandits so, with a certain sense of guilt given the short distance, we flew there with the
UN's Humanitarian Air Service, landing on a grass strip just outside
town. The climate was cooler than Juba's, with low hills all around.
Every imaginable variety of fruit grew in abundance. Sadly, because
of very poor transportation to market, much of it was left to rot: a
problem throughout the Equatorias.

At graduation in late 2015, thirty young men and women were
dressed in traditional black and turquoise academic gowns. At least
50 per cent of the midwives' graduating class were typically men,
because South Sudanese education was principally accessed by boys.
But, to my surprise, there was no stigma attached to male midwives;
pregnant mothers accepted their services without demur. I found
myself thinking how prejudiced I must be to find this odd.

The town band led the graduates in, and much of Kajo Keji was in
attendance, under tents and in the shade of the grounds of the residential College of Nursing. There was speech after speech, and the
hospital administrator took advantage of the happy moment to make
a desperate plea for international financial support for his adjoining
(decrepit) hospital.

The Reverend Janet, chief of nursing at Juba's College of Nursing,
resplendent in formal gown and a bizarre cocked hat, handed out
candles to each of the students and they recited the Florence Night-
ingale vow, a kind of Hippocratic oath for nurses and midwives.
Certificates were presented to much ululation and cheering, the new
graduates' friends mobbing them and placing garlands of tinsel
around their necks. Dancers performed between the ceremonial
events, a senior official oddly dressed in a black suit and red fez occasionally prancing in – as per tradition – to reward particularly impressive dancers with small cash prizes.

There was only one negative note, but it seemed churlish to be
concerned. When the graduates said a few words each of thanks,
many added that they hoped their new qualification would allow
them to go on to be doctors and to study abroad. I was happy for
them; who could blame them for ambition? But we hoped they would
all stay in South Sudan, however challenging their careers might turn
out to be.

The Canadian Office, Juba (2012). At this time there were four Canadian officers and two drivers. Catherine sits on the left, Caroline on the right, my desk in the centre. Unless otherwise noted, all images by Nicholas Coghlan.

Exterior, the Canadian office (2012). Most of the roads in Juba are made of dirt.

Alfred Taban, editor of the *Juba Monitor* and dean of South Sudan journalists.

Juba's main street: Airport Road.

SPLA soldiers, Akobo (2013).

Murle IDP woman and baby. Kongor, Jonglei State (2013). Her traditional blue and red headdress is in the colours of her husband's age set.

Women unloading relief supplies, Kongor, Jonglei State (2013). The women typically undertake all the heavy work in unloading and delivering supplies, under the direction of male chiefs, and paid by relief agencies.

General Roméo Dallaire in pensive mode en route to Pibor, Jonglei State (2015).

General Roméo Dallaire secures a commitment to release child soldiers from a
Cobra Faction general, Pibor, Jonglei State (2015).

The author, health minister Dr Riek Gai, and President Kiir at the laying of the foundation stone for a Canadian-financed maternity ward, Wau (2013).

Nuer girls carrying water home, Mayom, Unity State (2012).

Unexploded ordnance, Mayom, Unity State (2012).

Blowing up ordnance, Mayom, Unity State (2012).

Ajuong Thok: newly arrived refugee woman from the Nuba Mountains of Sudan (2013).

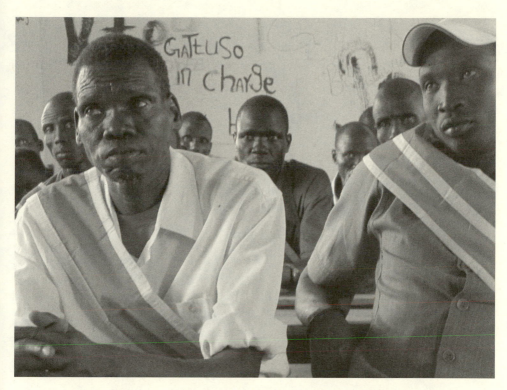

In Canadian-sponsored meetings, village chiefs talk democracy. Ulang, Upper Nile State (2013).

The county commissioner and SPLM ladies, on the Sobat River, en route from Ulang to Malakal, Upper Nile State (2013).

6

The Refuge-Seekers

Unity State, 2012–2013

Unity State was called Western Upper Nile until the administration of Sudan's president Nimeiri changed the name in the late 1970s. His hope was that the newly discovered presence of oil would serve to bring together the North and the even-then-fractious South. I'd visited frequently during the war years, as Unity was then the centre of the oil industry; you could guess an aid worker's instinctive sympathies then by whether they called it Unity or Western Upper Nile.

I flew up in November 2012 to the dirt strip at Rubkona, just outside the state capital, Bentiu. Justin Green, the stocky, bearded white Canadian/Zimbabwean who ran the operations of the Danish Demining Group that we were supporting, met me, and we hurried to his Land Cruiser. "Gotta step on a bit, mate," he commented. "The road to Mayom's not exactly lekker, we need to get there before dark."

The one-lane dirt track ran through tinder-dry yellow scrub and low brown-barked acacia trees. We were well into the dry season now; it hadn't rained for six weeks. But the big trucks that had passed when the track was still wet had left ruts in the heavy, black cotton soil that were a metre deep in places, and that had hardened like concrete. Notwithstanding the border officially being closed, every few kilometres we would come across an ancient Bedford, its Arabic-numeral plates identifying a trader from Sudan, tilted at a crazy angle and deeply stuck. Some trucks had shed their loads, and the disconsolate driver's assistant would be fanning himself languidly atop a pile of boxes of soap, while the driver stood wondering what to do. In one location, a gang of seven or eight men stood on a truck's lee side labouring to right it, but you could see that both sets of wheels

on one side were no longer touching ground, and they would have to
let it fall again. It took us four hours to drive seventy kilometres.

At last we reached Mayom. I recognized the wide-open space
where, eleven years earlier, I'd talked with some of the thousands of
women and children who had been driven into government territory
by rebel SPLA forces under Peter Gadet. I remembered one family
telling me they had built a thorn fence at night to protect themselves
from a marauding pride of lions. There was a long, low, brick church
and an abandoned clinic, but nearly all the other buildings were
straw-roofed *tukuls*. A light blue haze hung over the sprawling, quiet
town in the early evening. Large magpies perched in a few straggling
acacias or on fences. Incongruously parked among the *tukuls* at random angles, with drying underwear festooning their barrels, were
five T-55 tanks. Justin pointed out the one permanent, concrete building. "That's the home of Paulino Matiep ... he died just a month or
two ago, in August I think."

When I had met him in the old days, Matiep had generally been
aligned with Khartoum. In January 2006 he saw the writing on the
wall, ceded to the blandishments of the SPLA, and was promptly
appointed deputy commander-in-chief. More than 50,000 of his men
were attached to the regular army, but he retained some former militia soldiers (formerly SSUM, but latterly known as SSDF) as a large
personal bodyguard; confusingly, some splinter elements of his forces
remained inside Sudan, still opposed to the SPLA. With the evident
support of Khartoum, the left-over rebels still made pinprick attacks
into South Sudan close to Mayom. They also laid mines that had
killed upwards of twenty-five civilians in two attacks over the past
twelve months.

"DDG's been here five weeks now," Justin explained as we completed our short tour of Mayom and bumped over to his outfit's
straw-walled compound. "We're moving from site to site in Unity,
clearing old stuff and some new mines too. The compound's been lent
to us by a local women's cooperative and we share it with another
NGO, Non-Violent Peace Force. Not quite the company we ex-
squaddies normally keep," he added with a grin.

With military precision derived from his own career in the
Zimbabwean and British armies, Justin had divided his personnel
up into well-disciplined units: a medical crew with their designated
ambulance; the finance/accounts team; the vehicles gang; two teams
for mine-risk education; three ordnance-disposal teams. The first

evening I was in camp gave a good idea of the daily routine. The medical team reported four staff sick with red-eye; finance asked what allowance should be made for the Christmas party; the vehicles gang reported on diesel supplies, a radiator leak, and the state of one Land Cruiser's tires. The mine-risk awareness teams, with careful reference to a map, reported on their activities over the day: which villages they had visited, exactly how many people they had spoken with (160 women and children in the village of Cheng Chan), what information they had gathered on ordnance.

The three ordnance-disposal teams had so much to report that I had no time to write it down. My hurried notes have team leader Evening (his siblings, he told me later, were called Morning and Night, the times of their birth) accounting for fifteen 82-millimetre mortar rounds, twelve RPG rockets, two phosphorous grenades, one unexploded and semi-buried bomb, one 107-millimetre rocket, and hundreds of rounds of machine-gun ammunition. The other two teams had similar finds to report. All this had been gathered in only three days. Most of these objects, I learned, were found in buried caches left behind by militia groups. Much of the ordnance I later observed was rusty and crusty, but some mortar rounds looked to be quite new, with small cotton bags of gunpowder tied close to their fins to boost their range.

The work was done in close liaison with county-level officials and the local SPLA commanders. Team members commented that they found the SPLA officers well aware of their own government's prohibition of the use of anti-personnel mines (a great preoccupation of the Canadian government) and very happy to discuss the question. "They don't actively help us but they don't interfere either."

Next morning, I was first asked to give an official send-off with team photos to the DDG convoy as it began its daily rounds, each vehicle carefully spaced in radio contact with the medics bringing up the rear. Letting them get ahead, I drove with Justin to look at three or four medium-sized craters in the heart of Mayom itself. "These were munitions caches, the villagers pointed them out to us. A couple were actually inside *tukul*s, buried, so we had to blow the *tukul* as well ... but they're easily rebuilt."

We drove to the northwest for thirty minutes to catch up with the main convoy at the latest designated disposal site, in dense acacia woods 200 metres off a quiet red-earth track. Two large piles of ordnance had been brought there over the past several days for what would be the sixth controlled explosion in five weeks: dozens and dozens of mortar rounds of all sizes, rockets, a semi-exploded aircraft-dropped bomb, fifteen sacks full of large- and small-calibre ammunition. Over the space of the next hour, the remaining UXO was placed carefully in three adjacent pits. I was impressed at how methodically, carefully, and silently all the men worked under the quiet direction of Kons, who surveyed the scene calmly with his clipboard. Long pieces of red spaghetti-like detonating cord, each with a TNT charge at one end, were brought in from a separate location, taped together and laid down over the pits; sandbags were placed on top. With all the spaghetti in one bundle, it was stabilized and arrangements made to bring the end of the firing-cable close.

"Everyone go now," Kons quietly ordered, staying behind with only one assistant.

The next and most delicate step I followed by radio. With one of the pair standing well back from the pits and quietly talking over the radio, the other carefully attached the detonators: short metal tubes hardly larger than rivets. Back on the road, announcements had been made by megaphone, the vehicles all withdrawn, and the road cordoned off for two kilometres either way. All of this was accomplished without a single word from Justin. We assembled at the firing point, 800 metres from the pits. With everything ready, I was solemnly handed the small battery-powered firing box – alas, no plunger – with its little silver key in one side. "It's all yours, mate. Privilege of being a donor."

A slow turn, about a three-second pause. A single very large "crump" reached us, 150 kilograms of TNT going up in smoke. Seconds later, we could see a mushroom-shaped column of black smoke rising 800 to 1,000 metres. We walked back to the site, put out a few small fires, and inspected the now much larger pit. There was not a trace of metal left, just a few shreds of white plastic sacking from the sandbags flapping in the trees and a lot of newly fallen leaves on the ground.

By April 2013, word reached Juba that most of the rebels left behind by Paulino Matiep in Sudan had decided there was no future opposing the new government in the South and were ready to come in. A number of the press releases made on their behalf bore the name "Gordon Buay" and, oddly, an Ottawa phone code.

Sure enough, Mr Buay turned up one day at our garage-cum-office in Juba. We crossed the courtyard to my house and there, perched on the edge of an overstuffed sofa, he regaled me with all sorts of interesting news and gossip (not all well-founded, I would soon realize, but fascinating nonetheless). Buay hailed from Ulang County, Upper Nile, and was a Jikany Nuer. By his own account, he was quite well-connected: the mother of James Hoth (at the time, chief of the general staff) was Buay's aunt, and Paulino Matiep's former deputy-commander Gordon Koang (or Kong), who had stayed in Sudan when Matiep came in, was his uncle.

In 2007, in distant Ottawa, where he had emigrated as a refugee during the war, Buay named himself chair of the South Sudan Democratic Front/Canada, representing both the South Sudan Defence Forces militia that his uncle Koang led, and also the slightly broader SSLA. In this capacity, he subsequently helped negotiate safe crossing of the border for ex-rebels who were now camped out in two locations adjoining SPLA garrisons within South Sudan. There was one group of 3,000, primarily Bul Nuer, at Mayom, and another (numbering 2,000) of Dinka and Shillook loyal to Johnson Olony at Kodok, Upper Nile State. They all still had their weapons and even some vehicles, and were awaiting reintegration into the SPLA. None were being paid, but the regular SPLA troops were probably not being paid regularly either.

Buay was about to initiate negotiations on behalf of the SSLA with – on the other side – a military commission led by deputy chief of staff Lieutenant-General Thomas Cirilo. While demands would include integration into the regular army with existing or higher ranks, there would also be political demands. Notably, the SSLA would require that three MPs associated with their movement, who formerly sat in the Khartoum legislature, now be admitted to Juba's. By early October, negotiations had made some slow progress. Disarmingly, Mr Buay showed me his list of demands:

- One lieutenant-general
- Five major generals
- Six brigadier generals
- One major general and four brigadier generals in the police

Plus in the central government he was asking for one presidential advisor, one head of commission, two members of commissions; in

Upper Nile state, one minister and two commissioners; in Unity state, one minister, one advisor, two commission members. Two ambassadorial positions were also required. Finally, the rebels demanded that certain Shillook lands in Upper Nile state, left vacant when their owners went to Sudan to join the militia and subsequently occupied by others, be vacated again.

Later that month, Buay and (ex-rebel) Lieutenant-General Bapiny Monytuil Wecjang met with President Salva. Most of his demands had been met. The chief of the general staff, James Hoth, was especially determined that no new lieutenant-general position be created and warned the president, "This is a slippery slope." Most of his generals, who had earned their promotions through years of patient service, were bitter at seeing soldiers who had been fighting against them not only forgiven, but ranked above them.

"And is there a financial element to all this?" I asked Buay with false innocence.

"Of course," he answered immediately, with an enthusiastic grin.

As well as a substantial amount of cash, General Bapiny wanted compensation for the three houses he was leaving behind in Khartoum, and was threatening to sell his technicals to the highest bidder if no money was forthcoming from Juba. Buay modestly allowed that one ambassadorial position had been conceded – to him personally. This, I said to myself, was nothing to get excited about; South Sudan had at that time about fifteen embassies, but over sixty ambassadors.

Thus was concluded the reintegration into the regular SPLA of the last major Southern militia that had refused to line up in 2005 and 2006. The episode demonstrated pragmatism on the part of the central authorities in Juba but it also pointed to deep flaws in the SPLA, a reminder that this army was a fragile coalition of unintegrated militias that were, likely as not, commanded by generals who had insufficient knowledge and experience. Buay laughingly agreed. "Yes, it's true. There are now more generals in the SPLA than in the whole army of the USA."

At the time of independence, and as many had foreseen, two anti-Khartoum regions – Blue Nile and the Nuba Mountains (South Kordofan) – had been left stranded north of the new border that separated Sudan from South Sudan. The pro-South leadership in both areas (which were not contiguous, but which were easily reached through remote territory from South Sudan) reacted to provocation by pro-Khartoum troops by launching a new rebellion of their own, in due course striking an unnatural alliance with another anti-Khartoum militia based in Darfur, the Justice and Equality Movement (JEM).

The SPLM/A-North, as the rebels dubbed themselves when referring to both their political movement (M) and their army (A), could be frustratingly ambivalent in their declared objectives. To the outside world, they usually proclaimed that they wanted nothing less than full reform of the Sudanese state, along thoroughly secular, democratic lines. But to many ordinary people in Nuba or Blue Nile, the goal was to have Khartoum leave them alone in some form of ill-defined autonomy.

This war was sporadic but vicious. For much of the time, rather than risk direct confrontation with the well-disciplined SPLA-N – whose morale was usually better – the Sudan Armed Forces favoured high-altitude bombing from their Antonovs. The bombing was extremely inaccurate but it had the effect of driving farmers off their fields and disrupting agricultural life. By 2015, Khartoum was starting to use lower-altitude fighter bombers that had a more direct effect on population centers, and in several instances cluster munitions were used. Ground offensives were launched at the beginning of every dry season; typically, Khartoum would make serious inroads to begin with but the rebels would rally and push them back by the beginning of the Wet.

A year or so into the war, 250,000 civilians – disproportionately women and children – had fled into South Sudan, into two refugee camps that sprang up spontaneously. Yida, in northern Unity State, housed about 70,000 from the Nuba Mountains, while Maban, in Upper Nile, held 180,000 from Blue Nile (where, in general terms, the government of Sudan's campaign had been more successful). The site at Yida suffered from serious drawbacks, the first of which was apparent on my first visit in late 2012. The pilot of our white eleven-seater Cessna Caravan had to slam his brakes on hard when landing, so short was the runway. At its north end were the wrecks of two medium-sized cargo planes that had been on charter to MSF and whose pilots were not so careful. Happily, the only casualty inflicted by MSF was one dead donkey.

"You can't lengthen the runway," explained Karen, a young American staffer working for the UN's refugee organization, as she

greeted me off the plane. "In the Wet, there are lakes at either end; in
fact, the whole camp becomes an island." In November, only a month
into the Dry, it was difficult to imagine that it ever rained here. As we
bumped along a dirt track that wound its way past dozens of haphaz-
ardly arranged shacks roofed with white tarpaulins, we left a cloud
of fine red dust behind us. Every so often, we'd dodge two-metre-high
termite hills made of red earth and the odd acacia tree that had lost
its lower branches to foraging goats. Long lines of women waited
patiently with yellow plastic jerry-jugs at boreholes drilled by the UN
or partner NGOs; ragged children waved at us happily.

We came out into a more open area with two incongruously mod-
ern-looking warehouses. "The one on the left belongs to Samaritan's
Purse," Karen said, referring to the faith-based American organization that was delivering relief in Yida.

"And the other?"

She hesitated. I was already wading into controversy.

"The SPLA. It's where they store what you might call their 'non-
food' items."

Refugee camps are usually located at a safe location near to the
area from which people are fleeing, and are preferably easy to access.
"It's about twenty kilometres to Jau," Karen explained. "That's on
the border. And from Jau into the heartland of the rebel-controlled
area, it's a safe trip, completely under rebel control. But for us, for
UNHCR, this is a problem. It means that the SPLA-N come in and out
as well, and if you're looking at things from Khartoum's perspective,
that could make Yida a legitimate military target."

The problem was greater than this. Karen was being as diplomatic
as a UN functionary should be. It was widely supposed, particularly
in Khartoum, that Juba actively supported their erstwhile companions in the Nuba Mountains with shipments of weapons and vehicles,
and it wasn't that much of a stretch to figure that the large warehouse
we had just passed might contain some such material. For these reasons, the UN was adamant that Yida must move out of the swamp,
further from the border, further from the SPLA's supply routes. Until
quite recently, the refugee community and its leaders had refused.
Their argument was that, exposed as it might be, Yida (which had
been bombed in November 2011) was incomparably a safer location
than Nuba. Moreover, it was accessible to the Nuban people and its
health issues were non-issues to people who routinely had no access
to health care. Similarly, the expense of aerial supply into Yida from
Juba was irrelevant to the refugees.

A number of international NGOs were also quite hesitant, but not for reasons they always felt comfortable stating publicly. "The thing is," confided Dave, another American who worked for a large organization that provided basic health services in the camp, "if you move Yida further into South Sudan, you make it more difficult for people to go back and forth."

I must have looked quizzical. Are refugees supposed to go back and forth? He shrugged.

"It's an open secret that a lot of people come out of Nuba to pick up food here and then go back in ... You could say they're not really 'refugees' in that sense. But if Khartoum won't let any relief in at all from the north – and it won't – then this is an effective way of serving that population."

What the refugee leaders found unanswerable in the end was that Yida's overt use by the SPLA-N was dangerous to the civilian population and incompatible with humanitarian principles.

After a night in one of UNHCR's tents we drove thirty-five kilometres south to Pharyang, then another thirty-eight kilometres east past a place called Jam Jang to the proposed site for the new refugee camp at Ajuong Thok. It was in empty country, a little more sparsely wooded than Yida, but not liable to flooding. There was adequate road access and an air strip that could be rehabilitated. Jam Jang comprised only 500 or 600 persons. The geologists had yet to do their tests, but there was no reason to suppose that boreholes would not be feasible. All that remained was to negotiate an agreement with the local authorities.

Back in Yida, I spent two mornings observing the complex process by which incoming refugees from the north were processed and registered. The scene was frenetic and crowded. As well as dealing with a daily influx of three to five hundred new arrivals, UNHCR staff were simultaneously re-registering the entire existing population of the camp using biometric data. This exercise (which had lasted a month) was about to finish. "We think it will result in a net downward revision of camp numbers from seventy to about fifty-three thousand," Karen said. "The difference is because of double-dippers, persons passing their children from one group to another to boost their allocation. You donors should be very happy," she added. "It means 17,000 monthly rations saved."

I spoke through an interpreter to a number of new arrivals. Most were women and children from Buram and Um Dorain Counties in Sudan; the fit men had obviously remained in Nuba either to fight or to safeguard their families' remaining possessions. There were few very old people; the rigours of the journey meant that the infirm were unlikely to undertake it.

Nearly all clutched handwritten and stamped notes: exit permits issued by the SPLM-N leadership. Many had travelled with other families from their *bomas* (villages); within Yida, each family lived in parallel *bomas* with their kin and friends.

"Did you see the bombers?" I asked.

"Yes," people would shrug. "They come over the fields ... Almost the same time every day. We hear the engines, we go and hide in caves."

It was difficult to have anything like a political discussion, but everyone I spoke with said they wanted the independence of the Nuba Mountains, plain and simple. In the circumstances, they were surprizingly optimistic. "Morale is high," camp staff told me. "Much more so than in Maban" (the camp housing refugees from Blue Nile).

All life and death happened at Yida. Unfortunately, deaths were routinely concealed lest a family's food ration be cut accordingly. To discourage this practice, UNHCR was introducing bereavement kits: the offer of funeral shrouds, caskets, and a small one-time food allowance. Day-to-day discipline and policing were enforced by traditional leaders. Some of this tended towards the medieval (women were routinely imprisoned for the crime of having been raped) but there was growing acceptance of the South Sudan National Police Service (SSNPS), paid for by UNHCR. Disputes could occur around the camp's boreholes, where the lineups were perpetual and long; often these might involve members of the host community, who felt their rights had been usurped. There was an unexpectedly large and colourful market, with traders not only from Bentiu and Pharyang but from Nuba itself.

There were six major international NGOs working at Yida – Samaritan's Purse, CARE, MSF, Solidarités, and so on – under the coordination of UNHCR, and there were occasional tensions among the organizations. Paul, an Australian who worked for UNHCR, remarked, "You know one thing I really don't appreciate, mate ... It's when on a Sunday we hear those folks," and he gestured over the fence to the adjoining compound of a faith-based organization, "It's when I hear them praying for us ... I reckon I can really do without that."

Ten months later, I was back at Yida again.

One morning Cosmas Chanda, the amiable but slightly taciturn Zambian head of UNHCR for South Sudan, had a set of business meetings to attend to, so he loaned me a four-by-four and driver. "Just take a drive up towards Jau," he said. "I think you'll find it interesting."

We drove north, almost to Sudan, passing first a police then an SPLA checkpoint. In the space of twenty minutes we must have overtaken 500 persons – mainly young women, some with infants in their arms – trudging along a sandy track through the woods towards Jau with twenty-kilogram bags of grain or plastic containers of cooking oil perched on their heads. I saw one young girl leading a blind man with a stick. The monthly World Food Program general food distribution (GFD) had taken place a day or so before at Yida. All these registered "refugees" were now calmly heading back to the territory they had just fled, taking supplies to their men. 15,000 of Yida's registered 60,000 or so refugees now participated in this monthly phenomenon: they migrated south a day or two before the GFDs, back north a day or two later.

Back at the Yida biometric registration center at 10:00 a.m. (opening time), a hundred persons were waiting to have their data logged, having just come in the opposite direction, south from Nuba. All new arrivals were registered. Those in emergency need of nutrition received it, as did all infants, but only those willing to be transported to Ajuong received ration cards. I spoke with one alert-looking young man whose papers showed him to be seventeen years old.

"Where are your parents?"

"In the Nuba Mountains," he said.

"Why have they not come with you?"

"They want me to have an education ... so they have sent me here to school."

Last time I'd been to Ajuong Thok, it had been a stretch of unpopulated, sun-baked forest reached via a narrow track that petered out in the trees. Now it was a well-established camp housing 4,000 on well-drained and (currently) lush land with room for up to 20,000; the target was 10,000 by year's end, and the government had indicated that similar spaces could be made available a little way down the road. Several families were setting up camp. Most of the international NGOs in Yida had mirror operations here. There was a small but well-appointed and clean hospital ward, a birthing clinic, and a blood-testing lab.

Chanda (that was how he liked to be known) had already made a name for himself in Juba by seeking to eliminate duplication among NGOS working with the UN coordination by encouraging those with unacceptably high overheads to leave. Here I saw him in action. We wandered around a small birthing clinic being set up by the International Rescue Committee. It duplicated one we'd looked at barely fifteen minutes earlier, run by the designated health lead. Chanda looked at me knowingly and said to the chastened staff, "This needs to go ... let's talk about it later."

Ajuong's main attraction for the Nubans was education. There were 1,033 children attending primary school at Ajuong and 612 secondary students. At both schools, students were accommodated in large tents; at the primary level seating was on the dirt floor, but the PTA was beginning the fabrication of rustic benches at the secondary. Teachers were recruited from within the Nuban community under the supervision of the Lutheran World Federation. I asked one teacher, "How big are your classes?" "Hmm ... about 180, sometimes more."

A downside of the experiment was that, as everywhere in the greater Sudan, the Nubans tended to think education was wasted on girls: the primary school ratio was 733 boys to 300 girls. When I asked the secondary school students what messages they had for the people and government of Canada, one reply was, "Please talk to Omar (al-Bashir). Tell him we want peace in our country."

Before flying back to Juba, I met in Pharyang with the newly appointed county commissioner, Major William Deng Ayei, a former traffic policeman. Facing his office was the set of containers with a roofed-over space between them that the Canadian oil company Talisman had set up as a clinic years before. It looked to be disused, but it was often hard to tell in South Sudan. The commissioner's first gesture was to present me and Chanda with a sheep apiece. Mine chewed contentedly on my armchair as we chatted for half an hour, and contributed substantially to the dung on the floor. Subsequently I donated it to the refugees of Yida on behalf of the people of Canada; I suspected that within minutes of my takeoff it had been despatched to greener pastures.

These Are SPLM Ladies

Ulang, Upper Nile State, and Juba, 2013

We had a small fund at the embassy called the Canada Fund for Local Initiatives. The money always arrived from Ottawa frustratingly late – it had to be expended by the end of the financial year, with no latitude at all – and the approvals process was excessively bureaucratic. But this modest resource was the only means of initiating activities ourselves. In late 2012, we reached an agreement with MatMedia, a South Sudanese NGO, to hold discussions about grass-roots democracy in Ulang County, a remote part of Upper Nile State.

I flew with UNHAS up to Malakal, my first time back since I had been posted in Khartoum. The clear plastic chairs at the airport, I was impressed to see, were still there, though looking a bit scratched. I remembered once boarding a plane for Khartoum there that wouldn't start; the pilot got it going by bashing the starter motor with a baseball bat kept, for just that purpose, behind his seat.

Malakal possessed only one recommended hotel, a pleasant place with large airy courtyards off the dusty main street. It was popular with the local Big Men; their bodyguards' AK-47s, slung nonchalantly over their shoulders, would clang up against the stainless-steel serving dishes in the self-service restaurant. The Big Men would sweep in and out in large V-8 Toyotas with tinted windows; when the bodyguards rushed to open the doors, you could see that the upholstery was artificial fur, and ornaments dangled from the front-window visors. There was also a large group of Australian missionaries at a conference with local Evangelicals. They would loudly greet each other with appropriate biblical quotations from thirty metres or more away, and then embrace in a complicated ritual that must have been proprietary to their particular sect.

I tried to go for a walk along the riverbank to see if there were any barges like the one I had ridden past Fashoda years ago, but you couldn't get near the water anymore. Every road and alleyway was blocked and uniformed soldiers angrily waved me away; it seemed odd that Malakal was more militarized now than it had been when it was under siege during the civil war.

The following day, I took a taxi to the airport to board the Cessna Caravan that would take me to Nasir, the nearest place to Ulang with an airstrip. All seemed to go well for an hour, until we were right over Nasir and losing altitude. We made one pass low over the main dirt road, so low that startled men looked up and waved at us and a donkey bolted. Then another pass, heading out over the Sobat River at the end of the road where we could see a wrecked plane half-submerged in the water. By now the pilot and co-pilot were involved in an altercation, with the co-pilot repeatedly peering out of his side-window, consulting the chart on his lap, then remonstrating with the pilot. After the third attempt, we turned away. "Very sorry, now we are low on fuel, we need to go back to Malakal."

Back in Malakal the pilot tried to excuse himself by saying that visibility had been poor. This was laughable, as we had flown low enough to see the startled expressions on people's faces. Clearly, he had come in at the wrong place. Another night in Malakal, another hour or so's flying, and next day we were down on the correct landing strip, about half a mile away from the main street.

There was only one flight a week to Nasir. As there was no road out and I didn't fancy spending seven days there, I needed another plan and – with Chol, the MatMedia staffer who'd met me in his four by four, and who'd lived for years in Nebraska – we spent all morning executing it. I'd already contacted the county commissioner in Ulang to ascertain that he had a launch that could take me downriver to Malakal after the project was completed. There was only one catch. "There is no fuel, you see. You will have to buy a barrel of fuel in Nasir and bring it with you."

We spent hours driving around Nasir, following different tips we'd been given. Finally, an Ethiopian storekeeper obliged. Everything was discussed in a furtive manner, with lowered voices and much looking sideways, which made me nervous; I was even more so when the storekeeper required US$800 up front, and there was no barrel in sight. "It's all right," Chol whispered to me in his midwestern American accent. "I know this guy. And anyway, I'm a lot bigger than him."

Eight hundred dollars seemed an awful lot, but we'd checked around; anything for sale in Nasir had to come a very long way, through Ethiopia, so in general prices were several times higher than in Juba. There were additional expenses: the vehicle Chol had obtained was one of only four or five in the region and he'd had to pay a steep price for it, not to speak of the gas he'd wasted yesterday coming all the way from Ulang just to see me fly away. It was a good job I'd brought plenty of money. But I did wonder what the Ottawa bean-counters would make of the receipt we'd got for the barrel of diesel, written in Amharic characters.

It was a two-hour ride to Ulang, with our barrel in the back, along a very narrow and deeply rutted track in the dry forest on the north side of the Sobat River. We didn't see anyone else en route. In Ulang, life revolved around cows. In the late afternoon, when we arrived, what passed for the main street – a long, wide sun-baked expanse of black cotton soil – was serving as an informal corral for the five thousand or more head that had been brought in for the night. Their restless milling around raised a fine dust that obscured the sunset and all night their lowing could be heard as white noise. As elsewhere in the country, cattle were valued (and bred) not for their milk or their meat but as a form of dowry, or as payment in case of criminal proceedings, and for status. Chol told me that in Ulang an average bride would set you back thirty to thirty-five cows, but the price these days was rising and a girl from a good family would cost fifty or more. "If you have committed murder," he added without my asking, "then seventy or so will get you off scot-free. But you still need to worry about the victim's family; they might not go along with what the chief says." Chol also said, "But you know what? When I was a little kid here, just before the war, I can remember how people used to set off and walk their cows all the way to Juba, even on to Kenya … You see, Nicholas, they did sell them for meat in those days. What happened was, during the war, with the fighting and what not, you couldn't do that anymore. So folks stopped worrying about whether their cows gave good meat. Now they were only good for buying women … and so people started looking at their horns and their coats, more than anything. Crazy, I guess."

I stayed in a fenced compound on the edge of town belonging to the Irish organization GOAL. There were chickens in my bedroom and it took a few minutes to chase them out. In the evening, we sat in plastic chairs, listening to the cows lowing. The darkness soon became

almost total; there was no generator at GOAL, but you could hear
one or two in the distance. Across the river you could see a few camp-
fires, and occasionally a light puff of wind brought the smell of wood
smoke. "Remember Walgak, a few weeks back?" asked Chol. On
8 February, there'd been a massacre of about one hundred Nuer cattle herders; the fires were from the survivors of that raid.[1] The people
of Ulang blamed the Murle and Yau Yau. But Chol, the outsider
who'd only recently come back, admitted that the Nuer raided as
well. "Before, in the war you know, it was the Arabs. But the government can't say that anymore. It is our own people. And our army
does nothing to protect us."

Ulang and neighbouring Nasir were blessed with a limited but significant alternative to cattle-raising and herding. The Sobat was
abundant with fish (and consequently supported enough bird life for
an ornithologist to think he was in heaven, not that many twitchers
were found in these parts). As there was no possibility of freezing the
catch, it had to be consumed the same day or dried; racks of braided,
dried, and redolent Nile Perch lined the river bank, and dried fish had
become a vital dietary supplement.

It would be misleading to suggest that no modernity had reached
these distant parts. The Zain mobile telephone network had built an
enormous tower in Ulang three years earlier and every fashionable
young man and woman now had a mobile phone, the more cacopho-
nous its ringtone the better; Celine Dion was popular. Although there
was no mains electricity, one or two stalls in the market had genera-
tors that powered a few flickering bulbs at night and one of the shops
even had a satellite dish that was used to beam in the English Premier
League on Saturday nights. This single TV set, set under the brilliant
stars of a stygian equatorial night, with thirty adolescents following
every kick at Anfield, made a bizarre sight.

A positive development since I visited these regions a dozen years
earlier was the arrival of pit latrines. No longer were there segregated
stretches of the river bank dedicated only to defecation. In Ulang,
GOAL responded mainly to malaria and respiratory infections; there
were some cases of moderate malnutrition, but appropriate programs (also NGO-run) were in place. In this ultra-dry and hot climate, access to plentiful and clean water was critical, and in this
regard Ulang was lucky; its (NGO-drilled) boreholes provided good
water at an easily accessible depth. Fearful and perpetually hot and
thirsty foreigners such as myself were still advised to stick to bottled

water, though. Wherever Chol and I went, we'd attract legions of small children in our wake, waiting for us to finish and discard that one-litre PET bottle that we carried everywhere, so that it could become a water-carrier for their family.

And yes, politics had also reached Ulang.

With our sponsorship, 150 village chiefs, elders, and women from all eight *payams* (districts) of the county had come into Ulang. Some had walked all day in forty degrees to be here; some had camped out in the bush on the way. Hazards of walking in the bush included lions and tigers ("tiger" was the local word for leopard). Inconveniently, the only suitable location for this gathering was the extremely basic primary school. It was a tight fit to get seventy-five adults into each of two classrooms, at desks designed for twenty-five small children. The tall chiefs wore their red and white sashes and carried their sticks of office, the women their Sunday finery, ankle-length and body-hugging faux silk dresses that must have been an ordeal in this climate. Only a handful of the younger men (there was no age bar to chiefdom) knew how to read or write, and none of the elders. But interest was intense.

One chief summed it up like this. "We knew what we were doing when we voted for secession. And we are happy we have it. But we had no idea what we were doing at the last elections … we voted because they told us we must vote for relatives or for our clan; some of them promised us money … We elected four MPs for Ulang but we have never seen them since. We do not want to make the same mistake again."

There was open grumbling about the SPLM/A. Several people mentioned the perceived lavish lifestyle of top generals and VIPs (the term had become one of derision, explained my translator) and the perennial corruption scandals that were the talk of Juba. Let no one think the SPLM/A were universally revered in rural South Sudan, I thought to myself as the chiefs spoke. There was recognition that they had liberated the country, at enormous cost, especially to the civilian population (which was often overlooked by the still largely military leadership). But the war was over, and it was time to make progress. Most of the chiefs in the room saw none. Everybody understood that, in a democracy, you can always throw the rascals out – much nodding of approval here – but there was also nodding when, after an unexpected prayer for the delivery of all present, one outspoken woman said, "If they do not get the result they want next time, they will just change it. They have guns and we are afraid."

No doubt inadvisedly, I'd stated in some opening remarks (translated into Nuer) that anyone present should feel free to stand for public office if they felt they might do a better job than the incumbents. The interpreter took me to one side during a break and gently explained, "Mr Nicholas, of course you are right. But you see, to be elected, you have to speak English. Here there are maybe ten, no more than twelve who speak English, and none of the women."

Mostly I sat listening to whispered translations of what was being said in Nuer. At the end of a session, one young man provocatively turned to me and asked, "How many wives do you have?"

"One."

"So, what do you think about us? I have four. We all have more than one."

My hastily improvised reply that women should have as much choice as men brought a wave of enthusiastic female ululations and some clapping. But the underlying point was a serious one, and not at all off subject. The women of Ulang were strong, opinionated, not in the least shy; they would shake your hand as vigorously as any man and look you in the eye (unlike in Sudan). In contrast to the men – who all sported the six horizontal forehead scars of the Nuer – the younger women of Ulang had, like most Nuer women, rejected the extremely painful, sometimes dangerous rituals of scarification, and were quite modern in many ways. But they could not be village chiefs and they still had to submit to polygamy.

On the riverbanks, I saw hundreds of small boys playing happily. There seemed to be children everywhere – too many for the country's future good, surely. But talk of family planning was taboo in these parts, for a man's virility was measured by the number of both his cows and his children. You soon noticed that none of the children playing were girls, who had to stay home caring for their siblings or attending to domestic chores.

The commissioner – Ulang's Big Man – was not present for the sometimes frank discussions at the primary school. But I went to see him anyway (not least because I needed his boat if I was ever to get out). In the style of every commissioner in South Sudan and no doubt in imitation of his forebears – the legendary British district commissioners of the colonial era – Ulang's sat in a large open courtyard on a comfy chair, with acolytes at a respectful distance in less capacious plastic lawn chairs. On a small table at one side was his rod of office, along with two mobile phones, neither of which was quiet for more than two or three minutes at a time.

My grovelling request for the loan of his boat was met with what I soon learned was a characteristic silence, followed by a gentle "Okey." After this, he was much more at home speaking about American politics – he had lived for a decade in Chicago – than South Sudanese. Despite allowing that Susan Rice (then US ambassador to the United Nations in New York) had always been a good friend to South Sudan, he did not think that the just re-elected Democrats would take much positive interest in his country. But he argued that they should, if only because there were so many Americans ("like me") in South Sudan.

Careful enquiries in town had suggested that this commissioner was regarded as "Okey" in spite of the fact that – like the five others since independence – he had been appointed by the governor rather than elected as the constitution required. The unanimous favourite was the first incumbent, in 2005. He had insisted that all the civil servants who had decamped to the more comfortable Malakal return to Ulang to earn their keep. But he made so many enemies in this fashion that his tenure was short. When the current commissioner politely gave me his phone number, I asked him where I might usually find him. "Sometimes Juba, often Malakal," he said calmly.

On the last evening I was in Ulang, the pitiful wailing of a woman filled the night air for almost an hour. That afternoon, I learned, she had lost two children to drowning. They had been playing at the riverside.

Soon after dawn, as I bumped my way along the Sobat in the commissioner's speedboat, consuming my expensively bought fuel at a fierce rate, I was accompanied by the Big Man himself. He had jumped at the prospect of a free ride out to Malakal, along with his three armed bodyguards, two assistants, and two elegant women whom he described to me carefully: "These are SPLM ladies." We sat uncomfortably on the thwarts, but the commissioner had thoughtfully brought a comfy chair with him and balanced it cautiously amidships.

An hour out, one of the bodyguards flagged the driver to slow down. Among the lily pads, a dead body was floating in the water. We summoned the nearest dugout, paddled by two men in their twenties. They looked at it briefly. It was their father, who had disappeared

two days earlier. Gently, and without visible emotion, they took the
body in tow and headed for the shore. There was quiet shaking of
heads on board. One of the SPLM ladies took out her Nuer bible and
mumbled a short prayer. The commissioner flicked his swagger stick,
said "Okey," and the driver gunned the Yamaha 75.

Death never seemed to be far away in South Sudan.

Back in Juba, all the political attention had turned towards vice-
president Dr Riek Machar. His trajectory was an interesting one. A
portion of it, his relationship with and marriage to British aid worker
Emma McCune, was related in the best-selling book *Emma's War*.[2]
For many years the Big Man of the Nuer people, he had split from
what he termed the Dinka-dominated SPLM/A in 1991, allied himself with Shillook leader Dr Lam Akol, and sided with Khartoum for
much of the rest of Sudan's civil war. He returned to the fold in 2002
and had served as vice president since independence in 2011.

Riek, who spoke excellent English, held a PhD in "strategic planning" from the University of Bradford. He also had an American wife
as well as the more visible South Sudanese Angelina, was more outgoing than the less articulate President Salva Kiir, and had been much
more accessible to the international community – in part because
between 2011 and April 2013, the president had focused his attention principally on the complicated relationship with Sudan.

His perceived treachery in the nineties had not been forgotten.
Cynics suggested that it was in an attempt to re-make himself with
a view to advancing beyond the vice-presidency that in 2012 he
launched (or hijacked) the idea of a grand Peace and Reconciliation
Conference modelled on South Africa's Truth and Reconciliation
Commission. High-profile figures, including Archbishop Desmond
Tutu, were to be invited. This general idea had been mooted since
well before the Comprehensive Peace Agreement in 2005; during my
posting in Khartoum, UNICEF had held extensive consultations with
most of the parties concerned. But it had become clear that the conference was to be "forward-looking" (i.e. the sins of the past would
not be examined) and that the thorniest issues of reconciliation,
including the ongoing conflict in Jonglei, were not to be addressed at
all. In March 2013, Riek was forced to announce postponement of
the event, very likely at the president's insistence.

A week or so later, at an informal meeting of the elite politburo late one night over drinks at the presidential residence, Riek announced his intention to challenge Salva Kiir for the chairmanship of the movement at the upcoming Extraordinary Convention of the SPLM. Were he to be successful, he would automatically become the party's nominee for the presidency in the election to be held in mid-2015. Salva, the incumbent president of the country and chairman of the party would become a very lame duck. Even if unsuccessful, an open challenge to Salva by Riek would open various cans of worms and bring into the fray other men (and women) of ambition who might otherwise have kept their heads down: SPLM secretary-general Pagan Amum, Governor Nyandeng of Warrap, and Deng Alor (ex-minister for cabinet affairs) were the most prominent of these. Rebecca Garang, the widow of Dr John, could be a player too.

On 15 April 2013, it was announced on television that President Kiir had "removed" the vice-president's executive powers. It was not clear exactly what this meant, as those powers had never been specified. But the announcement appeared to remove Riek from public activity and allow him only a ceremonial role. Political speculation moved immediately into overdrive as everyone tried to figure out who could count on whose support, with analyses of ethnicity, personal friendships, and historical rivalries all thrown into the mix.

Salva Kiir seemed to have an immediate advantage tactically, since he could control the timing of the party convention at which the issue of the chairmanship would come up. On the other hand, it was speculated that, following the integration of Paulino Matiep's militia to the SPLA in 2006, the ethnic balance within the army (numerically) currently favoured Riek Machar's ethnic group, the Nuer, and while the Dinka held a majority of general officer positions, chief of the general staff James Hoth was also Nuer (albeit married into the Dinka community). Riek further had the ability to complicate matters in still-troubled Jonglei, if only by staying mum as Lou Nuer youth mobilized against the embattled Murle.

Dr Lam Akol, the Shillook Big Man then drifting in exile between Cairo and Khartoum, would also have read the papers' headlines with some interest. Might he be hoping for a phone call from his old ally Riek? Lam Akol had long wanted to return to South Sudan and pit his SPLM-DC against the mainstream SPLM, but Juba had thus far made it clear that he was not welcome; he was so identified with Khartoum in the eyes of many southerners that his credit might have run out.

Riek Machar bided his time. The annual celebration of Independence Day came: 9 July 2013. Avid SPLM watchers noted that Salva Kiir and Riek Machar did not speak to each other at the ceremonies. Then the rift between them seemed suddenly to shudder and widen again as the vice-president went public with strong criticism of the president for having sacked Unity State's governor, Taban Deng (a Nuer), whom Salva seemed to see as a threat. Other prominent politicians – including four more of the country's ten state governors – scrambled to line up publicly behind Salva. In an open letter to the president, eighty self-described Nuer "intellectuals and leaders" also backed him and called for Riek's complete dismissal. Members of the State Legislature of Unity first criticized Salva, but then backtracked to support him.

The man in the Texan hat, as was his wont, kept his counsel.

Ex-president Thabo Mbeki of South Africa paid a very low-profile visit to Juba and brokered a temporary truce: Riek and Salva agreed that neither would make any further statements concerning their political plans. There would be no further "administrative measures" (i.e. firings) but only until the next meeting of the SPLM's politburo, whose date remained unannounced.

Next it became evident that, two weeks earlier, Riek had visited Sudan to mend fences over a threat by Khartoum to cut off the South's access to international oil markets. Cynics suggested, with hindsight, that he had been chosen for this mission precisely so that it would fail. In mid-July, Juba received official notification from Khartoum, in the form of a letter to Foreign Minister Nhial Deng, that a shutdown would begin on 7 August; one of South Sudan's principal producers (Petronas) had already started sealing off wells, fearful that a sudden move by Khartoum might damage its installations.

All of this coincided with the advance and retreat of Nuer and Murle war columns across Jonglei. As I listened to a senior UN official delivering a briefing on Friday, 19 July, at SRSG Hilde Johnson's home, the skies darkened and lightning flashed. There was an inescapable sense of rising tension. I entitled a report to Ottawa, "Stormy weather ahead."

There wasn't long to wait. On Tuesday, 23 July 2013, Salva issued a presidential decree dismissing all his ministers, all deputy ministers (who were political appointees), Vice-President Riek Machar, and SPLM secretary-general Pagan Amum – the number two official in the party. Like Riek, Pagan had announced he would contest the chairmanship.

The news came mid-evening. In the Canadian office at the time were Brock, a junior military policeman on loan to us for a few days from the Canadian mission in Nairobi for the purpose of training our guards; a Canadian woman called Julie, who might or might not have been his girlfriend, and who was in Juba to advise the Constitutional Review Commission; and Pauline, an older lady sent to us by HQ to help sort our administrative systems. I found myself simultaneously dealing with panicky calls from Ottawa, investigating rumours of fighting on the streets, recalling melodramatic messages that Pauline kept sending to the Canadian foreign minister's office whenever I stepped out, and worrying what to do with Brock and Julie. The two youngsters had announced that they had had to leave their hotel – where they had separate rooms – because they were out of money. Julie appeared to be finding it all quite thrilling; this was just what she imagined and hoped life in the Canadian foreign service might be. Mercifully, neither she nor Brock seemed fazed when Pauline suggested the two of them spend the night on the two couches in her hotel suite.

By the next morning, Wednesday, there was an even greater presence of the army and central Juba was impassable because of road blocks, but things were otherwise quiet. The outgoing minister of information was spinning the affair on the radio as "a normal cabinet reshuffle." He recalled that in developed democracies, it was not unusual for an entire cabinet to be asked to tender their resignations for a "deck-clearing." (His complacency was later explained: he himself was to receive a promotion.)

It was the dismissals of Riek Machar and Pagan Amum that were neuralgic. Riek was the most prominent Big Man of the second-largest tribe in South Sudan, and his accusations against Salva Kiir (poor leadership, tolerance of corruption) resonated well beyond the Nuer community, even though Riek, as Salva's deputy, shared much of the blame. As for Pagan, he was an SPLM stalwart if there ever was. He could not command a significant ethnic vote in the same way Riek could (Pagan was from the smallish Shillook tribe, whose

loyalty was largely pledged to that other SPLM renegade, Lam Akol),
but the party intelligentsia and a number of old-timers would be dismayed to see him go. Pagan, moreover, was to be "investigated" by a
commission led by Parliamentary Speaker James Wani Igga. (Some
time later the commission reported publicly; it documented massive
incompetence and disorganization with the SPLM Secretariat, but
fell far short of proving that Pagan had benefitted personally and
financially from such mismanagement.)[3]

A major split in the SPLM now looked likely, I wrote to HQ. The
principal fear was that it could be on ethnic lines: Nuer vs Dinka.

8

The Knives Are Out

Juba, 2013

Most diplomats watched the political drama with detached interest; relatively few had anything more than a sketchy sense of the history of Southern Sudan and its key personalities and the majority were still infused with the euphoria of independence. There was brief excitement around the dismissal of Riek Machar and the cabinet. At home one night, Jenny and I listened to our double CD set of *Evita*. I was reminded of the years we had spent in Argentina in the late seventies: "Dice are rolling/The knives are out/Would-be presidents are all around."

But at work, the focus of our interest was the New Deal Compact, an evolving agreement between Western countries and the government of South Sudan according to which priorities for the country would be established by mutual consent, and benchmarks would be negotiated against which we would measure progress. There was much consulting on all sides. The government visited rural parts to hear the concerns of the population, while embassies contacted their capitals to see what part of the compact we could each support and each other to avoid duplication.

It was surprising that, in a country as underdeveloped as South Sudan, there existed no regular forum for embassies to meet, coordinate, and share experiences. I supposed that this was because the troika had fulfilled that role for a number of years and its members preferred not to relinquish their near-exclusivity of access. But with the compact at the top of everyone's agenda, there came into being an informal, self-selected group of countries and UN agencies calling itself the G6-plus, whose members met over a cold Nile Special and samosas in each other's homes every two weeks.

As 2013 advanced, the process became ever more intense. The principal interlocutor on the government side was the minister of finance, Aggrey Tissa Sabuni, an articulate, modest, and reasonable man with a low public profile. It was soon evident that commitment to and knowledge of the compact on the government side did not extend far beyond Aggrey Tissa and his director of aid coordination, Moses Mabior. Whenever we met with officials from other ministries, whose cooperation and participation would be vital to the success of the compact, it seemed that a different official was assigned every time, requiring a laborious process of re-education. All too often it was the outsiders, the foreigners who ended up chairing the working groups that were meant to be South Sudanese–led.

A particularly interesting finding of the in-country surveys was that most communities identified inter-ethnic reconciliation as their top priority for donor support (this with the caveat that polling and surveys are notoriously problematic in South Sudan). I was intrigued but not surprised by this after years of observing the civil war, which as often as not had pitted southerners against each other rather than against northerners. But for newcomers to South Sudan, this seemed aberrant. More to the point, how could you achieve "reconciliation" and how did you establish benchmarks? When we huddled with the government to reach a consensus over priorities, reconciliation shifted near to the bottom of the list.

Meanwhile, we were working with another branch of the Ministry of Finance to help the country organize its first international investment conference, an idea launched at a meeting hosted by the US government in Washington on 16 April 2013. Oversight was placed in the hands of a steering committee on which I sat with a number of other diplomats and government officials. This was another imperfect process, and many of the diplomats said to each other that it was folly to be thinking of attracting major foreign investment when a part of the country (Jonglei) was in flames. Perhaps more to the point, the country's capital had no electricity and no running water. We also pointed out repeatedly that it did not make sense to have a steering committee for a business event with no participation from the private sector, and that foreign participation would more appropriately be from Uganda, Kenya, and Ethiopia.

I was not optimistic that we would attract any serious interest from Canadian investors. In fact, I was not even sure that I would recommend they come here at all. Other Western colleagues gloomily agreed. But we also thought that the government should be given some credit for its optimism and sense of enterprise. So, we diligently reviewed with officials the legislation that we considered needed changing if foreign investors were to come, harped tactfully but insistently on the need to address corruption, and suggested that while it was good to promote yourself, it was not realistic to suggest – as did the minister of foreign affairs – that the investment climate in South Sudan was better than that of the United States. (There had just been a mass shooting at a military installation in Washington, and the minister scornfully said, "You see? Things like that never happen in Juba.")

One of the priority sectors identified was tourism. Rural South Sudan – especially the great swamp that is the Sudd – was one of the last great wildernesses of the world, and the annual migration of the kob antelope in Jonglei was second only to that of the wildebeest in the Serengeti. A rafting trip we had recently taken on the upper waters of the Nile had been adventure travel at its best. But all the hotels in Juba were run by foreigners, in large part because South Sudanese had yet to learn the basic art of unfailingly smiling at visitors. At the airport, you were far more likely to be greeted with a scowl, a sullen order, or a poke with a gun than with a friendly "Welcome!" The promotional literature for the conference actually warned that "it is illegal to take photographs in South Sudan without a permit," and appended a long list of things that could not be photographed under any circumstances. The list included "people" and "all government buildings."

In four years, I only ever met two tourists. One was on leave from a job with the United Nations in the Gaza Strip. The other was Levison Wood, a man who described himself grandly as an "explorer" and was walking the length of the Nile from south to north. In South Sudan, he had thus far only walked the length of the (tarmac) Nimule to Juba road, on account of the banks of the Nile being mined. Now he wanted advice on the way onwards. I advised him that he would find things difficult in Jonglei; he did, and had to fly over most of South Sudan.

In spite of these omens, the Investment Conference was actually something of a success. As 4 December 2013 drew near, investors, nearly all from Africa but some from China, flooded in. Although a ceiling had been set at four hundred participants, and a significant number of companies were turned away when the virtual registration rolls topped out, at least eight hundred packed Freedom Hall, the enormous white beer tent that was the conference site. This was by no means your average international junket. Temperatures were acceptable at 8:00 a.m., but by 10:00 the portable air-conditioning units could not cope with the massive crowd and the outside temperature of forty degrees. But most participants stuck it out, despite being slowly parboiled.

More irritating was the arrival of the president more than two hours late for the inauguration, for no apparent good reason. I knew that this phenomenon – the tendency of Big Men routinely to arrive extremely late for events and for their juniors to be too timid to start without them – was a feature of political life in South Sudan, but it did not impress the business community since an already packed schedule had to be compressed even further. Things deteriorated again on day two when events were held back for a cameo appearance by another Big Man, the prime minister of East Timor (who had actually come for the subsequent signing of the New Deal Compact).

There were presentations on roads and transport infrastructure, on the country's great agricultural potential, on oil, and on mining. When assessing the mining prospects in South Sudan, you had first to clear away the usual cloud of mystique that gathers whenever there looks to be gold in those hills. Gold there was in South Sudan – the SPLA drew upon the artisanal mines of Eastern Equatoria to help finance its twenty-five-year-long war effort – but the quantity was far from clear. The last reliable geological survey dated from the colonial period. However, both Finance Minister Aggrey Tissa and President Salva Kiir appealed, "Come now; it will be too late tomorrow."

Meanwhile, negotiations over the New Deal Compact were reaching a climax. A sticking point had emerged. Since the date of independence, the value of the South Sudan pound (SSP) had been legally pegged against the US dollar at 2.96 SSP to 1 USD. But a gap between the official rate and the parallel (black) market had slowly grown to the point at which, for ordinary citizens who did not have access to the official rate, a dollar now cost 4.5 SSP. Legal access to dollars at the better rate was controlled by the Central Bank, which issued a very reduced number of letters of credit upon application by business people.

The system was open to abuse, and it was hugely abused. Letters of credit went largely to a small circle of well-connected persons, many of them related to the governor of the Central Bank and to other top officials. These people were able to buy dollars at about three pounds, walk out on the street and sell them at 4.5 – and repeat the operation ad infinitum. The result was that the economy was undermined, with more and more of it operating at the unofficial rate. The government itself lost massively in that it deposited its oil-generated dollars in the form of pounds in the Central Bank at the official rate of three, and Western donors also exchanged their dollars at that rate; had the government been able to use the "real" rate of 4.5, it would have closed its budget deficit at a stroke, and if donors had the same privilege, they would have got fifty percent more pounds for their dollars.

Because of the de facto tax on aid dollars – a tax that went not to general revenue but to the bank accounts of a few well-connected operators – the European Union made its financial support for the compact conditional on the IMF approving a program for South Sudan. And the IMF, in turn, demanded harmonization of the exchange rate: either an official devaluation to at least 4.5 SSP to 1 USD, or a floating of the pound. Minister Aggrey Tissa understood why it had to be done and persuaded the governor of the bank. So, overnight, a devaluation to 5.0 SSP was announced.

With tragic coincidence, the governor timed his announcement for a day when there was a chronic shortage of diesel and gasoline in Juba because floods in Uganda had delayed incoming trucks. There was a perception that the devaluation had turned the fuel trucks around, and MPs and ministers (who had not been briefed by Aggrey Tissa) angrily summoned the governor to account in an emergency session of the National Legislative Assembly. Of course, he should never have agreed to appear, since the point of having a central bank is that it makes decisions independently of politicians. But after half an hour of shouting, abuse, and the throwing of paper aeroplanes, the governor reversed his decision. Parliament cheered. They thought this was a victory for the common people against the IMF. And the dollar profiteers (many of whom sat in cabinet) quietly smirked.

Simultaneously, the compact sank without trace.[1] And the prospects of the governor ever executing a successful devaluation in the future, having once caved before legislators, now looked very dim indeed. Poor Aggrey Tissa told a meeting of diplomats that "parliament is out for my blood" and that a petition was circulating to garner names for a vote of no confidence in his performance as minister.

I didn't ignore politics while all of this was going on. In November, a colleague visiting from Khartoum and I sought out the idle Riek Machar. Confusion over where he was living sent us first to a remote tract outside the city before we arrived – half an hour late – at his home on a large rectangle of walled grassland in downtown Juba. With his characteristic missing-tooth smile and dressed in a flowing pale-blue jellabiya, the Big Man waved us in; an assistant took notes and later on, a full account of our meeting was published on the electronic news site Sudan Tribune.[2]

Even though he had been removed from his role as vice-president, Riek remained an MP and continued to attend parliamentary sessions, though "only to listen." He was cautiously optimistic that the first in a series of SPLM party events, the National Liberation Council (NLC) meeting, would take place on 23 November, at which point members would discuss key party documents and undertake to vote in a simple majority on proposed revisions. "Our biggest challenge will be to ensure that voting takes place by secret ballot, not the open ballot the president wants. An open ballot always favours the incumbent," he said. "And we want the idea of the secret ballot to be carried through to the selection of the next chairman of the SPLM too."

Riek explained that when the time came, he intended to run on a platform of three main issues. "First, democracy not just in the country at large, but within the SPLM." He pointed to the blatantly illegal attempt by the president to gag ex–SPLM secretary-general Pagan Amum as an example of how the party lacked internal democracy. Any move against Pagan should have been properly debated, and a formal intra-party investigation launched; instead, the president fired him summarily and then decreed he could neither speak to the press nor leave the country.

"Then I'll be pushing for greatly increased federalism and better service delivery," he added. An improved federation, Riek insisted, was the only means of bridging the many ethnic fissures that split South Sudan. But public perceptions of the usefulness of federalism had been severely undermined by the government's inability to use the federal structure for the delivery of basic services at the state and sub-state levels.

Finally: accountability and governance. There was so much grumbling at all levels that we hardly needed to discuss this. Riek added, in passing, that people were ready to vote across ethnic lines as long as the security system allowed for it and voters were not intimidated when casting ballots.

We talked about the cabinet that had been named to replace that which he had led. Most members had a history of government in Khartoum, with two notable exceptions: Defence Minister Kuol Manyang and Information Minister Michael Makuei. "I think it's wrong to think these people have influence in Khartoum still," he said. "But Khartoum will be happy; the influence runs in the other direction."

With some prescience, Riek discussed feelings within the military at this time. After the cabinet shuffle, he said, he had "congratulated the army for staying neutral." But the president was not happy; "He had hoped the army would make a statement actively supporting him … Now he is travelling, for the first time, and making speeches to broaden his support base. But they are the wrong kinds of speeches, they are tribal."

We talked about Abyei, Jonglei, and in passing Riek complained that people seemed scared to come and see him. "Everyone was too afraid to accept the invitation I sent to my son's wedding celebrations." Winding up, and leaning forward to count on his fingers, he said, "I have two requests of you all … First, we need more active advocacy on the agenda of democracy, including the democratization of the SPLM as a party. Because whatever happens at the SPLM level is ultimately brought to the government. Second, you must do more to encourage multiparty politics. This is the only way we can break the idea that only the ones who fought the war can get in."

Riek came over as confident, talkative, eager to meet. Much of what he had to say to us made sense. But what he could or would not say was that as vice-president of the country and vice-chairman of the SPLM, he had had, for an extended period of time, the power to start addressing some of the ills he discussed with us. It was only in the spring of 2013 that his discontent with Salva Kiir's leadership started to be glimpsed. And until quite recently he had been simply silent on the need for internal transformation of the SPLM. If South Sudan was not in as happy a state as many of us hoped it would be two years from independence, Riek himself deserved some of the blame.

It was nearly Christmas. I knew from the previous year that Juba would almost empty itself of expatriates until mid-January in the New Year. Jenny and I were planning to splash out on a very expensive voyage to some remote islands in the Southern Ocean, leaving from Bluff, New Zealand. A friend and colleague, Robin, would come in to spell us for a couple of weeks. In the meantime, the rest of the office staff – Catherine, Caroline, and Nancy – had rotated out over the summer and were replaced by Jamie as head of cooperation and two female officers with their partners.

On foreign diplomatic postings, it is often not the hardship or physical danger that creates tension among the staff but ostensibly less important matters such as accommodation, even though the apartments and houses rented by the Canadian government overseas are usually quite a lot larger than people would have at home. I'd anticipated this. We had held a ceremonial draw to see who would get which apartment, even though all three were identical in size. Still there were issues, bad vibes between the two incoming couples, who were neighbours. But I was hopeful that with the Christmas break coming up everyone would get some much-needed rest and we would be able to get off to a fresh start in the New Year.

It was not to be.

After a long quiet spell during which the deposed vice-president kept his cards close to his chest, making only occasional pious statements about the need for democracy, it became obvious on Friday, 6 December, that Riek had not been idle. He was able to assemble a significantly large group of SPLM heavyweights for a high-profile press conference which he pointedly chose to hold not in the spacious grounds of his private residence but at SPLM House. It was about who was there, as much as what was said. Among these were:

- Rebecca Garang,* widow of the late Dr John Garang;
- Pagan Amum,* former secretary-general of the SPLM;
- Deng Alor,* former foreign minister and cabinet affairs minister;
- John Luk Jok,* former minister of justice;
- Taban Deng,* former governor of Unity State;
- Majak D'Agot, former deputy minister of defence;
- Peter Adwok Nyaba, author and former minister of education;
- Oyay Deng Ajak, former minister for national security;
- Madut Biar, former minister for telecommunications;
- Gier Chuong Aloung, former minister for internal affairs;

- Luka Monoja, former minister of health;
- Cirino Hiteng, former minister for culture/youth/sports;
- Ezekiel Lol, former (pre-independence) envoy to the US and UN; and
- Alfred Lado Gore, former minister of the environment.

(*) indicates members of the eighteen-member politburo, the top organ of the party, of which Machar was also a member.

Careful scrutiny told us that Riek Machar had at least one third of the politburo with him. But most informed estimates seemed to give Salva Kiir nearly the same:

- Kuol Manyang,* minister of defence;
- Nhial Deng,* former foreign minister;
- James Wani Igga,* vice-president;
- Anne Itto,* deputy secretary-general of the SPLM; and
- Paul Mayom,* minister of water.

The rest of the politburo looked to be undecided. One Big Man thought to be leaning to Riek Machar, if only because he had recently been dismissed by Salva Kiir, was our landlord, ex–finance minister Kosti Manibe.

The list of those at the press conference told us that Riek had recruited heavily among disgruntled ex-ministers; hardly surprising. Also unsurprisingly, the list was Nuer-heavy. But more significantly, the ex-vice-president had made inroads into the camp generally known as the "Garang Boys." These were old-time loyalists of John Garang (and thus ex-believers in the New Sudan) and for a period during the war they had been bitter enemies of Riek's SPLM/Nasir faction. The heavyweights from this constituency were Rebecca Garang, with all the history that accompanied her name, and Pagan Amum, who brought with him only part of the small Shillook vote but a lot of SPLM history. Riek would have been disappointed to have missed out on Nhial Deng, a Garang Boy if there ever was; he had recently been fired from cabinet for idleness, but Salva had evidently seen which way the wind was blowing and had seduced him back into the fold with the office of chief negotiator.

What was said was less important than the cast on stage. Riek criticized Salva for having abandoned the principles of the party founder,

John Garang; for ignoring the grassroots of the party; for ruling in an ever more dictatorial manner, and for flouting the party constitution. For good measure, he accused the president of wilfully covering up corruption. He concluded by calling for a meeting of the politburo before that of the larger National Liberation Council, "so as to correct the deviation from the SPLM vision and direction." Rebecca Garang and Pagan Amum also spoke. Pagan said that this press conference was only the first in a series of planned activities in the same vein; the next would be a rally on 18 December.

Why the emphasis on having the politburo meet first? Riek clearly believed he now had the numbers to defeat the president in the politburo but the NLC, with its bigger numbers and uncertain voting procedures, would be much more difficult to control and predict – unless, that is, the thinking of the politburo was already known.

The press conference passed off peacefully enough. But members of Salva Kiir's camp shot themselves in the foot by attempting, on Saturday, 8 December, to seize newspapers that had listed the names of those in attendance and printed Riek Machar's remarks. This was futile because Al Jazeera and Sky News had already recorded the event and the widely read online site Sudan Tribune also carried the news.

Forty-eight hours later, on Sunday, Vice-President Wani Igga was wheeled out by the president at the same locale for a riposte. He assembled a good crowd too, rejected Machar's allegations, and said that the ex-vice-president was seeking to profit from "disgruntled party members."

Tension in Juba was now rising by the day. My report to Ottawa on Monday 9 December was entitled "The SPLM starts to crack." The climax would come a few days later, when the president – after months of vacillation but now faced with the opposition's growing momentum – finally summoned the meeting of the National Liberation Council comprising about 200 senior party members. Salva Kiir's plan was to bypass the politburo, where his position looked shaky, and go straight to the NLC, where voting was by a show of hands and much more likely to favour the incumbent.

On Saturday, 14 December, the NLC meeting opened at the Nyakuron Cultural Center in central Juba. Its explicit objective was to resolve the internal differences that were threatening to fracture the party in two. Contrary to earlier rumours of a boycott, many of the SPLM members who had been at the previous week's press conference attended, including Riek Machar, his wife Angelina Teny, Garang's widow Rebecca, and Finance Minister Kosti. Notable by his absence was Pagan Amum, who was reportedly warned by the police to stay away. There was a strong presence of police and army, and the roads around the venue were cordoned off, but the atmosphere was initially relaxed and jovial.

The Catholic archbishop of Juba, Paulino Lukudu Loro, encouraged the NLC to "become more and more democratic," mentioned the "concerns, tensions and fear" in the population at large, and appealed to the SPLM members to respect the spirit of Christmas and to preserve peace and pursue reconciliation. He also suggested that it might be better if Riek called off a public rally he had announced.

Then came the keynote speaker. Salva Kiir harshly criticized those who had challenged him but extended an appeal to resolve differences peacefully through dialogue. He started off by paying tribute to Nelson Mandela, who had died a week earlier, and John Garang, and by reminding the gathering of the successful liberation struggle, of progress made since 2005, of "building state institutions where there were none," of the 2010 elections, and of the referendum for independence. Salva then stated, in an implicit reference to Riek, that some had abandoned the liberation struggle and "some comrades challenged my executive position." He said that "this takes us back to 1991" (when Riek had split from Garang and formed the SPLM-Nasir faction) and "I will not allow this to happen again."

He referred to the reshuffle in July, which he called a response to the popular demand to curb corruption and mismanagement, and explained that he was "determined to combat these evils." On a more conciliatory note, the president insisted, "there is room for everyone in the party," and emphasized the importance of resolving differences in a democratic spirit to preserve the party's unity. "The SPLM is a party of freedom of speech and everyone has the right to compete for every position."

He appealed to the NLC to "transform the SPLM into a living organization for all who uphold the revolutionary ideals ... as long as I am the leader of this party, I will continue to unite the people and extend a hand to those who fought us." This was the point at which deliberations were closed to outside observers. Late in the day, Riek and a group of thirteen of his followers walked out, stating the following: "Kiir's statements were of hostility, [and provided] no room for political dialogue. We attended the NLC meeting despite the fact that the Political Bureau did not convene. But there was no freedom of debate."

Next morning, a Sunday, diplomats gathered at the offices of the European Union. There was a sense of expectancy in the air. But it looked for now as if Riek – realizing he had not got the votes necessary at the NLC to challenge Salva's leadership formally – had conceded.

The NLC meeting continued for a second day in a mostly routine manner. Juba was quiet.

Later, someone said they heard the first shot at 6:00 p.m.; another person swore it was not until 11:00.

9

Juba Implodes

Juba, December 2013

As the sun rose in a cloudless sky on Monday, 16 December, the distant crackle of heavy machine-gun fire was interrupted with growing frequency by seemingly closer thumps. My small red Nokia cellphone was only showing an intermittent signal – the lines were obviously overloaded – but at 7:00 a.m. I called the two Canadian office staff in their apartments a couple of kilometres away to check they were all right, and to state what I thought was obvious: "Stay well way from the windows, hunker down."

The blithe reply came back, "Oh, but we've been watching it all from the balcony. What do you think is going on?"

Jenny turned on the radio, trying to find Miraya – the UN's station – while I unfolded my laptop and started the laborious process of keying in and waiting for a wi-fi signal. After a quick glance at message headers, I sent my very short e-mail to the watch unit at Foreign Affairs in Ottawa. I managed to get hold of Othmar, our Dutch security consultant, on the phone. He lived across town and reported that, in a brief foray outside, he had found all the streets blocked off and nobody moving. Then I tried Mandrea, our senior driver, who was always a good source of information. "I think it started at the Giada barracks. They are saying an officer was shot dead. But now the fighting is at Bilpam too," he told me.

Giada was one and a half kilometres in one direction from our house and Bilpam – the headquarters of the SPLA – was two kilometres the other way, so we seemed to be between two firefights. By 7:25 the noise was constant. Radio Miraya, perplexingly, had almost nothing to report, just Colonel Philip Aguer, the military spokesperson, stating that there had been some minor disturbances but all was now under control.

There didn't seem to be much we could do except wait. Jenny went to see that the guards had food and water; their shift change had, unsurprisingly, not arrived. She put on coffee and made some toast. As I munched, I called Mading Ngor, a Canadian/South Sudanese journalist, to see what he knew. He had just spoken to Information Minister Michael Makuei, who said the situation was "calming," and that there would be a press conference later in the day. Then I got back to my e-mail. There was a pro-forma message stating that the UN was suspending flights for the day, and the first wire item was now up, from the Sudan Tribune:

> December 16, 2013 (JUBA) – Military clashes have occurred between the presidential guards of South Sudan's president, Salva Kiir in the capital, Juba. The clashes occurred from about 10pm on Sunday evening in the old military barracks inside the capital and continued intensively for about one hour before one group was expelled.
>
> Sporadic gunfire rocked the new nation's capital overnight sending residents into a state of panic as movements were controlled by the military. The state-owned SSTV is currently off air while Juba airport remains closed. Juba residents also claim they have found it hard to make telephone calls since the morning.
>
> Military sources said the clashes between the Tiger special force occurred when one group predominantly of the Nuer ethnic group was suspicious of the deployment of another predominantly from the Dinka tribe. An argument between the two is believed to have led to the deadly clashes.

Things were quieter by 10:00 a.m., but I could hear tanks passing along a nearby main road and there was the occasional heavy detonation. Each phone call I made led me to a new rumour. One was that troops had entered the EU diplomatic compound in search of Riek Machar; another had him seeking refuge in the neighbouring US Embassy.

Apparently, the fighting had begun within the ranks of the Presidential Guard (Nuer vs Dinka), and had then quickly morphed into an attempt by troops loyal to Riek to take over GHQ at Bilpam. At 10:30, I interpreted the fact that tanks were moving away from Bilpam and towards the Nuer neighbourhoods of Jebel Kujur and Rock City as a sign that Nuer forces had been routed. The thousands of civilians fleeing to the UN compound at one end of the airport were presumably Nuer too.

Radio Miraya was playing festive Christmas carols.

I went back to my e-mail, and found this: "I would like to know what you have planned for me in the current crisis here in South Sudan. I am a Canadian citizen and would like to know what are your procedures in these circumstances." Good question. It was tempting to reply by redirecting the lady to the Canadian government website that warned against all travel to South Sudan, and that also stated, "Be aware that the ability of the Canadian office to assist Canadian citizens is extremely limited." But I had the feeling that more and more Canadians were going to show up, virtually or in person, and I started a chain of messages to suggest what we might be able to do. The airport was closed, so for the time being our advice was to stay home.

Around noon the president appeared on television, dressed uncharacteristically in fatigues, and delivered a statement:

Yesterday at about 6:30 p.m., during the closing of the SPLM National Liberation Council (NLC) meeting, an unidentified person near Nyakuron Cultural Center released gunshots in the air and escaped. This was followed later by an attack at the SPLA HQ's near Juba University (Giada) by a group of soldiers allied to the former vice-president Dr Riek Machar Teny and his group. These attacks continued until this morning. However, I would like to inform you at the outset that your government is in full control of the security situation in Juba. The attackers fled and your forces are pursuing them. I promise you today that justice will prevail.

Fellow citizens, let me reiterate my statement during the opening of the NLC meeting few days ago in which I said that my government is not and will not allow the incidents of 1991 to repeat themselves again.

This prophet of doom continues to persistently pursue his actions of the past and I have to tell you that I will not allow or tolerate such incidents once again in our new Nation. I strongly condemn these criminal actions in the strongest terms possible. Fellow citizens, your government led by the SPLM has articulated the ideals of democracy in the party as well as in the government and I will never deviate from them at any cost. The

SPLM is fully committed to the peaceful and democratic transfer of power and will never allow political power to be transferred through violence.

Fellow citizens, in response to the criminal acts of yesterday committed by this disgruntle [*sic*] group and for the sake of the security and safety of our citizens I declare curfew in Juba as to be observed [*sic*] from 6:00 p.m. to 6:00 a.m. with immediate effect from today, December 16, 2013, until further notice. Security organs are hereby directed to allow the residents of Juba to go about doing their normal work and move freely during the daylight hours. The security organs will also undertake full investigation into these incidents and the government will ensure that the culprits answer for their crimes before the appropriate law institutions.

From the beginning, almost no one believed that this was an attempted coup by Riek (the "prophet of doom"), although the government never gave up its narrative. Coup 101 theory was that when overthrowing a government, you made an immediate attempt to seize strategic locations such as the airport and radio/TV installations, and that you muzzled or otherwise contained the head of state and his senior officials. Nothing of this sort occurred. Indeed, many of those later alleged to have been among the masterminds had to be woken in their beds at home to be arrested. Riek fled Juba in a very undignified manner in the middle of the night in a black Hummer; it was later reported to have been found abandoned with pair of large red underpants on the back seat. The nail in the coffin of governmental propaganda came weeks later when, at the trial of several of those accused of conspiracy, Mac Paul, the director general of military intelligence, asserted that there was no evidence whatsoever for the theory. Ironically, he had been called by the prosecution.

So what did happen?

General James Hoth Mai, chief of the general staff and a Nuer, gave an account to investigators of an African Union Commission of Inquiry in mid-2014. He contradicted the initially prevailing theory that Dinka elements of the presidential guard had attempted to disarm their Nuer peers, presumably to pre-empt a Riek Machar powergrab after the meeting of the National Liberation Council:

We do not allow soldiers to go to sleep with their guns. There was no attempt to disarm anyone. We had 2 colleagues on duty that day. People mobilized to break the armory. There was no attempt to keep a particular group from being on duty that night. The Commander, a Nuer, killed his deputy, a Dinka, who was refusing for the armory to be opened. That same night, people came and broke open the armory.[1]

Hoth seemed oddly evasive about who the "people" who seized the armoury might be. But this account was generally consistent with that of Dinka major general Marial Chanuong Yol Mangok, commander of the Tiger Battalion (Presidential Guard). A different story was given to the commission by Lieutenant-Colonel Peter Lok Tang, the Nuer deputy commander of the 2nd Brigade:

On the 12th of December 2013, 740 [Dinka] soldiers were brought from Bahr-al-Ghazal, and taken to Luri. On 14 December, they brought them to Tiger headquarters at Giada. When they arrived, they [were informed] that their guns would be taken to the stores. On 15 December at 8 p.m., the Dinka component of Tiger Battalion [was] rearmed. I was there and inquired why the guns were taken from the store. They answered that they would take them back to the store. I waited for 30 minutes and asked again. At that time, Gen Marial Chanuong arrived, and ordered them to take more guns out. I went again to ask them why more guns were being taken out. This is when the bodyguards of Marial [Chanuong] began shooting. He started running back to his brigade headquarters, which is when his soldiers began breaking into the armory.

Lok Tang was asked, "Who fired the first shot?"
"I was shot at first – the bodyguard of Marial (a Dinka) fired at me."
Exactly who shot whom, and in what order, has yet to be established definitively, but the suggestions that a special unit of Dinka soldiers had been recruited in a semi-clandestine manner in Bahr-al-Ghazal, that a number had recently been brought into Juba, and that there was a Dinka/Nuer fight over the armoury were confirmed by a number of other witnesses who spoke to the commission's investigators. To the extent that there was a plot, it seemed to be not so much

an attempted coup as an attempted takeover of the hitherto bi-ethnic presidential guard by Dinka elements.

According to Majak D'Agot, deputy minister of defence, the force from Bahr-al-Ghazal had been assembled by General Paul Malong, governor of Northern Bahr-al-Ghazal, close ally of the president, and Hoth's eventual successor as chief of the general staff: "We did not pay for it from the Ministry of Defence, though they tried to get us to pay from our budget. The force was 15,000 strong, and was recruited in one area." Among people who gave roughly the same account, numbers varied from a low of 3,000 to a high of 15,000.

Riek Machar himself implicated not just Paul Malong in the plan, but also (self-servingly, it must be said) the president. "There were skirmishes in Heglig between our forces and Sudan in March, 2012," he declared. "This is when Salva started hard preparations. In Northern Bahr-al-Ghazal, I witnessed the mobilization of youth in camps. When Heglig finished, I was chairing the Council of Ministers. Nhial Deng asked the question: 'Why is there training of youth in camps in only one place in South Sudan?' I said I had no answer."

In the early afternoon of Monday, 16 December, I received a telephone call from the office of protocol at the Ministry of Foreign Affairs asking that I attend a briefing at J-1, the presidency. I was surprised, as gunfire could still be heard, but Mandrea took things very calmly. During the ten-minute drive, we found all shops closed, many soldiers sitting in the shade, the sunny roads almost empty of vehicles, tarmac chewed up by tank tracks.

The sound of gunfire picked up again as we approached the presidency. As diplomats gathered inside a large auditorium, we exchanged news. British ambassador Ian Hughes had seen people suffering from gunshot wounds being pulled out of a car in front of him; he added that there were seventy-plus police outside his home, presumably to deter asylum seekers and/or Riek Machar (whose home was close to Ian's). Everyone had seen large numbers of civilians walking along Airport Road from the Malakia/Nyakuron neighbourhoods of Juba (where fighting was thought still to be going on), heading for the main UNMISS compound at the airport.

Minister Barnaba Marial Benjamin and his grey-bearded deputy, Peter Bashir, stepped up to the podium promptly at 3:00. The 6:00 p.m. to 6:00 a.m. curfew was confirmed "until further notice …

but persons are asked to go about their normal business in the daytime (starting tomorrow)." Pausing occasionally as the building shook from distant artillery fire or as a tank clanked past, Barnaba talked at length about the possibility that some people might seek refuge at diplomatic premises. "You are perfectly free to accept such persons but you must inform the ministry, and you should also know that as soon as they go out on the street again they are liable to arrest; you know the story of Julian Assange."

The minister's narrative was of an attempted coup by loyalists of Riek Machar; he said those responsible would be apprehended, brought to justice, and tried openly. The minister said he did not know the whereabouts of Riek or of Pagan Amum, but jokingly said, "Some of you might know."

Deputy Minister Bashir went on to give a detailed account of the NLC meeting that had immediately preceded the "coup." He talked for fifteen minutes or more about how the committee he and James Wani Igga were on had been looking into alleged irregularities committed by Pagan Amum when he was secretary-general of the SPLM. Bashir dwelt in particular on two multi-million-dollar investments that had been "improperly managed." I was left with the impression that we were meant to conclude it was discontent with this report that had provoked Pagan, Riek, and their followers to attempt to overthrow the government. But we were not to worry; it was all a bit of a storm in a teacup.

Mandrea and I drove home again. As we pulled up to the black steel double gates at the entrance of our compound, I saw a body lying in the dust a few metres away. I got out of the grey Toyota Land Cruiser, looked both ways up and down the dirt road, and crossed to where a neighbour was standing in his doorway, looking at me.

"What happened?"

He hesitated, looking around and chewing on his thumbnail. "It was about twenty minutes ago. This man …" He gestured at the body. "He was walking along that side of the street. Some men came the other way."

"In uniform?"

"Yes, SPLA, in a green pickup. They stopped and spoke with him. Maybe five or ten seconds. I don't know what they said."

"And then what?"

"They shot him. They drove away."

I didn't need to get too close to see the distinctive horizontal scars on the dead man's forehead. He was Nuer. Either the soldiers had seen his scars, or they had asked him something in Dinka, and he had not been able to reply.

At 6:00 Emmanuel, our senior guard, came in to relieve his friends who had been on duty for twenty-four hours. His home near Giada seemed to be at the epicentre of things. "The Nuer attackers, they have light weapons. The Dinkas are inside, in the barracks. I saw a tank run a person over. Many houses have been destroyed. Many civilians have been killed, I think."

As darkness fell, I tried calling our Canadian colleagues at their adjoining apartments. The phone lines were jammed, so I sent a short e-mail: "Quiet here (I think; can't hear over the generator). Enjoy your sleepover – have you got marshmallows? Turn out the lights and tell each other ghost stories."

Any hope that things might be over faded in the late evening. At 10:00 we heard a lot of small arms fire, quite close by, and bursts continued throughout the night. Our fellow Canadians at the UAP apartments reported the same. In the morning of Day Two (Tuesday, 17 December), judging from the direction of detonations, activity had moved into the centre of town: the Thongping area in which most government buildings, including the presidency and the ministries, were located. We heard an artillery or tank round explode at 10:00 a.m. within a kilometre of our house.

Meanwhile, as my sporadic telephone reception went in and out, there were reports of Nuer civilians being executed on the streets, of soldiers at roadblocks interrogating persons as to their ethnic identity, and of soldiers entering compounds to search for alleged rebels. Heavily escorted convoys of VIPs had also been seen heading in and out of the presidency. We soon learned that a number of ex-ministers associated with Riek Machar had been arrested and were in detention at the residence of the inspector general of police; they were the core of the group that had stood on the platform at the press conference Riek held on 6 December:

- Oyay Deng Ajak (ex–minister for national security);
- Gier Chuong Aloung (ex–minister for internal affairs);
- Majak D'Agot (ex–deputy defence minister);
- John Luk Jok (ex–minister for justice);

- Cirino Hiteng (ex–minister for culture, youth, and sports);
- Koul Tong Mayai (ex-governor of Lakes State);
- Ezekiel Lol (ex-ambassador to the US);
- Deng Alor (ex–foreign and cabinet affairs minister);
- Madut Biar (ex–minister for communications and postal services);
- Kosti Manibe (ex–finance minister).

Riek Machar and four other wanted persons, said Information Minister Makuei, were still at large:

- Alfred Lado Gore (ex–minister of environment);
- Pagan Amum (ex-secretary-general of the SPLM);
- Taban Deng (ex-governor of Unity State);
- Peter Adwok Nyaba (ex–minister of science, higher education, and technology).

Rebecca Garang remained at home. Although Riek's whereabouts were not known, my Japanese colleague let me know by e-mail that heavy explosions were coming from the site of his house.

In the early afternoon of the second day, as a lull developed and with other diplomatic missions starting to discuss evacuation plans, I decided to move our fellow Canadians (two officers and one spouse; the other spouse plus Jamie were out of the country already) from UAP to the residential and office complex known as the Joint Donor Office, where our security officer, Othmar, resided. They hurriedly packed bags, Othmar made a reconnaissance trip, and by 4:30 they were relocated. The new site was significantly closer to the airport, but the advantage was moot as JIA was still closed.

In lulls and in anticipation of the airport reopening at some point, we started to feed Ottawa with as many names of Canadian citizens in Juba as we could find. Canadians were routinely asked to sign a system called the online register of Canadians abroad, but dual nationals were invariably lazy about this; they felt at home in their native countries, and many seemed to suspect that their information might end up with the taxman. We only had twenty-seven persons officially registered in this way, but by going through the mission visitors' book we were able to find the names and numbers of about 150 more.

In the afternoon, the UN's top official, SRSG Hilde Johnson, sent a message to diplomats summing up what her staff had learned:

Today the violence has penetrated into more locations in town, and into townships and neighbourhoods of Juba, with greater impact on civilians (included some incidences of ethnic-motivated violence). In some cases, some of the clashes, and the "sweeping" of the areas where there have been pockets of resistance, there has been intense gunfire. In the afternoon today, the fighting seems to have died down, and the situation seems to be contained. Nevertheless, whether there is a regrouping happening, oriented towards a resurgence of fighting during the night and in the early morning remains to be seen. The most recent statement by the Minister of Information on radio this afternoon announced the re-opening of the airport and urged people to report to work tomorrow, conveying that the Government is in control, may be an encouraging sign.

In a telephone call with the Minister of Defence this afternoon, he indicated that Riek Machar and Taban Deng had escaped from Juba and that the security situation is under control with no fighting. When I expressed serious concern about the incidents of ethnic violence, he attributed these to "criminals." The Minister of National Security indicated that the concerned people involved in the ethnic related violence had been apprehended, and included SPLA and other criminal elements. In terms of fatalities, the Defence Minister indicated that ICRC has collected 260 bodies (we have yet to verify with ICRC), whilst the SPLA had 70 bodies.

UNMISS had today seen 4,000 civilians seeking refuge at their airport base in Thongping and 8,000 in UN House, a few kilometers outside the city on the road to Yei.

At 9:00 p.m. we learned that when the airport opened the following day, the US would fly in a pair of C-130 Hercules military aircraft to evacuate their nationals and, as a secondary priority, foreign diplomats. We reserved some seats. Coordination between Western capitals was kicking in. As would become the pattern for days, "friendlies" announced flight plans and bids for seats were pooled. In due course, the US, the UK, the Netherlands, Germany, Italy, and the EU would all lay on flights, predominantly for their own nationals but open on a priority basis to Canadians as well. Although Canada's Department of National Defence offered to pitch in with a C-130, this offer was declined by Foreign Minister Baird, a disappointment that left us having to take embarrassing advantage of the generosity of others for many days to come.

Last thing at night, the US announced that it was starting a drawdown of its diplomatic personnel to leave only essential staff in place. As staff woke up in Canada, I was engaging in a bout of bureaucratic brinkmanship with HQ. Jenny and I were already booked to travel to New Zealand and the Southern Ocean on 20 December; although I was, under the circumstances, determined to stay, I was not enthusiastic about forfeiting several thousand dollars. It was only when I announced that I was packing my bags that I was able to obtain written assurance that I would be compensated.

Through all this, our local guards had stayed faithfully at their posts. We had been reduced to using dehydrated camping meals to feed everyone, which was certainly a novelty for them. Emmanuel told me that two men and a woman had come to drag away the body in the street. The second day of fighting came to an end.

Over the next few days a routine quickly set in, with Jenny's and my time spent very largely at the airport.

JIA reopened on the morning of Wednesday, 18 December, and a pair of USAAF Hercules were the first planes in. The streets being quiet, Othmar took me down to the JDO compound where we hustled our three Canadians to get ready. Although instructed to bring just one small bag, each had heavy suitcases, and we wasted valuable time as they repacked.

It was a three-minute ride to the airport on an empty road. Stopped by aggressive SPLA men at a roadblock we claimed diplomatic immunity, pointing at our red and white plates, but – with the whining engines of the C-130s now audible – it didn't seem the right time to resist their perfunctory search. We turned through the military gate to the edge of the tarmac. I helped our colleagues with their bags, pointed them to the aircraft visible through the knee-high grass, and they left for Nairobi, where a team from the Canadian High Commission would meet them.

Now it was just me and Jenny left. Although she had been ordered out too, I told HQ that no seats were to be had; it was already evident that if I was to be useful on the ground, I would need some help. But, at Othmar's urging, we did agree to move from our normal home to temporary accommodation at the JDO compound.

We carried on to the main terminal, where many thousands of people were milling around the small red-dirt parking area in front of the arrivals and departures doors and out onto the main road. The US had just organized a total of three flights, evacuating not just our diplomats, but Europeans, many US and USAID officials, and 150 to 200 American civilians. The EU evacuated forty-nine on a charter and had plans to take out another thirty-six the next day; Germany was planning to bring in a military aircraft to leave the day after that for Entebbe, and the Netherlands had received authority for an evacuation aircraft on Thursday. The US Embassy had drawn down its staff to "essentials" only, the UK and the Netherlands to four, Norway to one.

I spent a couple of hours informally booking seats with the friendlies for Canadian nationals, then, in anticipation of the 6:00 p.m. curfew, we took a quick tour around town. Traffic was circulating but at a much-diminished rate; you could see where tank tracks had chewed up the tarmac. There were many roadblocks in place, and the area around the presidency was sealed off. There were large numbers of soldiers and police on the streets, many in an aggressive, truculent mood. Bullet-ridden vehicles were pushed to the sides of the roads but a few shops were still open and vital blue water-tankers (Juba had no mains water supply) were circulating in the afternoon heat. We tuned the car radio to Radio Miraya as we drove. The first casualty estimate was 400 dead in Juba; later we learned that the number was a lot higher.

At the JDO that evening I called Hussein Mar, an old friend and now acting governor in Bor, Jonglei State. There had been serious infighting among troops at the main barracks in Bor the previous night, and there were fears that heavily armed youths were in town. Perhaps most worrying were rumours that the perpetually disaffected but highly effective Nuer general, Peter Gadet, was leading an armed contingent from his homeland in Unity State to renew the fight against the mainstream SPLA in Juba, and to avenge what was now looking like a purge, perhaps even a genocide, of Nuers. There was confirmation that Riek Machar was alive; he had spoken by telephone with the Sudan Tribune and denied any involvement in the "coup."

At 8:45, as Jenny and I were settling down to a camping meal in our sparsely furnished bungalow, I had a call back from Hussein. Clearly a crisis was developing in Bor. My old friend, ex-governor

Kuol Manyang, had just arrived there to try to control things, and staff were briefing him in the government compound when they came under heavy machine-gun fire from persons in auxiliary police uniforms. Some of the attackers seemed to have come from the north by boat. Gadet was the prime suspect. Hussein said they had lost many of their defenders. He and the governor had fled to the UNMISS compound by the airport where I could hear shooting over the phone.

Hussein himself was Nuer. I wondered which way he would jump.

As night arrived and Ottawa came on line, we began drawing up lists of Canadians, matching them to possible flights for the next day. It was past midnight when we went to bed. Miraya had now moved onto reggae Christmas carols, with "The Little Drummer Boy" repeated every twenty minutes or so.

———————

Thursday, 19 December, and subsequent mornings, we arrived at the airport by 8:00. We had a tiny red and white Canadian flag, intended for the Land Cruiser when the ambassador came from Nairobi, and we placed it prominently in the branches of a small neem tree in the parking area of the airport.

As each morning went on, more and more Canadians of South Sudanese origin found us. Some had been alerted by phone from Ottawa overnight as volunteers worked their way through our visitors' book; some had contacted us directly; some found us by word of mouth. My job was to match them with the seats we were offered by allies (who were also maintaining similar informal offices around the airport), check their paperwork, and shepherd them onto planes. My most helpful contact on the ground was Lizzie, a young first-posting political officer from the US Embassy who was singlehandedly running the complex American effort; she wore a tee-shirt, shorts, and a fluorescent road-worker's vest, and had one foot encased in what looked like a large ski boot. At the recent Marine Ball, a very heavy marine had stepped on and broken her foot.

The hot days passed, and we became more and more aware of the nature and gravity of what had happened. Several times we drove CD-1, the office Land Cruiser, via a long and roundabout route to the far end of the airport where 20,000 Nuers were crammed among the facilities of the UN logistics base. We would locate our Canadian by repeated phone calls, pull him into the back seat, and make our way back to the airport through thousands of desperate people. Usually he (it was always men; they'd left their wives and children back in Canada when they came to South Sudan) was quite terrified. Many of the men asked to borrow my baseball cap to cover the tell-tale Nuer markings on their forehead; one had me hold his hand to the very ramp of the aircraft. Twice we had to brazen our way through, pushing past heavily armed soldiers demanding to know where we were going and indicating I should let go of my charge.

Much of the time people's passports were expired or lost and – almost certainly – they had no incoming visa, having used South Sudanese documentation to enter. After fighting our way to the front of the lineup, I'd slip the languid immigration officers – who seemed unaware of and uninterested in the mayhem around them – a US hundred-dollar bill for each non-existent visa, for which the Canadian citizen would sign a promise to repay. As for the missing documents, we would spend hours on the phone with Ottawa as HQ searched their computer records and gave us authority (or not) to issue emergency travel papers.

We'd been worrying about Peter Pal and his daughter for days. They had witnessed a neighbour being killed in front of them and had been told by Dinka soldiers to get out and never come back. Peter had a passport but his six-year-old's was lost. They had no possessions at all. They stood patiently in the forty-degree sun as I spoke into my cellphone to Ottawa, where it was midnight and thirty degrees below freezing.

We were at an impasse, the little girl having no proof of citizenship. Then the Christmas spirit seemed to take over and a bureaucratic miracle took place. "Well," came the hesitant, distant voice over the cellphone. "Does the daughter look like him?"

I looked from Peter to his daughter; she was holding his hand, sucking her thumb, looking up at me.

"Yes, she does …" I said tentatively.

"Well, go ahead then. Issue the emergency travel document. We'll verify things later."

An hour later Peter and his daughter were winging their way to safety in Entebbe. He borrowed a phone to call me that evening from Uganda and thank me. "No problem," I said. "It's our friend in Ottawa you should really thank."

In many cases, the men we evacuated were leaving one wife behind to rejoin another in Canada, which gave me mixed feelings. They had left their families safe and sound in Canada, the children at good schools, to return to South Sudan a few years earlier; here they would find another wife and have more children. The South Sudan–born children were eligible for Canadian citizenship papers; the new wives were not necessarily. Depressingly often, when we ran the men's passport details through the computers, we found that child-maintenance payments were outstanding. This was normally grounds for passport denial, but given the threatening climate in Juba, I had no qualms about getting people out, at least to Kenya or Uganda.

As we helped Canadian citizens to leave – every day there'd be half a dozen with the Netherlands or four with Germany, a few with the UK, dozens with the US – we'd phone names and passport numbers to the plane's initial destination: Nairobi, Dubai, Addis Ababa, Entebbe. In those places, other Canadian officials would take over and decide if onward flights were needed. If passengers were going all the way to Toronto or Vancouver, social services and voluntary agencies would be alerted to be on hand with warm clothes at the Canadian airport.

One morning driving down Airport Road, Mandrea accidentally cut off a tank crew who were riding to work at high speed. They wore distinctive caps with padded ear flaps and very cool reflective shades. In an instant the four men had leapt out of their pickup and had us surrounded, weapons cocked and pointed at my head and Mandrea's. "Fuck you, man!" one of them shouted hysterically as he rammed his gun barrel against the driver's window, racking the weapon. We held up our hands in the classic gesture of apology, they sneered at us again, then jumped back in and tore away. My heart was pumping very fast.

Thursday, 19 December, was the busiest day of all, and the most dramatic. British Ambassador Ian Hughes confirmed that the Royal Air Force was sending an enormous C-17 transport jet from Brize Norton in the UK and he'd have at least fifteen seats for us.

By noon the apron in front of the terminal building was absolutely crammed with aircraft of all models and vintages: grey American C-130s; camouflaged C-130s belonging to Egypt, Kenya, and Uganda; Antonov cargo planes; an old DC-3; a dozen or more white UN de Havilland Dash 7s and 8s. There was a constant whine as most of the aircraft kept their engines running, looking for a quick turnaround. But from outside you could only get glimpses of this. There must have been 10,000 people or more trying to force their way into the small, grubby departure hall no larger than a classroom.

Then for a long period everything seemed to stop. There were no incoming flights, nothing outgoing. Ian was looking worried, making phone calls continuously. Someone passed me a smart phone that showed what I couldn't see through the tightly packed crowd: an orange, blue, and white Fly Dubai Boeing 737 had crashed nose-down in the middle of the runway, blocking all take-offs and land-ings. Nobody had been hurt but no one could figure out how to move the aircraft out of the way.

As Ben, the British defence attaché, phoned around to find a fork-lift or a crane, Ian was talking directly to the C-17 pilots by radio. The great grey four-engine jet roared overhead at a mere 200 metres, the shadow passing right over the parking lot, and I imagined the pilots craning to look down. Then it was gone.

Ten minutes, fifteen minutes. Ian went over to the three hundred desperate travellers standing by their bags in the declining afternoon sun and told them, "It looks as though they're not coming back. I'm terribly sorry."

Then the big bird was back! Turning and unmistakeably dipping now, coming in for a steep-looking landing. A great cheer went up; the evacuation was on again.

The RAF made a combat landing, using the only half of the runway available. But a new problem loomed. It was now 4:30; the aircraft absolutely had to take off by 6:00 when the curfew would come into effect, and at least 180 passengers still had to be processed and loaded. An executive decision was made. There was no time to scan bags, so no bags could be taken. "You must decide if you are really in danger of your lives or not," Ian grimly told his protesting compatriots.

A few angry clients walked away but most just abandoned their suitcases. Several people gave me bottles of whisky in an attempt to lighten their bags; others struggled into as many clothes as they pos-sibly could, and waddled out to the aircraft, sweating profusely. Ian graciously let thirty Canadians on board. At 17:45 there was still a line of passengers leading to the giant plane's rear door, but we had to leave or risk being shot after curfew. As we made it to the gates of the JDO at 6:00 p.m. on the dot, we heard a heartwarming roar: the C-17 was up in the air again, lumbering south to Entebbe.

Up-country, things were no quieter. Nuer rebels led by Peter Gadet seemed to be in control of Bor; a glance at the map confirmed that he could be in a position to threaten Juba. Deeper into the Nuer heart-land of eastern Jonglei State, a mob of Lou Nuer youth had overrun the UNMISS compound at Akobo, possibly in search of Dinka who had taken refuge. Two Indian peacekeeping troops were killed in the attempt to defend the compound, as well as eleven civilians.[2] Two days later, on Saturday, 21 December, I would attend a ceremony at Juba Airport where the coffins of the dead peacekeepers were cere-monially loaded aboard an outbound aircraft.

Riek Machar had popped up too, in another radio interview. To the disappointment of many – who had been hoping he would disas-sociate himself from the violence being perpetrated by Nuer militias in response to the initial wave of killings in Juba – he called openly for the armed overthrow of Salva Kiir. It may not have been a coup to start off with, but to all intents and purposes this was now a full-scale rebellion.

By Sunday 22 December, a week after the crisis had begun, central Juba seemed almost normal. But when I got hold of Roman, the Pole who headed the EU's humanitarian arm, ECHO, he told me, "I think that I will not exaggerate if I say that what we seeing is simply hor-rific. I would not dare quantify anything, but some parts of Juba are completely deserted. We see mutilated bodies (beheaded, bodies without arms, etc.), burnt and looted houses, cars, etc. By one word, heart-breaking." People had seen trucks piled high with bodies. Many had been thrown into the Nile, but in outlying areas corpses still lay on the streets and the smell of death was overpowering.

Extractions of civilians and foreign nationals from rebel-controlled Bor had been dramatic. An Australian who got to Juba told me that the helicopter on which she was travelling was bloodstained and that a woman had miscarried en route. The US despatched three Osprey vertical take-off aircraft directly from Djibouti to bring out American citizens from the Bor UN compound where 20,000 persons had assembled. All three were fired upon by rebel forces, taking more than a hundred impacts. The crew sustained injuries but – in an inspired feat of flying – the planes limped to Entebbe without having been able to land. For a few hours, a deeply angered and worried US State Department considered shutting down the American Embassy, which would have been a signal to the entire diplomatic community that it was time to leave. But logic prevailed. The attack was by

rebels, so why "punish" the government of South Sudan? The evacuation order was rescinded.

Deep in the hinterland, things were scarcely any better. At a remote
location called Werkok, three hours' drive (in the dry season) north
of Bor, a group of our Canadian/South Sudanese doctors (trained
through the SSHARE program) were hunkered down in their tiny
clinic, giving whatever remedy they could to the hundred or more
patients crammed into their single ward. The clinic had been overrun
by Nuer White Army youth flooding to support Gadet in Bor, but as
the rumour spread that Gadet would abandon Bor and the White
Army would retreat through Werkok, the team were appealing to
be evacuated.

Ajak, the team leader who had fled Bor as a small boy in the civil
war and who had earlier told me his life story, later wrote to me again:

> I did not imagine to run again from my hometown of Bor like
> what happened in May 16, 1983. However, Riek Machar forced
> us out while we were fulfilling our duties in the hospital with my
> colleagues. The shooting begun around 4 PM in the front door
> of the Bor State hospital, it surprised us during working hours.
> We did not know what to do in operating room. Mabior and
> Benjamin were doing a laparotomy on a wounded patient in the
> stomach. They remained there and I went to take care of my
> wife and sister in the hospital compound, I met them crying very
> panicked. It was an overwhelming situation, I felt very sorry
> for them. The shooting continued until 11 PM. It was difficult
> to have anything eat, neither drink on that day.
>
> Then, early morning the war restarted around 3 AM. Everybody
> left hospital exactly at 4:23 AM without clothes, no bags or doc-
> uments. We walked a long distance, about 45 KM in the bushes
> alongside the Nile, we drank that bad water but the weather was
> very hot and without food. Moses, Benjamin, Mayom arrived to
> Werkok first. And my wife and sister, Dr. Anthony, a group of
> 15 children and women, myself arrived to Werkok around 7:50
> PM because I was showing them the road to go as I have worked
> in that area for the last 4 years.
>
> Those guys of Riek Machar, they have been killing everybody:
> children, women and all civilians, no matter you are a soldier or
> not, they do not care. Also they have been destroying the town
> and burning houses and looting every place including hospitals

plus our hospital compound. They are like wild animals, drinking badly and raping foreign and local women, which is a very nasty thing. Crazy man is better than them. It's look like Rwanda at this time.

We will keep praying for the peace and asking you to keep praying for us. I hope in Lord our Savior Who is a provider of everything. Have great week.

The state minister of health, Jehan, appealed to me in an emotional message: "In God we Live, Move and Have our Being, Amen. Just as in the book of Matthew 24, rumors of war and destruction are all around South Sudan, complete devastation of human lives, property and land! But in all these we're more than conquerors in Christ Jesus. It will be good if those in Werkok are evacuated, both doctors and wounded citizens."

Samaritan's Purse, the NGO that had helped the doctors set up in Werkok in the first place, came to me asking if the embassy could front the US$5,000 it would take to charter a light aircraft. They assured us that the money would be repaid in Ottawa by the organization's Canadian branch. We could and we did; the evacuation a few days later went smoothly.

At Nimule, south of Juba, Ugandan troops had entered South Sudan and were moving towards the capital. Confused reports indicated that Ugandan helicopters had also been assisting the SPLA in taking on the rebel Gadet in Bor and had received incoming fire. Later I would learn that a Canadian–South Sudanese doctor had been killed by a helicopter-fired rocket.

Riek Machar was thought to be in Bentiu; he stated he had full control of Unity State and held "much of South Sudan." He added that General Gadet was under his command, and that oil production in Unity had ceased. Riek Machar said he would talk to President Kiir as long as the latter released the twelve political detainees associated with him.

The slightly surreal media coverage by domestic outlets continued. SSTV reported that evening:

The minister of information and broadcasting, Michael Makuei Lueth, says the massive movement of people, foreigners, rather, and nationals from Juba has no connection with the recent failed coup attempt, describing it as a Christmas routine where people go and celebrate in their villages and outside the country. The minister says the massive departure of people out of the capital is a normal routine. The minister further denied any ethnic fighting between the Nuer and the Dinka tribes.

Christmas Day, Jenny and I had a quiet lunch with Kees, the Dutch ambassador, and Christian – my EU colleague – at Kees's house on the JDO compound, where we were living. Bor had now been retaken by the government but there was a pocket of rebel forces near Terekeka, two thirds of the way from Bor to Juba and only forty kilometres short of the capital. After our meal Ine, a rather humourless colleague who was now the sole remaining Norwegian diplomat, burst in breathlessly. "The White Army … didn't you hear? They're coming: they could be here by this evening!"

The airport was closed. There really didn't seem to be anything to be done. We persuaded Ine to calm down and stay for a glass of champagne. Next morning it was back to JIA for the usual round of assisted evacuations. Ottawa was getting difficult, though, and on 26 December an e-mail arrived ordering me and Jenny out "immediately." Although our caseload was as heavy as ever – the more people we flew out, the more seemed to appear from nowhere – HQ would not listen to our appeal to stay and help desperate people to escape. The director general for security wrote back rather shortly and in a manner that did not lend itself to misinterpretation, "Decision is not/not changed."

On 27 December, with a great deal of reluctance, we took the last plane out. Even before Air Uganda had landed in Entebbe, Ottawa issued a "flag-lowering" statement:

Canada Temporarily Withdraws Canadian Staff from South Sudan

Minister of State (Foreign Affairs and Consular) the Honourable Lynne Yelich today issued the following statement:

The Government of Canada takes the safety and security of our diplomats abroad very seriously. Due to operational challenges, including the unpredictable security environment in Juba, the

Department of Foreign Affairs, Trade and Development has authorized the temporary suspension of operations at our office in Juba.

Canada's Head of Office in Juba will temporarily work out of the High Commission in Nairobi until appropriate measures are put in place to respond to the changing operational environment.

A Fight in Your Living Room

Nairobi and Juba, January–March 2014

The Tribe Hotel, in a green suburb of Nairobi called Gigiri, is one of those places described as "boutique." Its public areas are decorated with strange and slightly sinister-looking sculptures made of heavy black wire; the couches are peculiar in shape and have either no backs or backs three metres high; in the evenings, the lighting is so dim that you cannot read. The swimming pool is also oddly shaped and includes a swim-up bar that waiters can only reach by making small over-water jumps, frequently with disastrous results. Each bedroom provides only one chair, and an uncomfortable boat-shaped bathtub sits out in the open; the en-suite toilet area is screened by a faintly frosted glass wall that leaves little to the imagination.

But the staff are friendly in the extreme, and the place is conveniently close to the expat-favoured Village Market mall and both the Canadian High Commission and the US Embassy. On this account, for weeks – starting in late 2013 – the Tribe was crammed with idle diplomats and aid workers who had been evacuated from Juba and were in a kind of administrative limbo, desperate for news from South Sudan and with no defined program of work.

Here Jenny and I rejoined the Canadian staff who had earlier been evacuated, and our little posse was reinforced first by Robin, the former colleague who had initially been slated to replace me in Juba over Christmas, then by Eric O'Connor, on loan to us from the Canadian High Commission in Pretoria. Our first task was to consolidate all the outstanding consular issues on one large spreadsheet. The caseload went up and down, but for the next several weeks we had between ten and thirty-five active cases running, some including multiple family members. We tried to keep in touch with all needy

Canadians in South Sudan on an almost daily basis and to triage which cases needed to be evacuated most urgently.

Meanwhile, I engaged in lengthy and tedious negotiations with a risk-averse HQ with the aim of securing permission to return, even if only for very short periods, to bring more citizens out. With great reluctance and only after recourse to the foreign minister's office, we obtained permission for a one-day (no overnight!) visit to Juba, on condition that we demonstrate the urgency of the cases in question and that we check in on an hourly basis.

Thus began what would become another exhausting routine. Once a week, Robin or Eric and I (Jenny was forced by HQ to stay back, running the phones into South Sudan and passing us instructions) would get up at 4:15 in the morning, trek across Nairobi in the dark in a high commission armoured vehicle, and board the Kenya Airways flight that would get us into Juba by 9:20. Often we were the only passengers going there but flights out of Juba were still full. We'd spend a frantic few hours meeting South Sudanese Canadians at the office, then escort them on the afternoon flight back to Kenya. Usually we'd meet up with Colonel Dave and Major Ken from the Canadian UNMISS contingent, who also had citizens to refer to us. These had typically arrived at Canada House, the residence of the Canadian troops, thinking it was the embassy. They were looked after there (quite unofficially; HQ would not have approved) until we could take over.

On one of these visits, a young man called Biel presented himself. Aged about sixteen or seventeen, he was as tall and thin as the stereotypical Dinka – about two metres – and as off-hand as many adolescents. "Yeah man, I'm Canadian. I guess," he said laconically. He produced a slightly damp blue Canadian passport that looked as though it had been through a washing machine. From the blurry photograph, you could see that his now thin face had once been very fat indeed. It took nearly an hour to get Biel's story from him.

Biel had gone to Canada as a very small boy. He'd grown up in Calgary where, by his own admission, he'd become excessively fond of junk food, and Mom and Dad decided to send him to see his relatives in Bor for a few months to reconnect with the family, learn some Dinka ways, and lose a few dozen kilos. He'd arrived in Bor only days before Peter Gadet's rebels and the subsequent recapture of the city by government troops, helicopter gunships and all. With his local family, he'd half-swum and half-waded across the Nile, dodging hippos and crocs, to an informal settlement of displaced persons that within a couple of days had grown to 50,000 or more persons.

What then? "Well, I kinda hung out for a while, you know ... I looked for a ride but, you know, nothin' doin'."

So, with a couple of teenaged friends, he had walked the 200 kilometres to Juba. And here he was. Biel mumbled his thanks as we organized his way to Calgary; after he got there, he sent us a selfie trying out for the school basketball squad. Being the age he was, we guessed he'd probably brushed off his friends' inquiries with a variation of his favourite phrase, "No big deal, man."

Then there was Ezekiel. Just prior to one of our weekly visits I had a call from Ian, the British ambassador. He'd been at the airport the previous evening to meet a UN flight from Malakal that had some British citizens aboard needing to be evacuated. Among them was a strangely taciturn young man of maybe sixteen, who said his name was Ezekiel, that he was Canadian, and that he had nowhere to go.

Ian took him in for the evening – the curfew was imminent – and I went around to pick him up the next day. I managed to winkle out the name of his Canadian father, who was up in Nasir, the place I'd bought my oil drum a while back; it was now in rebel hands. Ezekiel's father was very evasive on the phone, and I deduced that he might have "gone over" to the rebel side. But he asked us to look after his son.

Ezekiel was so quiet that I thought he was disturbed and, as we fussed around all day in the office on other cases, I kept a close eye on him lest he suddenly take off. On the afternoon plane out, though, he visibly relaxed. By the time we reached Nairobi, he was behaving like a normal teenager. We took him to the YMCA while we hunted for the most economical airfare to get him home to wintry Waterloo, Ontario, and some friends of the family kindly took him shopping one day for warm clothing.

When Eric took Ezekiel to Nairobi's Jomo Kenyatta airport to board the plane for Toronto, he asked him if he'd be warm enough. "Sure, man," said Ezekiel. And he pulled out a black and yellow woollen cap. Eric laughed as he told the story. "In great yellow letters it said, 'Fuck You.' He said his Mom wouldn't mind. But I told him the Kenyan immigration officers would, so he agreed to take it off."

A case that worried us for weeks was that of Sally and her three boys. She had been born in Malakal, in what is now South Sudan, but her boys were Canadian-born and English-speaking. They'd come back in late 2013 to find out what had happened to their dad, who had returned earlier to Malakal only to disappear. As Malakal was alternately taken by the government then re-taken by the rebels, Sally and the boys would be flushed out into the bush to fend for themselves, only very occasionally coming back into the range of a cell-phone tower to contact a relative in Uganda. The relative would alert me that the family was alive and needed assistance. Then we'd lose them again.

It wasn't until March, by which time I was back living in Juba, that Sally made it to the UN Protection of Civilians site that had now sprung up next to Malakal airport, a kind of impromptu safe-haven with basic services such as water and rations. Here she'd worked for Médecins Sans Frontières for her keep and a few extra pounds until seats could be found on a flight down to the capital.

We met Sally and the kids at Juba airport. They'd been helped along by a UN staffer who had given her an American hundred-dollar bill out of his own pocket, the only money she now had. "But we have some family here in Juba who may be able to help," she said. "Can we go and see?" We drove out to the suburb and the street she remembered. The street was a ruin; the house was empty and ran-sacked; no one would talk to her. Someone finally called out, "You'd better go away. And don't come back."

Back at the office, I sent Mandrea out for some take-away chicken with chapattis. The boys sat cross-legged on the floor, grinning from ear to ear and eating so much I thought they would be sick. "In the bush," said Sally, "they just had to eat whatever we could get. But they weren't used to it. All they knew was hamburgers and fries. And they really missed their TV." In the late afternoon, I took the family to the airport for the plane to Nairobi, where the high commission staff would meet them and arrange for passage home. Thoughtfully, Sally said, "You know ... my boys. I want them to have something better than all this. That's why we went to Canada, and that's why we're going back."

Of all the individuals and families we helped, only Sally had fol-lowed the rules and kept her return air-ticket as you're supposed to. It was sweat-stained and dog-eared after three months in a pouch around her waist. She had the ticket, one hundred dollars in an enve-lope, and a bible with golden-edged pages. Nothing else. The last time I saw her, she was sitting on a blue metal chair in the chaotic airport departure area. She had the bible open on her knee and was running her finger across the tissue-thin page as she read.

By the end of February 2013, when we formally re-opened the Canadian mission, Ugandan armour was parked in a defensive posture at either end of the Juba airport runway: two tanks and a truck-mounted heavy machine gun at the western end and at least four tanks at the east end, where three Ugandan attack helicopters were also visible. On the streets in the daytime, the situation was ostensibly normal. At night, gunfire was still sometimes heard, not all of it of light calibre.

Thousands of Nuers had fled their Juba homes and made for the closest of two UN camps: one, at the end of the airport runway, called UNMISS/Thongping, the other at UN House, outside Juba proper. Although security in the city seemed to be stabilizing, their numbers were not declining and were now around 43,000; in these extremely crowded impromptu camps, outbursts of fighting were common. The curfew in Juba had been moved to 8:00 p.m. but foreigners were careful to be off the streets by dark (7:00); few of the formerly busy restaurants favoured by diplomats and UN workers were open in the evening at all.

Following the first formally signed cessation of hostilities in late January 2014, up-country fighting declined a little, but each side accused the other daily of infractions. There was major conflict, including the use of artillery by the government, near the hometown of Riek Machar, Leer (Unity State); taking this town (which had reportedly been "flattened") was a propaganda coup for government forces. The rebels alleged that outside forces from JEM (Darfur) and the M-23 (Congo) participated on the government side. Médecins Sans Frontières abandoned its 240-staff hospital in Leer, fleeing with ambulatory patients into the bush.

I met Health Undersecretary Makur, who had just finished a tour of damaged health facilities, and he told me that the twin cities of Bentiu and Rubkona had been absolutely devastated while the hospital in Malakal was unusable, being crammed with upwards of 4,000 IDPs. However, the hospital in Bor was under repair and would soon reopen. "The windows of your (Canadian-financed) maternity ward were all smashed, all the bedding stolen, but medicine cabinets have not been looted and the walls and roofs of the hospital are intact." Makur added calmly that he had seen the bodies of patients shot in their beds, presumably by anti-government forces.

The Nuer chief of the general staff, James Hoth, had been completely marginalized – possibly on account of his now-suspect ethnicity – and was telling anyone who would listen that he simply wanted to come out of this alive and retire to Australia. At one point, he actually packed up his personal possessions and left his office, but he was back a day or two later. Hopes that he might emerge from this crisis to play a political role as the only unscathed and credible Nuer leader looked increasingly unfounded.

National Security Minister Obuto Mamur was now in charge of the government's military campaign. Interior Minister Aleu also seemed to have the ear of the president. "I saw him last week," mused my UK counterpart. "As I was waiting in his anteroom, a white South African with an armed SPLA escort came out of his office. He looked a bit embarrassed to be seen." Rumours were circulating that South Africa was supplying military equipment and/or advisers, and that the ultra-light "Mini-Mokes" – large Go-Karts with heavy machine guns attached – that had been seen on the streets of Juba were South African imports.

On the outbreak of fighting, a number of prominent political figures associated by the government with the "coup" had been arrested, with – as far as anyone in the diplomatic corps could see – little justification. After a lot of pressure, seven were released to the care of President Kenyatta and were now minor celebrities in Nairobi. There was speculation that some or all of them – plus Rebecca Garang – might emerge as a third force, rejecting the path of violence taken by Riek Machar but disavowing the leadership of Salva Kiir just as emphatically. The most likely candidates to lead such a force looked to be (Nuer) John Luk, minister of justice until mid-2013, and Madame Rebecca, who was talking in increasingly mystical terms of herself as the spiritual heir of her husband. The group was known first as "the Detainees," then "the Former Detainees."

When not speculating over scenarios and betting on the next SRSG to succeed Hilde Johnson, whose term was expiring, the donors were trying to figure out where we had gone wrong. When conducting the year-long exercise to develop a New Deal Compact with the government of South Sudan, we should have taken the fact that the government placed national reconciliation at the top of its list more seriously. We had discounted the church-led National Peace and Reconciliation Commission as a vehicle for possible support because, from 2012 through to early 2013, it was hijacked by Riek Machar for transparently political purposes. That was not incorrect, but once he had been deposed in mid-2013, we should have taken another look at it. We had also considered the National Constitutional Review process worthy of support, but most of us thought that if the national government was to be made responsible for anything at all, it should be its own constitution. One or two of us had earlier thought that the SPLM's feckless, half-hearted attempts to reform could do with assistance, and the US and the UK had tried to be involved in the transformation of the SPLA: both of these causes seemed increasingly urgent, but peace was a pre-requisite.

One issue that preoccupied the denizens of Juba's Le Bistro was this: how would reconciliation and justice be balanced? Could or should there be any political future for the protagonists of this tragedy?

As international attention to South Sudan increased in December 2013, the government sought scapegoats. Its first target was the UN. In January, there was rage on the part of government ministers over the "refusal" of UN peacekeepers to allow Information Minister Michael Makuei access to the UN compound in Bor, crowded with thousands of IDPs. Makuei had turned up accompanied by fifty heavily armed bodyguards; he was told he could come in without them, as was normal UN practice. This did not prevent the video of the "outrage" being constantly re-run on state-controlled SSTV, so that some viewers believed that there had been several such incidents, not just one. The UNMISS official responsible for denying Makuei access, Ken Payamo, was (shamefully in my view) sent on R&R by the UN.

Another "discovery" was that of weapons in rebel hands stamped "UN"; the UN, of course, has no weapons of its own and the designation belonged to the manufacturer. This fact did not stop rumours alleging that Hilde Johnson was arming Machar. In mid-March 2014, the campaign reached a new crescendo with newspaper headlines quoting the ubiquitous Makuei declaring, "UNMISS management must prepare to leave."

SPLA soldiers had searched some innocuously labelled boxes of UN matériel being transported by road to the Ghanaian UN contingent in Bentiu, near Rumbek. These boxes were found to contain weapons (automatics, pistols, and ammunition), but the media reported they contained anti-personnel mines, even artillery, supposedly being shipped to rebel forces. The UN's internal practices did require that such items be transported by air; and there was no doubt that the boxes were improperly labelled. There had definitely been a cock-up. But it was cynical and absurd to suggest that SRSG Johnson and the force commander were involved in it, or that the weapons were intended for rebel forces.

The UN's multiple humanitarian and development agencies were also subject to state-sanctioned hostility. Deputy SRSG Toby Lanzer told me that a panel of ministers had said to him, "You hate us ... OCHA [the UN's humanitarian arm] is waging a media war against us ... we have caught vehicles in their tens ... anything you move will now be checked." Only in the last minute or so of the meeting had there been some respite with the grudging remark, "but the president has instructed us to cooperate with you."

On the ground, World Food Program convoys were now being stopped, unloaded, searched, and reloaded at random locations. To add insult to injury, truck drivers were required to pay for the exercise. When some hapless drivers stated that they had no funds, this was construed by the governor of Warrap State as "they refused to be searched." I interpreted this antagonism as the product of government frustration that the international community did not believe it had been the victim of a carefully planned military coup. There was also a perception that the West liked Riek Machar more than they did the current leadership. If we did relate more easily to Machar, this was because until July 2013 he had been not only the vice-president but also the designated government interlocutor for donors. In addition, there was anger – mixed with humiliation and embarrassment – at Western accusations that gross human rights abuses were committed by agents of the state in December 2013 (a reality).[1]

And finally, there was a sense of betrayal. During the war years, the West was with Southern Sudan. That support (and among the South's most ardent supporters was Norway's minister of international development, Hilde Johnson) was unconditional and unquestioning, but now tough questions were being asked, criticisms made. UNMISS kept presenting opportunities for attack. The hapless SRSG was a particularly tempting target because of her gender in this macho country; accompanying the public campaign against her was scurrilous whispering concerning her private life. She was hard done by. Appointed on the basis of her knowledge of South Sudan, her friendship with its leaders, and the assumption that this was a supportive government, she was like a teacher who tries to be friends with her students, then cannot impose discipline when they turn on her.

On 11 March the government brought to trial, out of the eleven politicians it had arrested in December 2013, the four it had retained in detention, considering them to be hard core. These were Pagan Amum, former security minister Oyay Deng Ajak, former deputy defence minister Majak D'Agot, and former envoy of the Southern Sudan government to the US Ezekiel Lol. The charges were various: inciting the masses, subverting a constitutional government, insurgency, causing disaffection among the police and the army, publishing or communicating false information, undermining the authority of or insulting the president, and treason (which carried the death penalty). Over several sessions I attended the trial, in a hot and cramped courtroom around the corner from our new office on the JDO compound. The evidence brought forward by the prosecution was thin:

- The transcript of a press release bearing the signature of the four (among others) that had followed the well-attended press conference/rally earlier in December 2013, which in turn criticized the president for his lack of vision, poor leadership, corruption, and general mismanagement of the country;
- The flag of a very minor (legal) political party that was found in Riek Machar's house and that – it was claimed by the prosecution – was to be the rebel flag;
- An allegedly incriminating audio-recording of a telephone conversation between Oyay and Taban Deng, in which "arming the bodyguards" was discussed.

The defence (led by the brother of ex-minister Deng Alor, one of the seven on bail in Kenya) made short work of this. The prosecution was asked whether any of the accused had been found in possession of weapons. The answer was "no," which effectively demolished the treason charge. The flag was laughed out of court as the defence asked, "Did the searchers also find a flag of South Sudan?"

"Yes."

"Did they also find a copy of the sheet music of the national anthem?"

"Yes."

As for the telephone conversation, the prosecution was unable to produce data showing when the call took place, nor even what telephone numbers were involved. The judge asked relevant and probing questions of both sides, and firmly refused the prosecution's request that the proceedings continue in camera. Things were relaxed, with the smartly suited defendants waving cheerily to friends and family; a good number of jokes were cracked.

Eventually, Justice Minister Paulino Wanawilla announced that the treason charges against the Juba Four were to be dropped following a directive from President Kiir; similar charges against those in Kenya were also dropped. The release took place at the same courthouse. Pagan Amum said he would have preferred the process to continue and a not guilty verdict to have been rendered. He insisted that it had been clear for some time that there was no evidence against the accused and suggested indirectly that the government was seeking to make the most of a bad job by appearing magnanimous.

In its own way, and against all expectations, this trial was a triumph for South Sudan's oft-impugned judiciary. From the beginning, the presiding judges made it clear that they were not going to be cowed; they refused prosecution requests for proceedings to be held in camera and threw out all evidence produced by the Ministry of the Interior when the minister refused four successive requests to appear before the court. It was clear that the charges could not be substantiated and that the case would be dismissed.

There were two other outcomes to the saga. First, the official narrative of a coup against the government on 15 December was discredited. The director for national intelligence, General Mac Paul, who had testified that there was no evidence to support the theory, was fired almost immediately. Much later (two years on), the senior justice who presided over the case was also dismissed with no reason stated. Pagan said, "We are going to dedicate our time to work hard for peace and engage between both the Government and SPLM/A-in-Opposition to end this senseless war that kills our people in our country."

———

By late March 2013, the rebellion had the SPLM/A-in-Opposition or the IO ("Eye-Oh"), as it was now known, in command of unconnected, largely rural areas in Greater Upper Nile (the states of Unity, Upper Nile, and Jonglei). Bentiu, Malakal, and Bor (respectively the three state capitals) had all changed hands several times and they had been virtually destroyed, their value now symbolic only.

But it was thought that Riek Machar's men would now steer clear of Bor, because it was within reach of Ugandan helicopter gunships (stationed then in Juba, later in Bor itself) and Ugandan land forces. Military analysts concurred that the Ugandan intervention had been the SPLA's strongest card, likely saving Juba from being overrun in the early weeks. Accordingly, Riek Machar was adamant that Uganda must leave. The government (less publicly) was equally anxious that they stay; it was not just that Uganda brought professionalism and muscle to their largely ill-disciplined and ill-trained SPLA forces, it was that the Ugandan presence in Juba meant that the bulk of the SPLA could be sent to fight in the North. If the UPDF pulled out, the SPLA must fall back. While the international community had been critical of President Museveni's intervention, my counterpart at the Ministry of Foreign Affairs asked me rhetorically, "How is this different from the French intervening in Mali?"

It was becoming clear now that both sets of leaders would struggle to supply their forces adequately as the rainy season set in. Juba had a significant national income, but most of its oil revenues were pledged to debt repayment. Granting the army retroactive double pay for the last three months of fighting had probably quietened some discontent but it had severely depleted reserves. Riek, meanwhile, had little or no income. He was constantly sending emissaries to Khartoum to call in debts from old friends in Sudan's government, but it seemed improbable that President Bashir would countenance major backing even if he had the funds to spare.

Motivation on either side was difficult to assess. The mainstream SPLA had something tangible and well-defined to defend: the elected government of South Sudan. But it had been demoralized and weakened by mass desertions, its reputation was low and the men knew it, and pay was irregular. In March 2014, one hundred veterans just released from hospital held up downtown Juba for several hours to demand their wages. Meanwhile, Riek's men were feeding primarily on a sense of injustice and a desire for vengeance. He failed to inspire them, although he made sporadic attempts to suggest he was fulfilling a Nuer prophecy and even, for a period, made a point of sleeping on a leopard skin. On both sides, the primary motivation was ethnic loyalty, with the possibility of booty as well.

But it was more complicated than Nuer vs Dinka. The Equatorians were also asking to be heard. The most prominent of these, Vice-President James Wani Igga, had emphatically cast his lot with the government, but he had never been popular with his own people and many other Equatorians were calling a plague on both warring ethnicities. Meanwhile, the governor of Central Equatoria made a comment that led him to have his knuckles rapped by the president. "Sometimes I feel that there are two grown men having a fight in my living room. They are breaking all the furniture, but I can't get them to leave." Amateurs of the history of South Sudan were recalling that the first civil war ended with a three-way accommodation – not two-way – and the consequent division of Southern Sudan into the semi-autonomous regions of greater Upper Nile, Bahr-al-Ghazal, and the Equatorias. The rebel-controlled area corresponded to Greater Upper Nile, the Juba-loyal to greater Bahr-al-Ghazal, with the Equatorias sitting on the fence.

And what was Machar himself up to? My friend Sven, the EU ambassador, told me a story, laughing. "We were travelling with our European humanitarian team to see the situation in Nasir. When it was time to leave Nasir, we found the plane had a flat tire. Nothing serious, but it would take us an hour or so more to fix. So the county commissioner said, 'Would you like to come and see Dr Riek?'"

"What, you mean he was right there?"

"Yes, it was incredible. No one had said anything. So, we drove off into the bush for fifteen minutes. There was this little camp, just some straw *tukuls*. Someone told me it's where he used to live with Emma; that she's buried there. And there he was. Sitting on a green lawn chair in his fatigues. And you know what?"

Sven paused for dramatic effect.

"He was reading a book. It was called *Why Nations Fail*. I asked him if he had found out why. He said no. He'd only just finished chapter one."

––––––––––––

In Juba, life went on.

Over the years, many Canadians who'd worked at the office, who'd been posted with the Canadian Forces, or who had served as police officers with the UN in South Sudan had found time to make their way to the unmarked compound in the Hai Cinema neighbourhood of the capital that housed Confident Children out of Conflict (CCC). This was a home for girls (and a few stray small boys) who had been the victims of sexual violence. CCC was run by Cathy, a dynamic Ugandan nurse who had made it her life cause, with the help of a succession of international volunteers and a small cadre of semi-professional staff. Cathy was devout and the home was quietly Christian in an entirely positive way. Despite this, the church on whose land the structures stood was seeking to evict CCC and take over the buildings for itself. I'm not a practising Christian myself, but I'd never seen a more truly Christian project than Cathy's.

About forty of the girls lived on site and they would proudly show us around every time we visited. The rooms were immaculately clean and tidy, each girl's teddy bears and stuffed animals neatly arranged – much more so than any Canadian teenager's would be. On special occasions, they would sing for us; more informally, they'd play football or volleyball with visitors. Once we took Canadian general Roméo Dallaire to visit and he loved dandling a tiny one-year-old on his lap. The Canadian soldiers worked with us, with the help of some Canadian government funding, to build a new outdoor shelter for CCC. One of the majors who rotated through Juba supported, out of his pocket and those of his friends, basic computer skills instruction for the children.

It was scarcely believable what the girls had been through. Some had been prostituted as early as six years old, often for five or six pounds (two dollars) a time; the city cemetery was a favoured locale for assignations. Many had been beaten and had permanent scars on their legs and arms. One precocious eleven-year-old flirted with all visiting men; she spoke excellent English but was HIV-positive and needed to take her anti-retrovirals daily. Often she would take off for days and Cathy would trawl her known haunts to try to bring her back. Another resident was seventeen-year-old Lina, the victim of attempted rape by her own father. Possibly egged on by a supportive relative, she'd come to the embassy claiming to be a Canadian citizen requiring transportation home. When the truth came out she apologized for lying, but she could not go back home. So Cathy took her in.

Lina wasn't the only one with living parents. Sometimes these parents said they wanted their girls to come home when they were of marriageable age and worth some dowry. There were three or four very small boys as well. Cathy had found one of them abandoned on a rubbish dump when he was only a few days old. He had developmental problems and was nearly four before he spoke, but he was making real progress. His mother had appeared after a year or so; she would not allow Cathy to adopt him legally but was perfectly happy to have him looked after until he was grown up.

An officer with the Toronto police, Tracey, had been seconded to UNPOL, the police-training and liaison unit of the UN Mission in South Sudan, in 2011. In her spare time she volunteered with CCC and back in Canada, she couldn't forget the kids. She raised funds from her friends and relatives and at work, then saved up all her leave to spend a month each year back in Juba. With the conflict in full swing, she brought her boyfriend Brad, also a police officer, who helped with some of the more practical projects at the orphanage.

Brad and Tracey decided to get married in South Sudan, and Jenny and I were invited to the ceremony at All Saints Cathedral. It was alternately moving and unintentionally hilarious. As is traditional even for Christian weddings in Sudan, Tracey was covered in intricate henna designs, which worried her. "My boss back home, I don't know what he's going to say ... It's an absolute no-no ... tattoos are for gangs!"

She and Cathy had negotiated with a hairdresser to have a very fancy hairdo, but this was traumatic as well: once it was done there had been the inevitable argument over the price, and the two of them had had to flee into a waiting taxi. Brad had bought a shiny grey suit at the market for a very reasonable twenty dollars US but was worried that, if he moved too much or even sat down, the seams would rip. And then there were the lessons read out in the airy All Saints: one harped on about the evils of divorce (both Tracey and Brad had been married previously) for what seemed like a very long time, while another seemed to authorize wife-beating.

Throughout the ceremony, the women in the congregation ululated and cheered, and other members walked around the happy couple and the priest, looking for the best angle to take selfies. Back at CCC there was the party of the year – sans alcohol, of course – and Tracey and Brad looked a little overwhelmed. Cathy was simply beaming. Later someone told us this was the first in-country wedding of two Westerners in the history of South Sudan. "In fact, you could say it was the first white wedding!"

My friend Mading, a Canadian of South Sudanese origin who had been a DJ in Calgary, also got married while we were in Juba, but this was a much more solemn affair. Mading belonged to a very important Dinka family from Bor; his bride-to-be, Rose, was from the other major Dinka community in South Sudan, centered on Warrap and Bahr-al-Ghazal. Rose was the sister of a government minister and something of a prize but Mading, as an educated member of the diaspora and sometime journalist of repute, was a prize as well.

Negotiations between the families were long, arduous, and almost completely out of the hands of the young couple. Eventually, one hot Saturday, we were invited to the meeting of the two families and the pledging of cows in the grounds of the Home and Away restaurant. The auguries were not good. Only a few days before, there had been a massacre of twenty or more Bor Dinka, allegedly by Murle raiders, at a place called Jalle. Many of the community leaders were either in mourning or investigating the killings, so attendance was modest and very muted. About four hundred chairs had been set out under tents in a field adjoining the restaurant in two blocs, facing each other. One was for the bride's family, one for the groom's.

As at Western weddings, the groom's family arrived first, the bride's fashionably late. But neither bride nor groom had any part in these ceremonies. An MC summoned, in turn, twenty or so men to speak from the groom's side. Everything was in Dinka, so I understood little except that they lauded the character and wealth of the groom. The keynote speaker on Mading's side was a large man called Deng Dau, a regional politician of clout who clearly had national ambitions. Although he too spoke in Dinka, his speech was littered with English words such as "national legislature," "constitution," and so on. Nobody, least of all Mading, seemed fazed that this stump speech went on for at least thirty minutes.

As Deng Dau was wrapping up, Mading – seated impassively a few metres away in a smart suit – sent me an SMS saying, "You're on next." Having had no indication as to what the protocol at these affairs was, I had brought along a small gift just in case: a nicely wrapped tin of maple syrup. I'd found that playing the ignorant but genial foreigner (the *khawaja*) was a good tactic in such circumstances, and it worked this time. I handed the tin to the slightly bemused MC and delivered a few light words in English.

The serious part of the ceremony was the pledging of bride wealth. In this instance, the price was a steep three hundred cows, to be paid by Mading's family to Rose's. This was one of the highest sums I'd heard of; eighty or ninety was quite common but anything over two hundred was rare. Rose, as a minister's sister, was clearly a good catch, but her family had cannily calculated that Mading, a returned diaspora member, could be tapped for much more than the usual amount. When I saw Mading a few days later in the company of a Bor elder at Le Bistro, I jovially asked how married life was treating him. He did not smile. He was meeting with the elder to discuss tactics.

"They've moved the goalposts," Mading said grimly. "The other lot. We'd agreed that some of the cows would be delivered in the form of cash, at a price of 2,000 pounds each. But now Rose's family are upping the price to 4,000."

I'd often ribbed Mading about being a modern, Westernized man who had fallen back into "tribal" ways. He really wasn't happy now. "Only last week, I went to Dubai and spent the rest of my money on gold bracelets for Rose. I don't have any more money left ... Maybe we should just go to Canada and forget all this."

Waiting for takeoff
aboard the RAF's
C-17 at Juba
(19 December 2013).
Courtesy of the
British Embassy,
Juba.

At the first meeting in Juba of the Joint Monitoring and
Evaluation Commission: author between the Ambassador
Cleland Leshore of Kenya (left) and Ambassador Jamal
Al-Sheikh of Sudan (right), November 2015. Courtesy of
Radio Tamazuj.

Nuer children in the Juba Protection of Civilians site (2014).

Meeting with IDP women, Bentiu Protection of Civilians site (2014).

UN light tank, defending the Bor Protection of Civilians site. The defences of the camp were strengthened after a gang of youths overran the camp and fifty-eight persons were killed in April 2014.

The author inspects the Presidential Guard prior to presenting credentials to President Salva Kiir.

Pallets loaded with grain aboard the Ilyushin 76, en route to Nhialdu (2014).

Women with traditional cradles, Thaker, Unity State (2016). Some had walked for days to pick up food from the air drop.

Air drop under way, over Thaker, Unity State (2016).

Swamps near Leer, Unity State (2015). For nine months of each year, much of central South Sudan is flooded and the population must seek high ground, along with their cattle.

Children greet the humanitarian country team's Mi-8 helicopter at Nyal, en route to Leer, Unity State (2015).

The humanitarian country team at Leer, Unity State, moments before gunfire starts (2015).

Gatwech's reunited children, Akobo (2015). Fighting had broken up the family early in 2013, and Gatwech's wife died; it was two years before the children were traced.

Dinner at Tearfund, Motot: Mary the cook with half a kob (antelope), 2015.

War Child Canada flag, Malakal POC (2016).

Sign on Airport Road, Juba, welcoming Riek Machar back (April 2016). Left to right: Vice-President James Wani Igga, Dr Riek Machar, President Salva Kiir.

The Echo of Mille Collines

Bentiu, Bor, and Juba, April–December 2014

In April 2014, after a lull of a few weeks, fighting picked up again.

An attack on Bentiu, Unity State, by the SPLM-IO began to gather force on Monday, 14 April, following the rebels' seizure of Mayom (to the west). Before dawn on Tuesday, IO forces under Peter Gadet engaged the SPLA at its divisional HQ in Rubkona, then seized the bridge across the river to Bentiu. By noon they were in control of the centre of town. Brigadier General James Koang of the IO made a broadcast on Radio Bentiu on 15 April. UNMISS reported – oddly – that the SPLA did not make use of its tanks in the defence of the town; it turned out later that their commanders had defected and placed the armour in rebel hands.

At the outset of the fighting, Mongolian peacekeeping troops rescued ten expatriate oil workers from the small Safinat refinery under construction twenty-five kilometres to the northwest of Bentiu; two were now in critical condition. Meanwhile civilians flooded into UNMISS's Protection of Civilians (POC) compound, which was soon housing 12,000 (up from 4,500 two weeks earlier). Once again, the ethnic demographics had shifted dramatically. Before, it was Nuers seeking shelter; now it was Dinkas fleeing from the Nuer-dominated IO. There were some reports that even some Nuer individuals in Bentiu had been shot on sight for "not celebrating."

This event would soon precipitate further violence several hundred kilometres to the south. Three days after the fall of Bentiu, on Friday 18 April, a 300-strong group of armed Dinka youth approached the UNMISS compound at Bor where 5,000 Nuer displaced persons had taken refuge. They initially presented a petition calling for the removal of these persons from Jonglei State. But this was just a front for the group to force its way into the compound. UNMISS peace-keepers fired over their heads to drive them back. In the ensuing fracas, fifty-eight people were killed: forty-six internally displaced civilians, two national staff members of the International Rescue Committee whose base was by the entrance, and ten demonstrators. UNMISS called for support from the SPLA but they arrived too late to be of use.[1]

There was evidence that the Dinka youth were egged on by government authorities, possibly even armed by them: weapons included rocket-propelled grenades. Minister Michael Makuei, no stranger to the Bor UN compound, was quick to muddy the waters by stating that the youth were "provoked" by reports of Nuers (whom he termed "rebels") celebrating the fall of Bentiu, and by suggesting that UNMISS was to blame for the whole incident.

Then the focus swung back to Bentiu, where atrocities were committed by troops and irregulars loyal to Machar. A UN team that visited the city accompanied by an Al Jazeera camera crew was dismayed to find hundreds of bodies littering the streets. A few clips aired internationally showed corpses being moved by a bulldozer.

The centre of the horror was the town's main mosque. According to preliminary testimony, insurgent rebels encouraged civilians to take refuge there "for their own safety," robbed them of all their belongings, then shot 200 dead. The total death toll in Bentiu was estimated by the UN to be as high as 1,500. Among the bodies observed by the UN were children clutching automatic rifles. Most significantly, there were multiple reports that in the hours following the rebels' arrival, Radio Bentiu had broadcast messages calling upon the insurgents to rape, kill, and mutilate Dinkas and (Muslim) Darfuris.

"Radio Mille Collines," mused a friend when we heard the news. "Remember Rwanda, 1994, wasn't it?" The UN carefully reconstructed the timeline. There was no doubt that these broadcasts occurred once the rebels were in control. This was the first time there had been explicit incitement to murder on an ethnic basis by either the IO or the government. As such, to borrow the carefully measured expression Deputy SRSG Toby Lanzer used, Bentiu was "a game-changer," an echo of the Rwandan genocide.

Why were the Darfuris targeted? It had been common knowledge for some time that members of the Darfur-based JEM rebel movement had been fighting alongside the regular SPLA; Bentiu was known to be an unofficial base for JEM commanders on R&R in South Sudan. The JEM and the allied SPLM-N (rebels fighting Khartoum, based in the Nuba Mountains) also frequented the refugee camp at Yida. But while allegations of JEM fighting alongside the SPLA were likely true, there were also credible allegations that the 10 had launched one arm of their attack on Bentiu from Sudan with the full knowledge and connivance of the authorities. Regionalization of the crisis was creeping in.

If there was any good news, it was that UN human-rights investigators and other international officials (including Lanzer) were allowed entry to Bentiu, asking questions without hindrance. But 10 commander James Koang casually denied knowledge of any bodies at the mosque with an innocent-sounding "Is that so?" and Riek Machar, quizzed by phone, denied that his troops could in any way be responsible and improbably suggested the 10 had been set up by the government.

The fall of Bentiu prompted the government to change the top brass at last. This was when the well-educated and articulate Hoth ("a soldier's soldier" who had held office since 2009 and was seen as impeccably neutral on the ethnic front) was replaced by Paul Malong. Malong had been governor of Northern Bahr-al-Ghazal since 2008, but also held the rank of lieutenant-general and had considerable combat experience. He was a classic South Sudanese Big Man, a Bahr-al-Ghazal Dinka like Salva Kiir, reputed to have forty wives and over 200 children. He spoke poor English and was far more comfortable in Dinka; many said he was illiterate.

In the first week of May I accompanied Lanzer and some journalists, including the BBC's Alistair Leithead, on a two-day visit to the POC site near Bentiu, which had swelled to a population of 25,000. Driving the five or six kilometres north from the Rubkona airstrip, we saw a large number of wrecked vehicles and burned-down houses. The BBC crew that visited Bentiu later the same afternoon found the town quiet, although a small market was functioning. The piles of dead bodies filmed by Al Jazeera two weeks earlier had largely been cleared away. In the mosque – scene of the massacre – there were heaps of clothing, scattered possessions, and some visible bloodstains. The hospital, which had been the scene of more killings, was functioning again, though mainly serving the military.

With some trepidation (for the general was reported to be furious about the Al Jazeera coverage) the reporters met with the 10 commander, James Koang. Koang did react with hostility, but only towards the *New York Times* reporter, who was of Sudanese origin and whom he immediately accused of being a member of the JEM. Once this misunderstanding had been cleared up, Koang made a routine denial that his forces had committed atrocities and said that "two or three" of his men had been detained and would be investigated on this account. This was Koang's last day as commander in Bentiu; he had been transferred by Riek Machar, presumably on account of the very bad publicity incurred by the rebels in their attack on the state capital, to be replaced by Peter Gadet. Not long after this interview, the town was lost to the SPLA again.

The Bentiu POC at this time (it would later grow) was a city in two large, fenced compounds on flat but very muddy ground. The rains had come early and they had been heavier than normal. IDPs were removing sections of the wire to go seek firewood and/or privacy for defecation. A Mongolian battalion was struggling to expand the perimeter and to patrol it as more and more people arrived. This was a Sisyphean task, and the troops badly needed reinforcing.

POC 1 was largely Nuer; this camp had steadily filled over the past two weeks, notwithstanding the IDPs' sharing the ethnicity of the rebels in command of Bentiu. It seemed to me that this revealed the disillusionment of locals with both sides of the conflict. POC 2 was more mixed, including 600 Sudanese traders (and possibly some Darfuris and/or runaway members of the JEM), Shillook, and a few Dinka. Most Dinka had by now fled to neighbouring Warrap State. The Sudanese complained of discrimination (not very justifiably, I thought) and were appealing to the UN to repatriate them. As the border was only thirty or so kilometres away, and they had come under their own steam, the UN was not sympathetic.

Housing in the POC site consisted of bamboo-walled shacks with white UN-supplied plastic sheeting for roofs. With the rains so strong and disease a serious threat, the main focus of the agencies was sanitation and clean water. The daily water ration had been upped from a frightening one litre per day per person to around eight, the ratio of latrines improved from one per 353 persons to one per seventy (the UN standard was one per twenty-five). Food distribution had thus far been minimal, hampered by a chronic shortfall in pipeline funding and severe logistical issues. On the day of my visit, seventy World Food Program trucks (each carrying ten to twenty tons) were still stuck across the front line on the other side of Mayom. They had not been able to move for two weeks.

With so many people crammed into such a small area and with arrivals and departures so unpredictable, there were many problems.

Water was often the focal point for conflict and camp leaders were understandably furious that UNMISS engineers had terminated the sewage outlet from the military camp in the middle of the IDP camp; the scene was not a pleasant one. The non-governmental organization called Non-Violent Peace Force, along with UNICEF, had opened rape-counselling centres and UNICEF was seeking to bring in dignity kits, but with cargo space at such a premium there were bitter disagreements among agencies as to what their priority should be. Weapons searches were conducted with frequency; one was due the morning I left, but another was postponed in anticipation of change in the control of Bentiu.

Various Canadians participated in the relief effort: two with Médecins Sans Frontières, one as the director of operations for the International Organization for Migration, and a fourth – Solomon, of South Sudanese extraction – as a UN volunteer. Solomon, who had been here for two years, was the star of the camp: he spoke multiple local languages, had developed excellent relations with all the community leaders, and had made himself "Mister Fixit" for every INGO and UN agency.

Toby and I met with two large groups of community leaders, one at each POC site. The men, predictably, produced their (long) lists of requirements and exhibited the familiar sense of dependency and entitlement. But once the men made way for the women, the message became – counterintuitively – more political: "Don't just send us relief … We need a quick response to this cancer that has led to so many deaths. You managed to end the civil war. Now, because of the mistakes of our leaders, we need your help again."

Condemnation of both Salva Kiir and Riek Machar was unanimous and balanced. One woman, who had lost two sons over the past four months, bitterly asked, "Where are their children, Riek's and Salva's? If they were on the front lines like our children, things would be different. Why are we dying for two people?" Another woman asked Lanzer to pass a video-recorded message to both President Obama and the secretary-general of the UN. After careful preparation and rehearsing in English, she solemnly intoned, "Tell this to Obama from Christina in Bentiu: we want peace."

All the relief workers were fatigued but positive. They pleaded with Lanzer for more airlifts, more food, more non-food items – more of everything. Most felt that the POCs were here to stay, at least until the next dry season (they were right; by December 2015, the Bentiu POC was home to 127,000 displaced civilians and the second-largest city in South Sudan after Juba). The Mongolian forces that protected Bentiu were respected, notwithstanding "Sewage Gate," and it was acknowledged that they had performed to the very highest standards by rescuing 500 people from Bentiu hospital two weeks earlier, when the town was under attack by rebels.

Toby was tired as well. Like Hilde Johnson, he had received threats against his life and travelled with close protection. While in public he appeared ebullient, confident, even domineering. In private, and off the record with the journalists, he was thoughtful and nuanced. In an off-camera confession that left the hardened Leithead and the NYT journalist briefly silent, looking at the floor, he said that some evenings since the crisis began in December, he cried.

Next morning, as we prepared to board our outgoing helicopter, Leithead was torn as to whether or not he should stay. He was frankly disappointed that he had arrived in Bentiu too late to capture the same kind of grisly footage that Al Jazeera had run for days on end. Now there was a rumour that the SPLA was set to re-take the town. It could make for a good story – or he could sit here for days and nothing might happen.

He decided to stay.

As we prepared to leave the compound, our preparations suddenly became hurried. I was told peremptorily to put on my flak jacket and was bundled into the back of an armoured UN personnel carrier. With me was Joanna, Toby's young, blonde, and glamorous Dutch assistant. We lurched as we set off and she inadvertently put her hand on the bottom of the ruddy-faced Mongolian peacekeeper who was manning the gun turret. Both faces went even redder.

At the airstrip, the Mi-8's rotors were already turning; we were pushed in and took off. About one hundred metres into the air, we banked to one side. I could see that four or five technicals had just drawn up at the airstrip. The men were pointing up at us, but for the moment did not look hostile. It was the SPLA, in the process of recapturing Bentiu. Leithead got his story.

As fighting continued longer than expected, and as one "cessation of hostilities" after another was broken, the need for an international monitoring mechanism became evident. By late May, the Monitoring and Verification Mission (MVM) was operational in Juba, with teams partially operational in Bor, Bentiu, Malakal, and Nasir.

There were some serious structural issues with the MVM. It was a subset of the regional political body known as IGAD: the misleadingly named Intergovernmental Authority on Development that brought Sudan, South Sudan, Ethiopia, Eritrea, Kenya, Djibouti, Somalia, and Uganda together in a loose political bloc, and that was attempting to mediate the crisis. One problem was that Uganda was both a member of IGAD and a party to the conflict. Ugandan troops had not been involved in direct fighting since January 2014 (when infantry, gunships, and tanks were all deployed in combat, with significant losses) but they were still the primary defence for Juba airport and for Bor, both of which were in rebel sights. It was conceivable that the teams could find themselves reporting ceasefire infringements not just by the two principal parties but by the Ugandan army – an awkward situation, to say the least. Sudan was also a member of IGAD and a participant in the MVM. While not a direct party to the conflict, it certainly had an indirect and not necessarily helpful hand in things. I doubted it was for reasons of comfort and/or tourism that Sudan chose to have all its team members assigned to Malakal, close to the Sudanese border and very close to havens for Sudanese rebels.

In the event, the MVM did a decent job of getting out and reporting violations. But two further issues gradually rendered the utility of the mechanism questionable. First, each team was meant to have representation from both the rebels and the SPLA. But the IO claimed that its personnel would not be safe in government territory even within UN bases, so they never participated. This undermined the credibility of many of the MVM's reports. Secondly, and more importantly, while reports of violations were dutifully posted on IGAD's website and even published in paid newspaper ads, the political parties were never presented with the violations, let alone challenged to respond to them and/or penalized in any way. It all seemed a colossal waste of money and effort.

I spent the middle of 2014 in a kind of diplomatic limbo, part of it in Ottawa. A decision had been made to finally upgrade the status of the Canadian office in Juba to that of an embassy. Nothing very substantive would change in the short term; I would keep my job, but with a new title: ambassador. I would now be allowed to fly a small Canadian flag on the official vehicle, and my apartment – unchanged – would now be known as the "official residence." Host-country officials

would be henceforth required to address me as "Your Excellency."
Less positively, from my point of view, as an acting member of the
executive category of Canadian government civil servants I would no
longer be able to claim overtime either in the form of cash or time off,
and would thus be confined to around twenty days of annual leave.

Appointments of Canadian ambassadors, nominated by the
prime minister and officially designated by the governor general,
are meant to be kept secret even from family until the last minute.
Nominations are very occasionally retracted when some unforeseen
objection is made to a candidacy. While the bureaucratic wheels
moved slowly I took extended leave, then spent a month in an
Ottawa hotel with Jenny, trying not to let anyone – even my poor,
tiny team back in Juba – know what was going on. Whenever we
had brief stays back "home" like this, there was some cultural read-
justment, including catching up on all the hit TV shows: *The Big
Bang Theory* that summer.

At last, following a chance encounter in an elevator, a staffer in
Foreign Minister Baird's office saw fit to expedite things. A press
statement was issued naming me the first resident Canadian ambassador to South Sudan, and in October 2014 Jenny and I headed back
to Juba. I had an impressive gold-leaf charter in my pocket along with
a set of letters of credence to be presented to President Kiir, in which
the governor general assured the president that I was trustworthy.

On the JDO compound, we were no longer squatting in a pair of
bungalows borrowed from the British but had our own small building, pending the resolution of complex negotiations for a five-way
sharing with the Netherlands, Norway, Sweden, and Denmark. Our
new embassy was, in fact, several shipping containers bolted together,
with their inner walls removed, but by Juba standards it was not bad.
It was set among the trees, had a sloping green roof, and had the
Canadian coat of arms (rarely recognized by most of our Canadian
visitors) by the door. Uniquely for a Canadian chancery – the correct
name for an embassy building – it was bullet-resistant, with two-
centimetres-thick windows.

Unfortunately, reinforcing the building had stretched the budget to
the limit, so there was no money left over for the Department of
Foreign Affairs' standard communications set-up, known as SIGNET,
let alone the more sophisticated equipment that would allow us to
transmit sensitive ("classified") material. We would have to make do
with wi-fi with very limited bandwidth, fed to small laptops. We still

relied on our cellphones and the old voice-over-internet spider-phone. Unfortunately, the nature of the material used to reinforce our walls meant that it was difficult to receive a cellphone signal inside the office, so many calls had to be received or made outside while pacing up and down under the trees.

We also had to make do with the cheap Chinese furniture we'd used ever since we opened the office in the converted garage three years earlier. And as before, I had no office of my own; we would all four share the same open space. But in honour of my new status, I kept the Canadian flag in my corner of the room.

It was some time before I was able to present my credentials to President Salva Kiir. The big day was put off several times until a critical mass of other would-be ambassadors, nearly all of them resident in Addis Ababa, were on hand. In a prior meeting at the Ministry of Foreign Affairs, we were briefed as to the protocol to be followed and each given a time slot for the following morning.

My allocated time was improbably early: I was asked to be on hand at the embassy at 8:00 a.m. Not surprisingly, it was nearly 10:00 before I had a panic-stricken warning from our guards that two large, black Toyota V-8 cars were impatiently honking their horns, waiting to get into the compound. They screamed in, grabbed the small Canadian flag I was clutching, and put it on the lead vehicle. I was pushed into the back seat and we were off, sirens blaring. It was only about a mile to J-1, but we seemed to cover it in less than thirty seconds, with all other traffic held back by sunglass-wearing police on white motorbikes with blue flashing lights.

In the gardens within the gates, the blue-uniformed presidential guard stood in the sunshine. Escorted by a senior officer dripping with braid, I solemnly inspected them, not quite certain whether I was supposed to march in step with him. We then retreated to a podium and stood to attention as the two national anthems were played. This was a nervous moment, as the band could not have had much practice with "O Canada"; they played it too slowly, but not in such a way that non-Canadians might have noticed.

Inside, I was ushered along red carpets into a large curtained room lit by chandeliers. Standing in the place indicated, I offered up my letters of credence and of the recall of my Nairobi-based predecessor along with a short formula of greeting. I was ushered to sit at the right hand of the president in a red gilt chair while Jenny and another embassy staff member observed from a discreet distance.

President Kiir was apparently in good health and – although subdued and soft-spoken, as he always seemed to be – friendly and responsive. He was wearing his Stetson, of course; I wondered if he ever took it off. Without reference to notes, he spoke of the long history of Canadian support for South Sudan through our high commission in Nairobi and expressed gratitude for the large number of civil-war refugees Canada had accepted. He said that those returning from the diaspora had a critical role to play now, with their superior education and training.

Kiir was interested when I mentioned my early years in the greater Sudan, and when I said that I had long ago visited Mapel, near his birthplace, he jokingly dismissed it as a place of "no importance compared to Kuajok" (his actual hometown). He recalled that we had met before, when we had jointly laid the foundation stone of the maternity ward at the Wau hospital.

We had a small celebration with colleagues and friends at the newly official embassy a couple of days later. The undersecretary of foreign affairs made a long and rather rambling speech in which he misleadingly indicated that he was available "at any time of day or night," whatever needs the diplomatic corps might have. After he left, my Australian colleague, who had come from Addis for his own ceremony and had been kept waiting five days, asked for his number. He impatiently swore he would take the functionary at his word and call him at 2:00 a.m.

I went back into the field where I had left off: travelling with Toby on one of his self-styled road trips. Last time we'd been to a UN Protection of Civilians site. But not all civilians sought the sanctuary of the UN; in fact, the vast majority, a million or so, had congregated in informal settlements where there was some other form of protection whether ethnic or geographical. A further half-million had fled the country entirely.

The largest informal site, at Minkamman in Lakes State, had two advantages for Dinkas: Lakes State was 100 per cent Dinka, and the Nile formed an effective barrier to Nuer-dominated Jonglei. By late 2014, over 70,000 IDPs had fled there from Bor as the rebels repeatedly attacked and sacked the town. Minkamman had been a way-station for our young Canadian friend Biel on his odyssey from Bor to Juba.

The village was the seat for Awerial County and normally a very sleepy place. The permanent population of the county was only 7,000, so the IDPs, encamped in white-plastic-roofed shelters over a wide expanse of dry and lightly wooded ground, now outnumbered the locals by at least ten to one. But the young and dynamic county commissioner assured us that relations between the two communities were good. In fact, he was delighted with the influx because it had attracted traders from across the state and a wide range of humanitarian services to which the permanent population also had access.

Because the displaced community was in friendly territory, no perimeter fence or other security was necessary and the camp had almost unlimited room for expansion. There was also good access to unused agricultural land. The only serious issue was Minkamman's location where, in the dry season, cattle herders brought their vast herds to water. This was not necessarily a benign phenomenon: the youth who looked after the cows were well-armed and aggressive, and there were fears as to what would happen when the dry season set in, in January.

Separating from Toby's entourage, I spent an afternoon talking to women IDPs. They patiently listed their tasks. "We build the houses … we help with the food distributions, we do the cooking, we look after the goats. We fetch the firewood. We look after the gardens."

"And the children?" I asked.

"Yes, of course, we look after the children too. There are very many."

"So what do the men do?"

There was a puzzled pause, then some giggling. If the ladies weren't so black, I'd have sworn they were blushing.

"They make babies."

"And how long does that take?" I ventured, when the laughter died down.

"Oh, about a minute or two…"

I didn't actually see any men making babies. They were generally playing cards, drinking tea, or on the phone to their friends. Very few of the women had phones.

The World Food Program distributed subsistence packages to a registered IDP population of 100,000. There were concerns that a significant proportion of those registered – maybe as many as 35,000

– were double-dipping: commuting to Bor whenever there was a distribution in that city, on the other side of the Nile. The technical solution to this problem was simple: biometrics. But the hardware required to conduct biometrically based registration was in demand elsewhere in South Sudan and it would be some weeks before it would reach Minkamman.

There were the usual gripes: a preference for beans and sorghum over lentils and much lamenting that milk (on which young Dinka and Nuer are traditionally raised to the age of five or six) was not available. But the chiefs, as they watched their women loading fifty kilograms on their heads, conceded that things were pretty good.

The question I asked everyone was, "What will it take for you to go back to Bor?"

Most answers were surprisingly personal. "When Riek goes back to Juba, we will return to Bor." (By this I assumed they meant that he must call off the rebellion and re-enter normal life.)

"And what do you think about President Kiir?" There was some grumbling, but there was more loyalty among the Dinka here to the president than there was among the Nuer in Bentiu to Machar. The chiefs said they would not accept a political solution that forced Kiir out of office. Among the men, there was awareness of the Addis-based peace process now under way. (Wind-up radios delivered by Internews and UNDP were the main source of information.) But few seemed optimistic.

Crossing the river to Bor, through the swamps and multiple channels of the great Nile, made for a blissful interlude, a break from the stories of human want and family tragedies. Hippos eyed us from among the slowly drifting islands of water lilies; pelicans and ibises swooped past; a croc lay on the bank. Fishermen in their dugouts, one wearing a red Arsenal football jersey and nothing else, greeted us with cheery waves. Toby wanted to go for a swim mid-stream but his Romanian bodyguards were agitated, so he shrugged and put his shirt back on.

We were brought back to reality with a jolt when policemen on the Bor waterfront tried to arrest the bodyguards.

First stop in Bor was a vision from hell: the half-abandoned site known as POC 1. Scarcely larger than two soccer fields, this lightly fortified UN compound at one time housed 17,000 civilians fleeing combat in the city. Fifty-eight had been killed here in the April 2014 attack. The previous week a torrential overnight downpour had

flooded the area, much of it waist-deep. Terrified IDPs had struggled
to hold their children above the water at 2:00 a.m. and most of the
informal shacks in which they lived were swept away. The day we
visited, there remained a vast stagnant lake with floating debris and
a few house poles still sticking above water level, and there was an
overpowering smell of raw sewage.

But to the UN's credit, this eventuality had been considered. POC 2
was almost ready, the day after the flood, to receive IDPs. The new
site was much larger and on dry ground, and it was heavily fortified.
There was one tank permanently stationed on each berm, seven
heavy machine-gun posts on salients, three circles of razor wire with
fifty metres of open ground between them, and a perimeter patrolled
every thirty minutes by armoured personnel carriers. The fort was
constructed by the Korean Engineers' battalion of UNMISS, and the
joke du jour was that defences were modelled on the DMZ between
the Koreas, though they were manned by Indian troops. When I
enquired discreetly of Hazel, the jolly South African focal point for
UNMISS, I was told that they had been instructed to harden their
earlier stance, which had contributed to the fatal ambush near Pibor
when they lost seven men. The extreme measures were on account of
the April 2014 attack.

Conditions inside the new camp were much better than in the old
one; they even included a playing field. But the mood among the
chiefs of the 2,500 or so Nuer who were still holed up here was grim,
in contrast to their Dinka counterparts in Minkamman. They spoke
with passion, conviction, and anger. "We have been the victims of a
genocide," they said. "We will never forget this." Nobody would step
out beyond the razor wire, let alone reach out to their former Dinka
neighbours, absent a firm and sustainable ceasefire. There was particular bitterness over the continuing presence of the Ugandan troops.
But anti-government feeling did not equate, for them, with pro-Riek
sentiment. A number of the women called for a plague on both their
houses, in contrast to the Dinka chiefs at Minkamman who were
much more supportive of their man.

Just outside POC 2 were two steel shipping containers that had
been adapted as makeshift jails. I spoke to a Finnish UNPOL officer
who said, "We use them for cooling off, though actually they're
pretty hot. If they fight, we put them in here for a few hours. But we
cannot hold them. You see, there's really no law about what we can
do when that happens."

In Bor town, things were more cheerful. The market that had been completely destroyed nine months earlier was being rebuilt and there was a buzz in the air. Nearly all the traders who were rebuilding were Darfuris, Sudanese, and Ethiopians. This was typical. At the best of times, the Nuer and Dinka were only inclined to run small-scale vegetable and produce stands. The gutted Kenya Commercial Bank was still adorned with graffiti from the (briefly) victorious rebels, but was being rebuilt.

Outside town, the facilities of Radio Jonglei had been completely destroyed and looted, with the loss of millions of dollars of recently donated equipment. The building was a haunted shell littered with ransacked files. Bats flew in and out. A typewritten notice on the wall called all staff to a meeting on 16 December 2013.

Bor hospital, I knew from Undersecretary Makur, was where some of the worst atrocities had been committed: dozens of patients were shot dead in their beds and octogenarian women were raped. The physical damage had now been repaired. I spent an hour in the Canadian-financed maternity ward, and you would hardly have known know there had ever been a problem there except for the single commemorative bullet-hole adjoining the plaque expressing gratitude to CIDA. Among the doctors was Ajak, whom I'd first met at our home in late 2012 and last spoken to by satellite phone in late December 2013 when he and his colleagues were on the run, their clinic at Werkok having been sacked by Machar's White Army.

Given all the fighting up-country and the deepening humanitarian crisis, it was easy to forget some of our earlier preoccupations with South Sudan. Reporters without Borders' latest press freedom rankings[2] had the country at 125th place, noting that government sensitivity about war coverage was increasingly limiting freedom of expression. An emblematic issue was that of the *Nation Mirror* newspaper, whose print run had been seized and which was not allowed to publish again. The ostensible reason was a banner headline on 28 January 2015: "SPLA Forces Withdraw from Renk as Rebels Launch Attack." The accompanying article did not support the headline. In correction, the paper next day ran another headline, "Upper Nile Government: SPLA has NOT withdrawn from Renk," along with a half-column apology and clarification. But this did not prevent the closure, which occurred one week later.

I visited the *Nation Mirror*'s editor, Wol Atak, to see what was going on and to express solidarity. Although agents from the National Security Service were outside his office and quizzed my driver, Mandrea, I was not denied access. The UK and US ambassadors had also visited recently. Wol did not believe the headline was the real cause of the paper's closure; he had spoken with the chief of the general staff, Malong, who said that the military had no issues with the paper. Rather, Wol suggested, the order resulted from an accumulation of issues.

Back in 2008, when he was a serving member in the National Assembly representing Tonj North (Warrap State) for the governing SPLM, Wol had tabled a motion for an investigation into a series of rapes and killings in Tonj, apparently committed by serving members of the SPLA. The motion was suppressed, and he was dropped from the SPLM's subsequent electoral lists. However, the governor of Warrap, who took the matter personally, was now President Kiir's advisor on local government. Secondly, late the previous year, at the time when the rebel IO was holding internal consultations in Pagak as mandated by IGAD, the *Nation Mirror* ran a number of reports about the consultations. Wol was reprimanded by authorities and also received an anonymous phone call saying, "Go back and join your president in the bush" (presumably a reference to Riek Machar). More recently, it had become known that the paper was preparing an in-depth series of articles on the genesis of the current crisis. This was not likely to back up the government's official line that December 2013 was a coup.

Other newspapers had been instructed by the National Security Service not to publish items concerning the paper's closure. Wol expressed disappointment with the attitude of his fellow editors. The local press association, AMDISS, did prepare a critical statement but then decided that discretion was the better part of valour and withheld it.

On 16 February 2015, Information Minister Makuei delivered a rant to journalists. The immediate object of his ire was the UN's Radio Miraya, which that morning had aired an interview with Rebecca Garang. He went so far as to say, "That UN, I will shut it down," and for good measure took swipes at the *Nation Mirror*, Gurtong (a media outlet), and Human Rights Watch ("bloodsuckers"). Cabinet Affairs Minister Martin Elia Lomuro, at the same briefing, described the human rights NGO as "bloodsucking mosquitoes."

A favourite place for foreigners to enjoy a leisurely weekend lunch was an open-air restaurant on the banks of the Nile called Da Vinci. It was one of the few places in Juba where you could sit by the wide and fast-flowing river, and the only one from which you could take a picture of the rickety Nile bridge, a hundred meters upstream, without risking arrest. Tables were set beneath large mango trees and occasionally a monkey would wander through, picking delicately at fruit or bread that you were careless enough to leave unattended.

It was also a popular venue for embassies to hold their National Day parties. The format was always the same. The government would nominate a VIP speaker but it was luck of the draw who you got. Almost invariably he or she would arrive very late, leaving the nervous ambassador to fret over whether he should abandon the speeches or go ahead anyway. After the speeches, there'd be the two national anthems and a toast, then everyone would start looking for the food.

Occasionally things were livelier. One Turkish National Day, the sound system ceased working for the jaunty South Sudanese national anthem. Touchingly, the South Sudanese who were present sang on, becoming slowly more and more out of synch with each other as the verses advanced. One German National Day, just after dark, there was a great disturbance, and I saw a knot of agitated people gathering around somebody on the ground. The person was thrashing and shouting and I thought, "Oh dear, someone is drunk already." But no; it was a soaking wet woman who had jumped off the bridge in an attempt to kill herself. One of the uniformed German police officers in attendance, assigned to UNPOL, had seen her falling and chivalrously dived in to rescue her. A strong swimmer, he successfully pulled her to shore. The trouble was, she did not want to be saved. Things became even more agitated when the private ambulance someone summoned arrived and nobody volunteered to pay for it.

In 2014, the Ministry of Foreign Affairs hosted a pre-Christmas dinner for diplomats at Da Vinci. Invited for seven o'clock, we made small talk for an hour as dusk was settling and mosquitoes biting, with no sign of food. Then at last drinks circulated: expensive Johnny Walker Black Label. Foreign Minister Barnaba stood up and invited all the Western diplomats to make a few impromptu remarks. We had the feeling he was killing time and that someone had forgotten to arrange any catering.

It was all quite congenial, everybody saying the right things about the somnolent IGAD peace process whatever our private doubts might be. Then from the car park appeared the always colourful figure of Interior Minister (and General) Aleu Ayieny Aleu, dressed in white silk with a headdress like a maharajah's. He had an ivory cane in one hand (I was told it was really a shoehorn, but it looked good). Aleu gently pushed Barnaba to one side and made a few inoffensive remarks about how we should all get to know each other better in informal settings. Then he launched into a tirade. First, he pointed with the stick at the hapless Stefano, Sven's replacement as ambassador of the EU. "You, Mr Ambassador! How much has the European Union spent on the IGAD talks?"

Stefano shrugged nervously, not sure if this was a joke.

"Fifteen million? Twenty? Euros or dollars? What a waste of money! You know what? We don't need your money. We can fix this ourselves ... just as we did in 2005."

He looked around for the ambassador of Sudan who fortunately had just left, tired of waiting for the food to appear. "And Sudan! Where is Sudan? You need to watch out, Mr Ambassador! You make trouble for us, we'll set our boys in Nuba onto you!"

After a few more digs, our host Minister Barnaba was visibly flustered, smiling a very sickly grin. But Aleu wasn't finished yet. He swung his swagger-stick dramatically in a wide semicircle. "You diplomats, you don't know what you are doing here. You have it all wrong. Juba will be the end of your careers. You'll see. This will be your graveyard!" There was a deathly pause. Then, just to be sure we had understood: "Do you hear me? This will be your cemetery, all of you!" Then he sat down.

It was certainly a memorable party. And I had the feeling that a couple of cables next morning would have the title, "From the diplomats' graveyard."

Communing with the Sky God

Unity State, Upper Nile State, and Juba, January to March 2015

A year after the events of December 2013, the opposition installed a de facto capital at the small town of Pagak in Upper Nile State, conveniently close to the Ethiopian border should government forces attack. An old friend from Sudanese days, Canadian academic Dr John Young,[1] observed the rebels' first serious attempt to come up with a political program, as mandated by the never-ending peace talks in Addis Ababa.

John was one of only two external observers who made it to the gathering. He said the atmosphere in the sprawling settlement was extremely open and friendly, with few armed men in evidence. There were no heavy weapons in sight but most of the rebel leadership wore uniforms (their old SPLA uniforms; as far as they were concerned, they were the legitimate army). If the rebels were feeling any pressure, they were not showing it. The consultations were organized state by state and were more democratic than parallel talks conducted in Juba, where pro-government figures simply restated their positions without discussion.

Contrary to earlier indications, all the top rebel generals participated in the talks, including Peter Gadet; there was no evidence of a split between military and civilian within the 10. The best-known Nuer prophet, Dak Kueth, was also at Pagak. While the bulk of the participants were Nuer, those keeping company with Riek Machar usually crossed the ethnic spectrum, including Dinka and Equatorian. Among the latter was Canadian/South Sudanese MP Henry Odwar, who a few months earlier had disappeared from Juba as I was in the process of issuing him a new passport.

The opening of the event was a keynote speech by Riek Machar. Oddly, this was delivered in English. The only portion that attracted any sign of internal dissent (after translation ...) was this: "We must be ready to exercise magnanimity. We must forgive atrocities committed against us and likewise ask forgiveness from those we have harmed." The address concluded with a ten-point platform:

1 The SPLM/SPLA calls for the institution of [a] federal system of governance in which the states and the local governments shall be devolved more political, judicial and economic powers. We have renamed our country the Federal Republic of South Sudan and immediately established 21 states based on the former districts during the colonial period instead of ten states.
2 The SPLM/SPLA shall implement Security Reforms.
3 Undertake radical reforms in the judiciary.
4 Administrative reforms at the local level.
5 Institute reforms in the political parties system to render them national rather than ethnic or regional in character.
6 Reform the civil service by depoliticizing and professionalizing it.
7 Promote economic growth by investing the petrodollars in agriculture.
8 Build modern physical infrastructure in cities, towns and villages.
9 Construct dams and hydroelectric power.
10 Encourage private sector as well as private public partnership to drive the development of South Sudan.

Not many of the above points were controversial. Point 1, however, bore careful parsing. By "devolution of economic powers" it was widely assumed that the rebels meant, "More local control over oil revenues." Those revenues proceeded exclusively from the three currently contested states. The renaming of the twenty-one colonial-era counties as states (in lieu of the present ten) would involve redrawing political boundaries on more ethnic lines, carving from the Greater Upper Nile those regions where there were significant populations of other ethnicities, notably Dinka and Shillook. John detected a very subtle and unspoken undercurrent around this topic: many of those present, he felt, would settle for an ethnically cleansed Greater Upper Nile (Unity, Jonglei, Upper Nile) either as an independent country, or as a nearly autonomous entity within a more decentralized South Sudan.

Generally speaking, there was a great deal of ignorance in South Sudan regarding the term "federalism." It seemed to be assumed that the more administrative units you formed and the closer you took these to the ground, the better; John Garang's mantra of "taking the towns to the people" was often quoted. But there was no understanding that this process would be meaningless unless the powers of these decentralized units of government were specified and the units properly and equitably resourced.

In subsequent discussions at Pagak, the masses showed little interest in the idea of power-sharing between Riek Machar and Salva Kiir. If Riek was permitted by his constituency to concede that Salva Kiir might remain president as long as his executive powers went to a new PM (Machar himself), it was only because it was felt that Kiir would not agree to this anyway. Nor did anyone believe that Salva Kiir would agree to the concomitant demand that, over the transitional period of thirty months, central government tolerate and pay for a separate rebel army alongside the regular SPLA. "Nearly everyone at Pagak," John noted, "really wanted justice (or revenge), Salva Kiir out, and restitution."

There was similar scepticism from the rebel rump over the Arusha process. This intra-SPLM dialogue was sponsored jointly by a Finnish organization called CMI and the ruling party of Tanzania (CCM). An initial week-long meeting in October 2014 in Arusha, Tanzania was successful in bringing together political elements of the rebel leadership with their brothers and sisters in the mainstream SPLM, and did achieve an admission of "collective responsibility" for the crisis. But the process had given rise to fears that it could distract from or undermine the mainstream IGAD peace talks. With this in mind, the initiative's sponsors had reached out to IGAD and to chief mediator Seyoum Mesfin in particular, to the troika, and to regional heads of state. A member of CMI told me, "Arusha's strength is its informality. We can treat Arusha as a test bed, a place to see where common ground might possibly lie."

At Pagak, the IO's military governor for Upper Nile, Gathoth Gatkuoth Hothnyang, a hard man even by IO standards, talked tough about Arusha. "The SPLM is a bloody party that has massacred its own people, lost popularity, vision, direction, and as such will never reunite its members and the entire nation of South Sudan.

Therefore, the [Upper Nile] delegates recommend creation of a new party that may unite people of South Sudan as well as lead our liberation movement."[2] The diaspora delegation (which included several Canadian citizens) was similarly sceptical, insisting that "the SPLM is too deformed to be reformed … it is the source of the current crisis. Therefore, it should be dissolved, and a new party should be created which will represent the values of the people of South Sudan."

Following the departure of the politicos from Pagak, the 10 generals stayed on to discuss strategy and coordination. John thought that the fabled White Army was developing into a more reliable resource for the rebels. Among its leaders now were persons with university degrees, along with diaspora members and even some women. He dismissed the idea that the White Army could be directed to do nothing but loot and rape; its leaders had a clear understanding of the strategic importance of keeping the Upper Nile oil fields open. They were also ditching their former tactics of stripping nearly naked and indulging in suicidal charges against heavily defended targets, recognizing that these tactics were not sustainable in a longer conflict.

What emerged from Pagak was that the rebellion was far from crushed. First, morale was high; Nuer generals laughed at the idea that they could be bested by Dinkas. Second, Machar was secure in his role as leader because the 10 saw no contradiction in his arguing for power-sharing while they pursued their agenda of revenge/justice. Third, the parallel rounds of consultations in Juba and Pagak had brought nothing new to the table. At the IGAD talks in Addis, the sticking points were still the powers of the prime minister and the more intractable matter of the security arrangements both sides would demand if a transitional government was formed. Finally, Arusha was still alive, but expectations should be modest.

In sum, all the indicators pointed to more fighting.

Over at the Ministry of Finance in Juba, there was gloom for other reasons. The country's oil production (which accounted for 97 per cent of the government's revenue) was now at 160,000 barrels per day, 50 per cent lower than pre-crisis levels. This was largely on account of surface infrastructure in Unity State having been destroyed and Unity's fields going off-line. International oil prices, moreover, were now at the fifty-five- to sixty-dollar level, the lowest in years, and likely to fall below fifty.

Sudan's take from South Sudan's oil was a fixed twenty-four dollars per barrel; this price reflected not only transit and processing fees, but – by mutual agreement – the paying off of a $3 billion liability in recognition of the fact that the South took the lion's share of the oil fields; indeed, it was envisaged that South Sudan would be a richer state than Sudan at the time of independence. Back then, when oil was priced at over one hundred dollars per barrel, it had seemed a good idea to agree to a flat rate in order to pay off the liability as soon as possible. If you also deducted from Juba's revenue payments due on loans taken out by the government over the previous year against future oil sales (precise figures unknown), you would be left with a very modest level of governmental revenue indeed.

Meanwhile, non-oil revenue throughout 2014 was down 22 per cent because of poor tax compliance in revenue collection and harmonization. By January 2015, there was a monthly shortfall of about 285 million SSP (US$95 million) on the 650 million SSP required for basic government functioning. The government was evidently making up the shortfall by borrowing that amount from the Central Bank – i.e., printing money. This was obvious on the street since new notes were in circulation for the first time in three years.

Also bearing scrutiny was the unofficial exchange rate of the South Sudan pound against the US dollar. It was now at 5.5 to 6.0 SSP per USD, which was almost double the official rate (3), and well above the 4 to 4.5 rate prevalent in mid-2014. Foreign-exchange reserves, so the IMF told us, were at US$379 million, or two to three weeks' worth of imports, down from five months' worth at independence in 2011. The IMF recommended that a country as fragile as South Sudan needed six to eight months' of cover. The prospects for external financing were very limited, given heavy drawdowns of the past few months and the uncertain political and security outlook.

There was widespread agreement among pundits that the government needed to stop holding the official exchange rate at 3 SSP, and either let the pound float or set a new price at or above the unofficial rate. The IMF reported diplomatically that "the rationing of foreign exchange allocations (at 3 SSP per dollar) entails a hidden transfer of resources from the government to those with privileged access to foreign exchange at the official rate,"[3] and added that this cost South Sudan a staggering 9.5 per cent of GDP annually. David Deng, the minister of finance who had replaced Aggrey Tissa, acknowledged the problem but told us that "political stability issues" made exchange-rate harmonization difficult. The implication was that the three or four hundred well-connected individuals who were making a killing from their specially licensed access to dollars – many of whom were related to the governor of the Central Bank – would not permit harmonization to happen.

It was widely speculated that the foreign-exchange reserves had been drawn down largely to finance defence spending, in replenishment of funds expended in combat over the past year, and in preparation for a new offensive. In support of this theory, four helicopter gunships flown by foreign mercenaries and amphibious tracked vehicles purchased from China became increasingly visible over the next few months.

In sum, and as the IMF put it to embassies, the government now faced the following choices:

- Stop paying salaries on account of dwindling revenue or continue printing money, thereby increasing inflation;
- Overcome vested interests to increase non-oil revenue or continue to see government revenues decline;
- Unify the exchange rate and boost GDP by 9.5 per cent or favour political stability by placating well-connected rent-seekers;
- Enact further austerity measures that will hurt ordinary South Sudanese by reducing basic service delivery or permit inflation – which will also hurt ordinary people;
- Cease defence spending, which will undermine the government's military advantage over the rebels.

Counterintuitively, negotiating an immediate peace deal would not necessarily help. Given such an agreement, a new transitional government would be under enormous pressure to deliver on a number of fronts, most notably the reintegration (yet again) of rebel militias into the regular SPLA and, simultaneously, demobilization. That alone would be an extremely expensive exercise. Disarmament/demobilization/rehabilitation (DDR) was a matter on which donors had been reluctant to engage even in better times, so costly was it and so liable to manipulation.

Although peace would allow the Unity oil fields to be restored and production in Upper Nile to be increased, this might take a year at least and, unless coupled with enactment of the much-delayed Petroleum Revenue Management Act, it was unclear how well revenues would be used. Peace could unlock a renewed disposition by creditors to make further loans, but it would have to be a pretty convincing deal.

The deteriorating economy would become increasingly worrying as the year went on and the government failed to make any hard choices. This had a direct effect on all of us in Juba, as living costs for ordinary people became unbearable and crime levels shot up exponentially. By mid-2015, we would still be observing curfews, not because we feared a repeat of December 2013 but because of the risk of extortion or worse by common criminals, frequently in collusion with unpaid security-sector workers.

The International Committee of the Red Cross (ICRC) had, for many years, been a regular recipient of Canadian funding for its humanitarian and related operations. Its reputation in South Sudan was as stellar and unsullied as everywhere else, although the cynics carped that it was the most expensive (for funders) of all operators. Early in 2015, I was excited when the ICRC invited me and Krista, an Ottawa-based colleague, to join them on a day trip to Kodok, formerly known as Fashoda, far to the north in Upper Nile. I'd last seen the place in 2003 from the deck of a barge as we drifted slowly past.

Fashoda had played a key role in the development of Africa. Here, in 1898, two of the greatest empires of the day – France and Britain – came within a hair's breadth of initiating a war. A tiny French detachment mandated with establishing east-west control across Africa under the command of one Lieutenant Marchand had planted the tricolour here. Meanwhile, from the north, Sir Herbert Kitchener came steaming upstream with four ultra-modern gunboats and thousands of marines, fresh from his victory over the Mahdists at the Battle of Omdurman. His objective: to consolidate British control over the Sudan and paint the entire Cape-to-Cairo route the pink of the British Empire. Marchand invited Kitchener to tea in his tent on the bank. They made small talk and the Frenchman wisely withdrew.

The Fashoda Incident, as it came to be known, turned out to be the high-water mark of the British Empire.[4] This was where the term "gunboat diplomacy" was born. It was also the moment at which France realized that Germany was the greater threat to its existence and that it was more expedient to accommodate than antagonize the British.

We boarded an ICRC Twin Otter just after dawn at Juba International. Cynthia, the ICRC's Canadian-born donor-relations officer who accompanied us, was very solicitous but also made clear that there were very strict rules to be followed, in particular, no photography, lest we endanger the organization's perceived impartiality. Just over two hours later we were descending over the Nile to a dirt strip close to – and aligned with – its west bank.

There was not much in the low, spread-out, and sweltering town to recall Fashoda's place in history. But high on the exterior wall of the county commissioner's office was a green/grey bronze plaque that simply read: "Marchand; 1898." With Malakal hospital in ruins as the city was sacked first by one side then the other, the ICRC had upgraded Kodok's clinic to a full-service hospital for the entire Upper Nile state. Verandahs on the principal buildings had been walled in to provide extra space, tents erected to serve as a *kalazzar* (river blindness) ward. All major medical services were now provided, including Caesarian sections and surgery, the latter at the hands of an expatriate ICRC doctor. On the day Krista and I visited, there were a dozen young men being treated for gunshot wounds.

"They were brought here by the SPLA after heavy fighting near New Fangak [Unity State], maybe six hours upriver," said the attending surgeon, Dr Apollo.

"All the wounds seem to be in the legs or feet," I commented.

"Yes," he replied. "About sixty to seventy per cent of the war wounds we treat are in the lower legs. We think it's not because the enemy are aiming like that; it's because the people who are wounded in the stomach, upper body, or head are either left to die or succumb on their way here."

The wards were immaculately clean, entry procedures well-established; the pharmacy was well-stocked. Some drugs still arrived from the Ministry of Health but the ICRC had had to supplement these meagre stocks several times over. A core of the more junior staff was employed by the ministry; the ICRC topped up their salary not so much to create incentive but so as to ensure regularity in payment. The hospital was busy, with more than half of the beds filled.

Kodok also served as a hub for ICRC operations throughout the southern part of Upper Nile. Much effort and time was expended in preaching international humanitarian law (IHL) to military commanders on all sides. The older generation, Cynthia told us, was particularly receptive to the ICRC because they remembered their work during the long civil war; many present-day commanders were at one time or another treated at the ICRC's hospital at Lopiding, near the major UN/OLS logistics base at Lokichokkio.

Staff members reported that receptivity was good, but they agreed that the current conflict had taken international humanitarian law abuses to new heights (depths?). The cyclical nature of the conflict (advance/retreat/advance again) meant that after each wave of attacks, greater apparently gratuitous violence was inflicted in revenge. Women bore the brunt of this: they were raped to punish "their" men and the more extreme the victims' ages (very old or very young), the more humiliating the punishment was perceived to be.

In May 2015, following the defection of SPLA general Johnson Olony to the IO, Kodok and the ICRC hospital were overrun by the rebels. All programs were shut down as the ICRC evacuated its staff.

Next day was another road trip with the same organization. As part of a wide-ranging negotiation with other humanitarian agencies, the ICRC in May 2013 took the unusual step of dropping relief supplies by air in South Sudan, the first time it had performed this kind of operation since Afghanistan in 1997. This decision was motivated by the organization's recognition that there were significant pockets of internally displaced persons that the UN's World Food Program could not assess and reach. Franz, the ICRC's delegate (i.e. chef de mission), told me quite simply, "It is an emergency of the first order; we have to do our bit." On account of its exceptional cross-lines access and credibility, the ICRC tended to specialize in dropping behind rebel lines.

Today's target was Nhialdu, Unity State, in the hands of – yes, him again – Peter Gadet. For security considerations, we had to witness the operation from the air, not the ground. So, for the second morning running, we were on the tarmac as the sun came up, among a crowd of much larger aircraft this time. Over the long grass adjoining the battered runway a light haze hung, and a flight of white cattle egrets flapped slowly away. As we waited, the Belarusian captain joined us. He wore baggy flannel track pants and a tee-shirt that could have done with a wash. We followed him round as he kicked the balding tires of his huge, oil-streaked four-engine Ilysushin 76. He shrugged and, through one of the crew who spoke a few words of English, said, "They're good for one more flight. Maybe."

You could see where they had cleaned around the giant Red Cross logos, inscribed "ICRC-Genève." Given that Gadet had shot down a white UNMISS helicopter a few months earlier near Nhialdu, it seemed a good idea to ensure that the insignia could be seen. A hundred metres away, an identical model Ilyushin with no markings was loading four armoured personnel carriers, no doubt also headed north as the government dug in and prepared its dry-season offensive. One of the drivers was gleefully performing whatever the equivalent of "wheelies" for tracked vehicles are called: sharp turns on the runway effected by halting one track and going full speed on the other. He was doing a nice job of chewing up the already rough tarmac. I was tempted to take a picture but Cynthia frowned at me intently, and I stopped.

On a run like this – 400 nautical miles each way – the Ilyushin carried thirty-five metric tonnes of grain, compared to the fifteen to seventeen that a Hercules C-130 could carry. But at this time of the year, with temperatures reaching forty-five degrees in the afternoons and greatly reducing lift, the aircraft could make only one run a day. We climbed aboard through the rear ramp. The sacks had been loaded on wooden pallets in two rows; although for most of the flight the sacks were chained down, the deck consisted of rollers so the pallets could be pushed around by hand.

We sat in the low-slung glass bubble under the nose for take-off. Krista, whose husband was an aircraft buff and who had passed on some of his enthusiasm to her, told me that these bubbles had inspired George Lucas when he was designing star-fighters (or whatever they are called) for the Star Wars movies. We taxied out and the roar of the jet engines grew. As the rubber-streaked pavement rushed below us at an accelerating speed, the noise became deafening; this aircraft would never have received permission to land at Heathrow.

The Belarusian crew spoke very little English. Once we were up, one of them gestured at us to climb the ladder up to the flight deck. These were seventies-era Soviet-built aircraft, and the pilots' station looked an awful lot less sophisticated than modern Boeings and Airbuses. The pilot and co-pilot communicated with the navigator in the bubble via a rotary dial telephone that rang with a tinny "brringg, brringg." The "digital" displays were rudimentary, glowing orange against a black background. A lot of items appeared to be held together with Scotch tape and coat-hanger wire. Everybody was friendly, and they kept offering Krista, Cynthia, and me industrial-strength coffee that looked to have been dredged from the bottom of the oil sump. Cynthia had warned us, so we went easy on the coffee and we did not inquire as to the toilet facilities.

As we neared Nhialdu, we dipped down and saw our speed slow from 320 to about 200 knots. Down the ladder again, this time into the cargo hold. Here, where there were no portholes, we sensed small shifts as the captain lined the plane up with the large white crosses that had been laid out on a one-kilometre stretch of dry land in the middle of a vast swamp. We made one dry pass at 150 metres. A button was pressed on a GPS up in the cockpit as we crossed the edge of the drop zone. We banked away for the first of three "wet" runs.

Each time the routine was the same. The loadmaster at the forward end of the cargo hold had one hand on a lever, the other on his earphones; he had to stand on his chair to peer backwards over the cargo, towards the rear door, where his buddy acknowledged the countdown coming over the earphones. The loadmaster gestured us to the back with a smile and a thumbs-up. We edged carefully past the loaded pallets. The rear crewman gestured to struts in the side, tightening his fist in a motion that obviously meant "hold on hard." Even if he had been able to speak English we would have heard nothing, so loud was the noise of the engines and of air rushing through the cracks around the rear door.

One minute out – we could tell by the emphatic arm-signals – the huge rear door eased open. A gale of hot wind blew in. Thumbs up from the door man, after a check to see that the pallets were free to run. Then there was a sudden lurch that had my knees bending involuntarily. The engines changed tone and we were climbing hard. Ten tonnes of grain, each sack wrapped six times over, slid ever so easily out of the back; now I could see the browny-green of the swamp rushing below us in a blur. It was a good job that we'd been told to hold on hard. After a few seconds, we levelled off and immediately banked hard to one side; there was another queasy moment, and we went around for the next run.

The operation was spectacular, and quite moving. I'd seen it all before, of course. It was over Nhialdu, likely the very same drop zone, that I'd had my very first sight of rebel-held Southern Sudan back in 2001. Those kids on the ground today, looking up at us, were probably the children of those I'd seen from the World Food Program

Hercules. The only difference now was that they were running from the SPLA, not from the Sudan Armed Forces.

The pilot made a final pass to assess his accuracy and we turned for home.

Later, I'd experience a food drop from the ground. We flew for the day to the tiny remote settlement of Thaker, Unity State, twenty kilometres to the northwest of Leer. This area was also under the influence, thought not absolute control, of the 10; there was little or no organized conflict in this part of Unity and there were no armed men in sight among the 10,000 or so civilians assembled to receive the first relief delivered in fourteen months.

Two Ilyushin 76s, carrying thirty-two metric tonnes apiece, were designated for the first wave of drops by the World Food Program, one flying out of Juba and one out of Gambella, Ethiopia. There was an aircraft parking problem at Juba International Airport, so WFP needed to use alternative locations for loading. As things turned out, bad weather elsewhere in South Sudan meant that an additional two planes were diverted over Thaker, so I witnessed a complicated aerial ballet of four aircraft each making five runs: one dry run plus four drops each, at eight tonnes a time.

One tonne fed sixty persons for one month.

The Russian and Ukrainian pilots, along with WFP's ground staff, had delivery down to a fine art. The jets came in at 200 knots, releasing their loads over a marked zone as they climbed at forty-five degrees, sans parachute. The white bags fell with a sound of artillery, clearly audible over the roar of the plane. Only one bag burst this time; the receiving population would sweep up every last grain. As this dramatic exercise was proceeding over half an hour, not a single child rushed to the drop zone to watch. In fact, few people even looked up at the big white planes circling low over their heads. This was partly on account of the fierce discipline imposed by chiefs, but above all because everyone already knew the drill all too well. Many of the adults present would have lived through the second half of the civil war, when OLS was despatching those Hercules C-130s from Lokichokkio every day.

Prior to and after the drops I met with the chiefs, women, WFP, UNICEF, and local staff of Samaritan's Purse, the NGO that would oversee the food distribution. Although Thaker was part of Mayendit County and therefore under the influence of the 10, SPLA-aligned groups had recently made off with hundreds of thousands of cows and taken them to government-controlled areas far to the north. It would be difficult to overstate the demoralizing effect these raids had had on the population. Young boys, the women reminded me, were raised on a diet of blood and cow's milk; both were now unavailable, so many locals were calling for WFP to prioritize cooking oil, as a mixture of oil and sorghum was considered an acceptable replacement. Last year, WFP had pioneered a technique of dropping cooking oil with mini-parachutes; the experts in question were due back soon.

At the height of fighting in mid-2015, people fled to a large island called Lang about seven hours away in the swamps. They returned to the area around Thaker in November; their numbers were bolstered by 3,000 IDPs coming in from government-influenced areas in Koch County to the northwest. Among the twenty-five or so women's leaders with whom I spoke, more than half were now heads of family. Their men were either dead or had disappeared. Many children had been killed, and when thanking the donors and WFP for the food to come, the women stressed that it would "allow us to become fat so we can have more babies, because we have lost so many." These were tough women; nearly all had walked a full day at least to get here, and they would trek home with fifty-kilogram sacks on their heads. There was the usual deprecatory laughter and gestures when I asked if the men would help them.

As always, the theoretical authorities – the chiefs with their red sashes, the county commissioner, 10 humanitarian commissioner John – were not necessarily the real ones. And even the young men with guns might not be where the action was. Amateurs (such as myself) should wade into South Sudan's anthropology at their own peril, but I had been interested to read Sharon Hutchinson, the leading modern student of the Nuer, and author of the authoritative *Nuer Dilemmas: Coping with Money, War, and the State*:

Contemporary South Sudanese Nuer prophets play powerful roles in interpreting the moral limits of lethal violence and weighing the legitimacy claims of rival government leaders. Their activities remain largely invisible to external observers investigating the making and unmaking of fragile states.[5]

Twenty-five kilometres southwest from Thaker was Thor, the home of Nyachol, at that time the second-most influential western-Nuer prophet, and the third historic prophet of the divinity Maani, indirectly of the Sky God. She shunned all manifestations of modernity, including telephones, cameras, watches, and modern clothes; she dressed in a grass skirt and leopard skin (if at all). On account of her abhorrence of modern clothes, very few Westerners – two, actually, one of whom was my good friend Diane de Guzman – had summoned up the nerve to meet with her. There was no question that she had played a key role in recent Nuer offensives in Unity. Hutchinson again:

> Nyachol provides local youth with added spiritual protections when they seek to guard cattle or acquire cattle from their Dinka counterparts. Nyachol ceremonially blesses offensive Nuer raids in advance by providing mustered youth with ashes taken from the central cattle-dung fire *(gol)* of *Maani*'s sacred byre. Nyachol's blessings allegedly protect her followers from bullets during cross-border cattle raids.

Of late, Nyachol had been playing a role in conciliation, possibly with the direct encouragement of Riek Machar (who himself, but more doubtfully, claimed certain religious powers). Rehan, a young staff member of WFP, had taken it upon himself to investigate further how and if Nyachol could be further engaged; Hutchinson had suggested as much, and I found myself wishing him good luck.

What a strange place South Sudan was, I thought. Huge white jets showered free food from the sky. But what grabbed the attention of the people of Thaker was a prophetess who lived naked in a straw hut, who communed with the Sky God and conferred immunity to Dinka bullets.

———————

As 2015 dragged on, there were military defections first one way, then the other. The most spectacular was that of Shillook general Johnson Olony from the government to the IO, along with three barge-loads of heavy weapons. A relatively minor defector from the IO was General Lul Ruai Koang, a young, articulate Nuer from Akobo, on the Ethiopian border. He came to see me at the embassy in

March 2015, in a smart dark suit, red tie, and crisp white shirt on whose breast pocket was embroidered in bright blue – just in case you had any doubt – "General Lul."

For most of the past fourteen months he had been the military spokesperson of the IO. His personal credibility had several times been cast into doubt, most notably when Radio Tamazuj accused him of never having been near a front line, but also when he claimed that a number of attacks on trucks on the strategic Juba / Nimule highway were the work of rebel militias only to have Machar's spokesperson refute him.

I started with the obvious question. "Why have you come back?"

Lul had evidently prepared his answer. Very quickly he replied, "My partner is here."

"What do you mean, exactly?"

"Well, my aim is a homeland for my people, the Lou Nuer. I think I have a much better chance of achieving this by working with the government in Juba than with Dr Riek."

Lul's vision was that the adjoining counties of Akobo, Uror, and Nyirol should be carved out of present-day Jonglei, given their own special status, and be made answerable directly to Juba rather than the state capital of Bor. His model was the Greater Pibor Administrative Area (GPAA), wrestled away from Jonglei after the three-year bloody insurgency of David Yau Yau and his Murle followers.

"Dr Riek," Lul went on, "does not share this idea. He wants twenty-one states, and he wants power in Juba. He's not interested in the welfare of the Lou Nuer people."

But what drove Lul into rebellion in the first place? "Pure anger … a desire for revenge," he admitted. From everything I knew, this drove most Lou Nuer still. Fifteen months on, Lul continued to believe that there must be full accountability for what happened in Juba in December 2013, and that Riek had failed to capitalize on the anger of the Nuer. He had shown little proactive leadership: "He left the bush nine months ago … there's no strategy, no guidance. We don't even talk by Thuraya. He's not been able to get more than a few weapons from Khartoum, and those only go into Unity, not Jonglei. We – the Lou Nuer – we can mobilize 40,000 men, but we have had no replenishment of matériel since June 2014."

This position of military weakness, said Lul, would force Riek Machar to cut a deal once he believed that no further concessions could be wrung from President Salva Kiir. Riek would be forced to accept that he would not be able to maintain a separate military, in parallel to the SPLA, for more than three or four months following a peace deal.

The young general tied himself into knots when assessing chief of the general staff Paul Malong, now thought to be impatient with the IGAD talks and ready to launch an offensive. "Malong, above all, does not wish to see rebellion rewarded," he declared. But reward was exactly what Lul's new comrade, the Honourable Yau Yau, had reaped from his rebellion. And historically, the SPLA had done little else than reward mutiny, most notably Riek Machar's first years-long revolt. It seemed to me that the only chance Lul had of a political (or even military) future in Juba would be if the government believed he could control the Nuer White Army and turn them against whichever enemy they wished. This did not seem to me a respectable way to launch a political career, which was Lul's avowed ambition.

Lul said there would be more defections, and added that he had been discussing his move with President Kiir as early as the previous November. What about Riek Machar's ace in the hole, (Bul Nuer) General Peter Gadet? Would he come in too? Lul would not be drawn, stating only the obvious, "Nobody trusts Gadet one inch."

In fact, a few months later Gadet would defect into a kind of limbo, in which he would spend months negotiating and machinating. And in March 2016, Lul would give up his political ambitions and accept the same job with the SPLA as he had held with the IO: official military spokesperson.

Maybe You Should Leave Now

Juba, Malakal, and Leer, March to May 2015

Soon after the crisis broke in December 2013, the African Union had committed to an inquiry into allegations of massive human rights abuses committed in Juba and other cities. An investigative team spent several weeks travelling the country and interviewing people. The creation of the commission of inquiry, or "CoI" as it came to be known, allowed the government to deflect a very stinging UN report on the same issues in May 2014. But the release of the AU version had been delayed ... and delayed. Top AU brass hemmed and hawed and said it would come out when the time was right; doubts grew as to whether the CoI would ever be published or the AU leadership was interested in seeing the principle of accountability triumph. The AU, after all, had elected Robert Mugabe as its chairman in January 2015.

Then, on 5 March 2015, as the two parties to the conflict were supposed to be wrapping up peace talks in Addis Ababa, a sixty-page document purporting to be the CoI report started circulating on the internet.[1] There were denials and prevarications all round. It emerged – after the simple expedient of switching on the track-changes option in Word – that this was only a dissenting chapter of the report by Professor Mahmood Mamdani, one of the five official commissioners.

There was shock at how frankly the leaked chapter apportioned blame to President Salva Kiir and his government for the initial wave of atrocities in Juba, and surprise at the political nature of the report's sweeping recommendations, which were far beyond what any foreign government had voiced publicly. The report explained many things we did not understand at the time, the major points being that there had been a catastrophic series of miscalculations on all sides throughout 2013, that personal ambition, ego, and ethnic loyalty repeatedly overrode national interest, and that there was no organized coup attempt. Key figures – notably the then chief of the general staff – were quoted apportioning most of the blame to the president for tacitly encouraging the worst atrocities and blocking attempts to investigate them. His hand was seen in the recruitment of the Bahr-al-Ghazal irregulars most likely responsible for most of the Juba killings, and current chief of the general staff Malong was deeply implicated as well.

Most of the blame for atrocities on the other side was laid on the White Army. A number of those quoted suggested that this Nuer militia was responsible to no one, and Mamdani concluded, "The SPLA/IO cannot be held responsible for the conduct of the White Army" (thus letting Riek Machar off the hook for the IO's worst abuses).

Before the thirty-page mark was reached, the report moved into historical analysis of the Comprehensive Peace Agreement of 2005. The critical role played by the "troika" (US, UK, Norway) in supporting IGAD and in pressing the parties to sign a deal was acknowledged, but a remark by one-time foreign minister but now opposition pundit Dr Lam Akol was highlighted: "The CPA gave the SPLM the power it could not have got by political means … The state became the SPLM, and the SPLM became the state." Taking this cue, Mamdani went on, "this was a make-believe state whose leadership was propped up and feted by important sections of the international community, key being the troika."

Recommendations were framed within the perceived need for "an Africa-oriented solution"; in Paragraph 173, a future role for the troika was explicitly ruled out because of its past errors. Strikingly, the entire cabinet of early July 2013 was held accountable, and Mamdani recommended that its members – including Riek Machar and Salva Kiir – be excluded both from transitional arrangements and from any future political office. This stipulation would also exclude the so-called G-10 or "Former Detainees."

As a human-rights report, the document had serious shortcomings and did not offer many avenues for follow-up by judicial authorities. It did not compare in quality with UN reporting on the same theme. But the principal conclusions were clear and seemed, to many analysts, to be valid: Salva Kiir had a large hand in what went on in Juba in December 2013; there was ethnic cleansing. The AU in Addis remained frustratingly silent, neither owning nor disowning Mamdani.

The next day in Addis, probably by coincidence, peace talks ground to a halt again. President Kiir had walked out, and no renewal date was announced.

For a number of weeks it had been an open secret that, were Salva Kiir to sign a power-sharing deal with Riek Machar as proposed by IGAD, his own military would bitterly oppose it. In February 2015, the SPLA had publicly spelled out its red lines, and when the president reluctantly went to Addis in early March for the final round of talks, Paul Malong brazenly convoked a middle-of-the-night meeting with his generals at his Bilpam GHQ to "discuss options." Kiir got the message, signed nothing, and obediently came home.

Instead of a peace deal, it was evident Malong wanted to have his way on the military front and finish off the rebels, preferably before the rains started in late April. He told Stefano, my EU colleague, "My men are ready; I can't hold them," and military spokesperson Philip Aguer said on SSTV, "the SPLA has observed that Riek Machar and his commanders are not listening to the regional bodies in the search for peace. Because of these violations, the SPLA forces will not be in their trenches and wait for the rebels to attack every time; the general command has now instructed the SPLA forces to have mobile forces. They will not have to wait for the rebels to attack them again in their positions."

As we sat waiting for a new uptick in fighting, the pundits in Juba pondered what had gone wrong with the peace talks. First among the most obvious causes of the breakdown was a set of disagreements over transitional security arrangements. The government wished ceasefires to apply to restricted "theatres of conflict" but the IO insisted on the ceasefire being decreed nationally, legitimizing the IO's claim to have a nationwide presence. On security-sector reform, the government wished to hold a review prior to the formation of a transitional government of national unity (TGNU) while the IO pressed for a committee to be formed by the TGNU. Most critically, the IO wished to keep the two armies separate for thirty months after signing an agreement whereas the government insisted on them becoming integrated immediately. On the other hand, the government would accept into this army only those who had deserted from its own ranks, not rebels from "outside."

The next set of disagreements was over governance. The bottom line here was that the government wished to maintain a president (i.e. Salva Kiir) with full executive power; the IO compromised to an extent, saying they could live with the president holding office as long as a first vice president or a prime minister (Riek Machar ...) had "almost equal" powers.

There were also more latent causes for the breakdown in negotiations. First among these was the matter of the succession to the presidency. As it became evident to most observers that the IGAD-mediated process had descended into a naked power struggle between two politicians, many began to think that a better way to address this issue would be to define how presidential succession should be handled within the SPLM (i.e. take away the names and ethnicities from the deadlock). But this had not been done.

It was also clear, in hindsight, that IGAD had allowed the mediation to become too exclusive. Although in the early days there had been some participation by opposition political parties, by women's groups, and so on, IGAD had allowed these groups to be excluded by the two parties with guns, both of whom came from the SPLM family. Finally, the international response to the crisis had been incoherent, within IGAD and more broadly. Within IGAD, the conflicting interests of some of its key members (Uganda and Sudan, for example) were well known, but others, such as Kenya, had not exercised the positive leverage they might have. Within the broader African Union membership, South Africa and Tanzania had engaged in the Arusha process mainly in solidarity with the beleaguered SPLM and not necessarily to support IGAD. China was not coordinated with anyone. Even the troika and the EU, which shared a common member, had not been as unified as one might have hoped.

The principal of subsidiarity by which the AU assigned regional issues to whichever of its eight "building blocks" was the obvious one – IGAD, SADC, ECOWAS – meant that IGAD must remain front and centre, at least nominally and to save face. But consensus seemed to be emerging that there needed to be an IGAD-Plus. This could be IGAD coupled with the AU High Implementation Panel with some other senior AU support mechanism, plus perhaps the troika.

***

Following the collapse of the latest round of talks in mid-March 2015, the president made a rare public appearance to explain himself. A rally was to take place at the usual venue: the John Garang Mausoleum. It was twice postponed, eventually to Wednesday, 18 March, for two reasons: first because it was feared the crowds would not be large and secondly because advisers counselled the president to rewrite his remarks and ease off on the anti-Western rhetoric.

I dithered for a while whether or not to attend; there was a risk that the president would deliver a rant. In the end, I went, and my only Western company was David, the German ambassador. The crowd was moderate in every sense, maybe 10,000 people, and on the quiet side. The Red Army band provided music. Allegations that the organizers would pad crowd numbers by bringing schoolchildren en masse proved unfounded; there was only an incongruous parade by forty boys and girls from the John Garang International School. Unusually, President Kiir came the last 400 metres on foot, with very heavy security. The temperature was enervating, even by Juba standards: forty degrees plus until the sun moved higher and gave us some blessed shade.

The warm-up acts were more rabble-rousing than the president's speech. Perhaps significantly, none of Juba's ecclesiastical dignitaries spoke, but an obscure cleric whom nobody seemed to know stepped up with a prayer that began by describing South Sudan as "wounded, broken," veered into the Annunciation to the Virgin Mary, and concluded with an out-of-place warning to the US, Europe, and China to "stop threatening us." Clement Wani Konga, governor of Central Equatoria, followed with a humdrum speech that ended with a less-than-catchy call: "Long live SPLM leadership consistency!" Then there was a South Sudan moment when Joseph Okello, who had oddly been invited to speak on behalf of the opposition, failed to show; without missing a beat, hardline Cabinet Affairs Minister Martin Elia Lomuro, nominally the head of a small party called the SSDF but the de facto prime minister, took up the baton, also claiming to be speaking "on behalf of the opposition."

He said to the president, "We hoped you would return on 5 March with peace," then went on to blame Riek Machar's intransigence for the president's failure. Lomuro also took swipes at IGAD. "They invited to the talks only those who oppose the government ... Who died among the IGAD countries for South Sudan? Let them not forget that three million of us died." There was another final shot at Riek: "Rebellion must not be rewarded ... there is no way we can accept Riek Machar as vice-president ... all he wants is our president's seat."

The president ad-libbed much of his one-hour speech, departing frequently from his English-language text into diversions and explanations in Arabic. He had never been a good public speaker, and people who took digs at him for wiping his brow from time to time didn't appreciate how hard it is to give a long presentation under the equatorial sun. He devoted three-quarters of his time to explaining and justifying why no agreement was reached in Addis, the final fifteen minutes to "the way forward."

The president's long review of every point of discord dispelled any idea that the parties might have been close to a deal pre-Addis. He made no bones about the fact that he had conceded almost nothing; en passant he admitted that, had he signed, he would have faced difficulties upon his return to Juba: "Some people said I would be forced to sign a bad agreement ... but I knew that would only lead to trouble for me." Salva's criticisms of Riek were not so much vitriolic as tired and impatient. The latter's history of rebellion was reviewed, and it was stated (not without reason) that "he just wants my job ... he might take number two, but that's just so he'll be positioned if something happens to me" (cue nervous laughter).

Discussing the future, he dropped the topic of Addis and his rival, seeming to suggest that, absent any prospect of progress, "*il faut cultiver son jardin*." The rains were nearly here, he said, and farmers needed to till the land; the Ministry of Finance should increase non-oil revenues and university lecturers call off their strike for the good of the nation. The anti-Western rhetoric that I had feared did not materialize, except indirectly in an off-the-cuff remark: "the only sanction that can work in South Sudan is if they speak to God and get him to halt the rainy season." The speech was not a game-changer. Much of what the president said about Addis was reasonable but disorganized and uninspiring. He seemed to lose his way more than once, made no concessions at all, and gave no hint of where – if at all – he might make any in the future.

A few days later, on 24 March, my sense that prospects for peace had receded and that the government was hardening its line was reinforced. In an emergency session, the National Legislative Assembly and the superior Council of States approved a bill that extended both the chambers' terms and that of President Kiir by three years. The bill passed with a large majority of 264 to 6. The mandate of the constitutional review commission was also extended, to December 2018. This development had been widely expected, although the extension was anticipated to be only for two years. Western countries, and many moderate South Sudanese, including some in opposition, had months earlier agreed that holding elections in July 2015 would be unwise. The conflict in at least one third of the country would have disenfranchised a large segment of the population. Even in more stable parts of South Sudan, tensions were so high that violence was likely. And in practical terms, we had six months earlier gone past the date that would have allowed for effective preparations at the height of the rainy season.

So, a legal formula needed to be found that would extend the life of both parliament and the president. This needed to occur before the end of March 2015, ninety days ahead of elections, when the current assembly would have been dissolved. An act of parliament was judged to be the most appropriate such formula. The critics cried that a tame legislature was rubber-stamping a power grab by the president. It certainly looked that way from outside. But both Salva Kiir and this assembly were elected in a process that, while far from perfect, was judged to have reflected the will of the people. However discredited the SPLM might be, this was the movement that brought independence to South Sudan. It still enjoyed a very considerable legacy effect, as did Salva Kiir.

Back at the office, I was finding that life in Juba was not for everyone. The evacuation of staff in early 2014 was followed by a decision in Ottawa to designate the Canadian mission as "unaccompanied"; neither spouses nor children would be permitted. This was to minimize the risk of anything happening to staff and their families in the event of another security crisis, and also to lessen the load in case a second evacuation became necessary.

As I had no interest in remaining in Juba indefinitely while Jenny languished outside the country, I declined to continue. Consternation at HQ. It would be very difficult to find a replacement at such short notice. So, an exception was made: Jenny would be allowed to stay as long as she worked at the mission and remained within the embassy's protective envelope. Bureaucracies being what they are, another department at HQ later got wind of this and said the contrary. There was no way she would be allowed to work at the embassy because of conflict of interest. By that time, of course, it was too late to reverse my decision … Jenny rather tiredly accepted the decree and started looking for work outside the embassy.

But the "unaccompanied" designation, which was not complemented by any compensatory measure to make the posting more attractive, greatly narrowed the field from which we could recruit staff. We soon began to pay the price in the form of unsuitable candidates applying and – *faute de mieux* – being accepted. Two arrived then left prematurely, and I concluded it would be better to leave positions unstaffed than appoint iffy people. This policy was naïve, since there were extremely few applicants who were even faintly qualified.

I'd thought that we might be able to take advantage of the large pool of Canadian diplomats who had passed through Afghanistan and might see Juba as equally challenging and professionally interesting but a few degrees safer. Not so. A friend at HQ commented, "The thing is, all those people who went to Afghanistan … It's 'been there done that.' They're now a few years older, they've moved up the ladder, they've got steady personal relationships, they don't want to do it again." It was also a fact that persons posted to Afghanistan enjoyed a special package that included not only the hardship allowances that accrued to the more difficult postings in the Canadian Foreign Service (at last count there were thirty-five or so Level 5s, the top rating) but also rest and recreation allowances: extra leave, air tickets, and so on. There was no such package in Juba; even the "accidental death and dismemberment" insurance to which we were entitled was, at this time, considered a taxable benefit.

The bald (but honest) explanation in Ottawa was that "there is no high-level interest in South Sudan like there was in Afghanistan, however difficult Juba may be." Our diplomatic friends in Juba were sympathetic. The entire UN system and nearly all the embassies were on rotations of six weeks in, two weeks out, with air tickets to Europe paid for each rotation, plus the usual generous European annual leave allowance of about six weeks.

Would a more attractive package have attracted more and better applicants? I thought so, but I wasn't sure. It seemed that the younger generation in the Canadian foreign service were not motivated by what had attracted me: the prospect of travel to exotic places, a whiff of danger and excitement, being a big fish in a small pond. They preferred the classic "cushy" posts – London, Rome, Washington – if they wanted to go abroad at all. A surprising number, mid-career, were perfectly content to remain in Ottawa. It was interesting, perhaps counterintuitive, that the two "stayers" in the short history of the post-independence Canadian mission in Juba were my excellent head of cooperation Jamie, a veteran, and myself, nearing sixty. This wasn't a place for youngsters, apparently. So we were perpetually understaffed, with Jamie and me always on the lookout to poach good people from elsewhere, always wondering what we could do to sell Juba without actually being misleading.

———————

All this time, my rounds of meetings went on, UN-hosted humanitarian country team meetings appearing most often on my agenda. As the only ambassador attending these meetings (this was a function not only of my interest but of our short-staffing), I had become the go-to expert on humanitarian affairs among the ambassadorial community. Similarly, I was the only head of mission to attend working-level diplomatic meetings on human rights. There was a natural synergy between the two sets of issues.

On 1 April 2015, we learned that a World Food Program convoy of three Land Cruisers had been held up in Akoka County, Upper Nile State, a region nominally under government control but with significant inter-militia (Shillook and Dinka) fighting. All contact with the drivers was lost but WFP was able to track the movements of the vehicles via GPS for several days. Eventually they were found, with significant damage: one with several bullet holes through the windshield. Dinka militias in Akoka said the vehicles had been used to attack them and were driven by uniformed personnel under the command of General Johnson Olony, a Shillook notorious for child abductions. But they could not say what had happened to the three WFP staff.

The agency immediately suspended its activities in Akoka and in neighbouring Fashoda (where Olony allegedly launched his attack) on two grounds: for safety of its staff, and to demonstrate its deep outrage. These abductions – they turned out to be murders – came on top of thirteen killings of humanitarian staff since the outbreak of the crisis; by October 2016 that number would rise to sixty-seven. Dozens more had been the victims of serious assaults.

I took part in an emergency meeting of the HCT to debate reaction to the WFP disappearances. The conclusion was deeply unsatisfactory but, as time went on, would come to typify the ambivalent, dilatory reaction of humanitarian organizations to attacks on themselves: there was a "recommendation" that agencies suspend services until at least a meeting had been held with the authorities to obtain clarification of what had happened. The group "recommended," not "required," because some international NGOs and organizations – MSF, ICRC – reserved the right to continue vital services. I could understand what motivated them, but the humanitarian community's inability to display solidarity (even in a restricted area and for a short period) was a fatal flaw in our collective attempts to hold the governmental authorities to account. We allowed ourselves to be morally blackmailed and our calls for accountability reaped steadily diminishing returns.

Not that it was always the government we needed to stand up to. In another incident, the IO forcibly evicted four international NGOs from their respective compounds in Pagak (Upper Nile), so as to take them over for a large intra-party event. As I saw it, all four should have objected vigorously and suspended services pending the return of their premises and an apology. But again, there was no solidarity. One of the NGO country directors said to me, "You need to understand that if we pull out, our donors will want their money back." I thought that this was disingenuous; certainly, in the Canadian case, we would have accepted a suspension of services for the greater good.

The most craven instance of agencies caving was when a very large convoy of World Food Program trucks carrying mainly food supplies north to the POC camp in Bentiu was hijacked and looted near Mundri, Western Equatoria State. When they were released, the drivers described their assailants as armed and uniformed. There was no doubt about where at least three of the trucks were taken; GPS trackers showed them to be inside the SPLA barracks in Yei. WFP supplied all donors with a list of the value of their goods that had been stolen; in the case of Canada, the total was US$300,000. But WFP insisted that we not make a public statement, let alone press the government for an explanation. They were more concerned with getting the trucks back intact – forget the food seized – and not endangering further their already difficult relationship with the government.

In the face of such passivity, government ministers merely increased their rhetoric. Around the time of the killing of the WFP staffers, Cabinet Affairs Minister Lomuro said at a press conference, "I want to tell you clearly that these humanitarian agencies are not interested in our development but want to involve politics because of our natural resources ... They [the NGOs] know we have oil and that is why they get involved in politics."

On 23 April 2015, shortly after killing the three WFP staff, the militia of Olony turned directly on the mainstream SPLA in Malakal. The SPLA deployed tanks on the streets to counter the threat and an unknown number of persons – reported as "dozens" – were killed. As of noon that day, Johnson Olony's men were in possession of the airport and most of what was left of the town following five waves of attacks the previous year, and were shelling the parts they did not control. Hundreds of civilians poured into the small POC site on the UNMISS base adjoining the airport and UN peacekeepers pulled back from the cyclone-fence perimeter to more robust razor-wire-topped berms, and humanitarians took refuge in Hesco bunkers.

Olony had, by default, gone over to the IO, and would henceforth become their most effective commander in Upper Nile.

Dr Riek Gai, the minister of health whom I had accompanied on my road trips to Yambio and Wau, was a stocky figure who always wore smart suits that were a trifle too tight. He was the most senior Nuer in the cabinet. I knew from engagement on the health file that he was one of the most effective ministers, and that he was close to the president. Dr Gai spoke English with an intonation that at times seemed oddly Scottish, favouring the phrase "Yer're rright"; he had studied in Scotland. His undersecretary and constant companion, Dr Makur, was by contrast a tall, rather forbidding British-educated Dinka. They were an interesting pair to talk to. During a number of long rambling discussions, Dr Gai spoke of Senator Mobina Jaffer, Canada's peace envoy to Sudan, whom he had met several times. His office in the ministries block was lushly furnished with deep leather armchairs, gold curtains with tassels, pictures framed in gilt. We sipped scalding hot sweet tea from glasses, and there was always a television on in the background that was difficult to ignore.

I spoke a lot about accountability. "Don't you think that Riek Machar's generals derive their oxygen from the perception of many Nuer in December 2013 that they were the victims of a pogrom? If they get no redress, they will continue to seek revenge – or justice – by picking up weapons." Gai agreed that "there was a very regrettable breakdown of order in Juba for which the government must take responsibility," but he insisted that Machar and his coterie had tried to subvert the government and a Nuer major had fired the first shot. "And, as you know, James Hoth Mai, the chief of the general staff at the time, was a Nuer. So, it's unfair of the international community to keep suggesting that Dinka elements in the government must take most of the blame."

I tried not to get drawn into the details of what had happened that night. The point was that the main government inquiry undertaken by Police Inspector General Pieng had yet to see the light of day and was presumably buried in a drawer in the president's desk while the authorized version of the AU's Commission of Inquiry into the same matter had similarly been buried, in this case by AU partners.

"But the president would like to see that report published," the minister insisted.

"Well, if he does, he has not stated so very emphatically."

Gai agreed (in principle) that in Southern Sudan, rebellions were typically rewarded with promotions, cash, and the life of Riley for warlords. Such deals bought short-term peace but were highly destructive in the long term. I went on, "These deals are still going on; look at Yau Yau in Jongei. And they tried to buy off Olony in Upper Nile, but it didn't last." Again, the minister did not demur. In fact, he enthusiastically agreed when I suggested that IGAD had mistakenly driven down the cul-de-sac of rewarding rebellion by allowing the talks to focus on power-sharing between Riek Machar and Salva Kiir.

What was the solution? The talks needed to be rolled back, I said, in such a way that the interests of the two Big Men were submerged in a broader discussion of how South Sudan should be led and managed in the years ahead. In a word, a constitutional review, whether you called it that or something else.

A strong, effective leader, I said, would not wait for IGAD but would publicly and generously acknowledge past errors – a "Gettysburg Address" in Juba – and boldly put forward a new plan for the country that would appeal to all constituencies, thus rendering Riek irrelevant. Perhaps Gai knew that Salva Kiir was not capable of a Gettysburg. Even if he were a decent orator (which he was not), he did not have the necessary vision or drive to break free of his venal advisers. When I hinted this, the minister displayed the instinct we had encouraged in all South Sudanese: to look to the outside, not the inside, for solutions. He took a dig at the troika and suggested that Canada re-enter the mediation game.

"What do you think about South Africa, Tanzania?" he asked when I immediately hedged.

"Maybe. But only if you're sincere. If it's to delay hard negotiations, to forum-shop, you won't get much sympathy."

The minister dwelt at length on the failings of IGAD chief mediator Seyoum Mesfin. "He's too ambitious, and he is openly in favour of the Nuer." He said that Mesfin had helped ensure that a large part of Ethiopia's UNMISS contingent consisted of Nuer soldiers from western Ethiopia (when I investigated, this assertion turned out to be false). South Sudan would have been much happier, he went on, if General Sumbeiywo of Kenya had been given the senior role over Mesfin. If the talks had to remain with IGAD, he grudgingly conceded, "Then why not give Djibouti the lead? That's the seat of the secretariat."

Gai and Riek, while of the same ethnicity, were old enemies and rivals. The minister seemed repeatedly to require reassurance that the international community had not "fallen" for Riek, and that it was not our agenda to put him in President Salva Kiir's place. "If we sometimes seem to feel at ease with Riek," I added, "it's not just because he is more articulate and funny than President Kiir, but because the president himself selected Riek to be his representative to the international community. For nearly three years, this was the man we were instructed to talk to and to trust."

More proactively and interestingly, Dr Gai returned to the idea of "depriving the rebels of oxygen" by discussing Sudan. Having served for years in President Bashir's NCP government (indeed he returned to Juba at the last moment, the day before the referendum), he was well-qualified in this regard. He pointed out that Riek had remained militarily alive because of the matériel and other support given to him by Khartoum. This was where their weapons came from, and 10 forces frequently retired into Sudan when being pursued. Gai thought, correctly, that we had effectively given up "doing anything about Sudan," but that a constructive – rather than a destructive – Sudan was key to building sustainable peace in South Sudan.

Those days, I found myself thinking a lot about accountability. The shabby deal by which war criminal Yau Yau had been bought off was only the latest case in point. Couldn't it be said that the IGAD talks – however well-meaning – by "blessing" the continuance of Salva Kiir and Riek Machar in office were now going to compound errors yet again?

Most of my diplomatic colleagues would give me a polite hearing in this regard. As the acknowledged humanitarian expert, I was a kind of conscience, after all, carefully deferred to at meetings of heads of mission, and I had a more detailed grasp of human rights law than most. I think a number of colleagues even agreed with me privately. But none were prepared to do much more than mumble about accountability publicly, let alone echo Professor Mamdani's suggestion that neither Salva Kiir nor Riek Machar was actually fit for public office. The fallback seemed to me rather defeatist: "Yes; you are probably right; but what guarantee do we have that their replacements would be any better?"

Meanwhile, Ottawa had encouraged its heads of mission to become active on social media. This was at our own risk, and at odds with the requirement that more formal statements on my part – i.e. longer than 140 characters – needed to be cleared at high levels. But after some hesitation, and following strong encouragement from the prolific Toby Lanzer, I plunged in – hammering accountability and human rights above all else. This required finesse, and I didn't always get it right. It would clearly not be acceptable for an ambassador to call for the head of his host country to be investigated for crimes against humanity, but the trick was to harp on commitments already made by the big players (for example, in various IGAD documents) on provisions within the Transitional Constitution of South Sudan, and so on, and to link tweets to strongly worded documents emanating from the AU and UN.

I thus assembled a following of 1,500 or so. But, as is the nature of Twitter, there was some abuse: a few calls for me to be expelled, one calling upon the Jieng Council of Elders (an unofficial grouping of Dinka dignitaries) to deal with me, one or two saying it was disgraceful for an ambassador to be making "insinuations" regarding accountability. One individual, not entirely without reason, suggested I was guilty of hypocrisy. He attached a photo of an armoured vehicle manufactured by the Canadian company Streit being used by the SPLA to attack rebel positions in Unity State. I followed up and the allegation was correct, but lawyers at HQ pointed out that the vehicle would have been manufactured at Streit's plant in the United Arab Emirates, and thus not liable to Canadian export-control legislation (which would have prohibited sale in South Sudan). The legal case was watertight; it seemed to me that the ethical case was not.[2]

Also, I found I was being turned to by Stefano and Philippe, my genial colleagues at the EU, as the initial "pen" on multinational local statements led by the EU, on matters of human rights and humanitarian affairs. Neither spoke English as his first language, and for reasons to do with troika internal politics, the other two main Anglophone countries represented in Juba – the US and UK – did not always participate in such statements.

Late in the dry season of 2015 (April onwards), government-allied Nuer militias launched a violent onslaught in Unity State from three directions. For the first time the conflict took on a Nuer vs Nuer dimension, which seemed – coincidentally or otherwise – to take depravity to new lows. There were reports of rape camps, of infant girls being defiled, of boys being castrated and left to bleed out to halt the breeding of future enemies.[3] Medical clinics were not just looted but the buildings systematically flattened. NGOs struggled to cope; several evacuated, returned for a few days, then found themselves having to leave again.

In late May, there was a lull. I joined a small delegation from the UN's humanitarian country team to show the pale blue flag in southern Unity, meet with IO officials (whose control in this area seemed solid), and help make a recommendation as to whether it was now safe to operate. After the usual delayed clearance from the SPLA at Juba airport, we took the Mi-8 first to Rumbek, in government hands, where we refuelled, then made a cautious progression to the north and into the rebel heartland. At this time of year, our stops were like stepping stones. One thousand feet below, as far as we could see to either side, was swampland, with small, irregular-shaped islands every few kilometres. It was a bright sunny day with just a few clouds; the reflections in the water made for a picturesque scene. A few of the more solid islands had palm trees; many boasted a shack or two, and you could tell the more recently occupied islands by the white tarps spread over the traditional straw roofs. Once or twice we flew over a man in a dugout. Who could tell where he had come from or where he was going?

We landed first at Ganyiel, then Nyal. From Nyal our Ukrainian pilot radioed ahead, "Leaving Nyal now. ETA Leer twenty minutes."

"Roger, we'll be waiting."

At Leer, we came to a noisy halt at one end of a long dirt runway; the town was at the other end but there were *tukuls* in the trees on either side. I was a bit surprised, as the rotors wound down and the pilot came aft to open the door, that no one had come out to meet us. Usually in South Sudan even unannounced arrivals brought out dozens of small children, but there was no one in sight. I stepped out and snapped a picture of the rusty shipping container near which we had parked on which some wit had daubed, in white paint, "Welcome to Leer International Airport."

We were seven or eight at the foot of the ladder. Esteban, the Argentinian team leader from OCHA, grimaced faintly, pulled out his Iridium phone, and dialled a couple of numbers. No answer. With a shrug and in his heavy accent, he said, "Let's go."

There was still no one to be seen. It felt like we were on the set of a bad Western movie. A few bundles of dried twigs blew across the dusty runway. I said that I expected to hear the theme music from *The Good, the Bad and the Ugly* but Anne, from the NGO Medair, didn't smile at the joke. She was looking worriedly at Medair's compound, 200 metres ahead on our right, whose gate was firmly shut. As we walked over there uncertainly, she dialled. Again, there was no answer.

Above the wind and dead ahead we heard a few pops, isolated at first, then a *pop-pop*-sequence, a bit louder. We paused. "I don't like the look of this," said Esteban (unnecessarily, I thought).

More pops. Now there was a cloud of dust approaching: a four-by-four painted with camouflage colours with a heavy gun on the back, ten or twelve AK-toting men crammed around it. For a moment, I thought they were firing at us and vainly looked for cover. There was none. The doors of the big white helicopter 300 metres behind were closed, and it looked very vulnerable with its motionless, drooping rotors. But the shooting was aimed into the apparently deserted straw huts fifty to one hundred metres away.

The pickup skidded to a halt and the men piled out, forming a rough circle around us, firing outwards as they stepped down. Their commander seemed to be a tall, thin uniformed man in a black leather cowboy hat. He spoke, but we could hardly hear him over the gunfire. He whistled perfunctorily a couple of times as if to quiet his men, to no effect.

Suddenly there was an explosion that seemed very close. I staggered, half in surprise, half in fear, and looked around. A sixteen-year-old in a red Manchester United football jersey and flip-flops was brandishing a smoking RPG launcher; he'd just loosed off a round and was laughing hysterically. It seemed to me the men were all on drugs; either that, or they'd just survived the fight of their lives.

A khaki-painted half-track lumbered up with two technicals and a more senior officer with a Tiger Battalion flash on his shoulder. Only now did I figure out that it was the SPLA, and that they had a few minutes earlier taken Leer. A man with only a sidearm strode towards us. He was the new county commissioner as of about ten minutes ago. The shooting continued, but he shouted over the din that he wanted us to come with him. That seemed to be a bad idea. One by one, at his prompting, we introduced ourselves. I just gave my name and said nothing about my job. During a lull in the gunfire, he looked at us thoughtfully and said, "OK; maybe you should leave now."

Rarely have I been more relieved. We quietly turned around and made for the helicopter, trying not to run. I even had the presence of mind to take a few pictures of the stately Ugandan cranes who had been observing everything from the long grass. The door opened, we clambered in, the engines caught with a cough, and the rotors began turning, too slowly it seemed. From my porthole, I could see the little military detachment. They'd stopped firing, and the commissioner was looking at us even more speculatively.

As we rose and banked away, headed back to Nyal, nobody spoke. Looking down, I could see women up to their waists, even to their necks, in the swamp, looking for refuge. One carried her baby on her head in a cradle made of reeds. I thought to myself, "It's almost biblical."

Snakes Are Available

Uror, Akobo, and Juba, June–December 2015

Late in August 2015, after much cliffhanging prevarication on the part of the president, the Agreement on Resolution of the Conflict in South Sudan (ARC) was signed.[1] A document of more than sixty pages, it laid out a complicated formula for national power-sharing that would restore Riek Machar to the vice-presidency. A timetable provided first for the formation of a transitional government of national unity – with ministerial positions to be split between the present government and the 10, other parties receiving a much smaller quota – and ultimately, thirty months on, for national elections. It allowed Salva Kiir to remain president in the meantime.

By most reckonings, it was a good deal for the 10. It legitimized their relative military strength in the east and northeast of the country (including, critically, the oil fields) by granting them political control. It was a poor deal for the legal, unarmed opposition, who would see their share of seats in parliament decrease, and most judged it a poor deal too for the Equatorias, who had patiently watched the Dinkas and Nuer tear the country apart. Kiir signed with visible reluctance. He attempted to qualify his government's ratification with a set of "reservations" but, unsurprisingly, the 10 did not buy these; nor did anyone else in the international community.

A month after the agreement was signed, I drove to Bilpam, the SPLA's headquarters outside Juba, and met with my old friend Kuol Manyang, formerly governor of Jonglei, now minister of defence. Bilpam was the lion's den, for this was where the crisis began. In addition, there were odd touches of the surreal. Adorning the grounds were a three-metre-long helicopter gunship made from the parts of scrapped cars and a quarter-size delta-wing fighter aircraft fabricated from tin cans and string by a whimsical SPLA sergeant, a story that had gone viral when the BBC interviewed the enthusiast ("all it needs is an engine," he had said).

You always have to start off meetings like this on a positive note. I congratulated the minister on his president's signature of the ARC, on the various subsequent statements of commitment made by senior members of the government, and, in particular, on the mature role played by senior officers during the preceding week's workshop in Addis Ababa on transitional security arrangements. For once, the government had the IO on the back foot: Juba had signed the minutes of the workshop but the IO were still hesitating and would continue to do so for some time. Kuol listened politely enough but did not respond directly, so I asked him where he thought there was most risk of things going wrong.

As was his wont, he launched into a very long recitation of recent South Sudanese history, focusing on a succession of "betrayals" of the Southern cause in the war years by non-Dinka. Indiscreetly, he stated at one point, "It was the Dinka who won independence, Mr Nicholas; you must never forget this; not the Nuer, the Azande, or anyone else."

The recent "rebellion" he cast very much in the context of a long chain of internal South-South revolts. The implicit message was that the rebels were welcome back and "we will accept them – as we have done so many times before – but we will not trust them." Also implicit was the suggestion that the international community would be to blame if it all went wrong. "You are forcing us to share power with Riek," he said, adding, "I don't mean you, of course; I mean the troika." Accurately, he noted that Riek Machar had recently lost his three most eminent generals and was left with only the unreliable Johnson Olony. He suggested that Riek was a busted flush, and the peace agreement was only of limited relevance because it did not include those three and their forces. Most notorious among the three was Peter Gadet. Kuol acknowledged the latter's history of extreme duplicity: "He has changed sides at least ten times in thirty years, to my knowledge." But he admitted that Gadet was a very effective commander and could be damaging if not brought in.

Kuol Manyang came over as bluff but not stupid. Noting that Sudan had played a significant role in perpetuating the rebellion by supplying arms to Riek Machar, he complained that the West seemed to have given up pushing for political reform in Sudan and that

"Bashir can get away with anything." He was particularly aggrieved that Sudan "keeps claiming we are supporting the SPLA/N in Nuba and Blue Nile" to justify its meddling in the South, "but this is not so."

In the medium to long term, he agreed that the two countries needed each other if they were to be sustainable, and this meant solving the border disputes that had been bedevilling relations even before the current crisis. Kuol then commented casually, "We now have the map." Anyone who had followed the history of Southern Sudan would have known immediately what he meant. "The Map," allegedly created before the independence of Sudan in 1956, was a document southerners claimed existed somewhere, showing the British-drawn line between the two administrative areas of what was then one Sudan.

If South Sudan indeed has "The Map," they are still keeping it under wraps.

On 2 October 2015, after a quiet period during which everyone mulled over the peace agreement and the parties struggled to reach a deal for the IO's return to Juba, President Kiir dropped a bombshell by creating twenty-eight states out of the current ten. These were grouped into three regions: ten states in Upper Nile, ten in Bahr-al-Ghazal, and eight in the Equatorias (see maps on page xiii).

The concept of dividing the country into units that were largely ethnically homogeneous was not new: it even had its own name, *kokora*, normally translated as "regionalism." Ethiopia was often held up as a model for emulation; the recently created Greater Pibor Administrative Area, within Jonglei State and effectively a Murle homeland, was an example closer to home. Riek Machar had long been an advocate of greater subdivision within the federation and the preamble to the peace agreement acknowledged that a more devolved form of federation was needed.

In general terms this decree, if enacted, would give the Nuer relatively homogeneous areas, but it engineered certain borders in such a way that governorships in the oil fields would go to Dinkas. Other groups were more blended. The manner in which the states were allocated per region (ten-ten-eight) gave greater weight to the Dinka (Bahr-al-Ghazal) and Nuer (Greater Upper Nile) than to the third region in South Sudan: the Equatorias. But what was most provocative was not the idea itself but the fact that it was being imposed unilaterally, in an anti-constitutional manner, and outside the ARC agreement explicitly based on ten states. Riek Machar's carefully worded statement of reaction acknowledged the IO's longstanding ambitions for a more devolved federation, but called Salva Kiir's announcement a clear violation of the ARC.

It was an open secret that the proposal came from the hard-core, reactionary Jieng Council of Elders. In fact, at the end of the televised announcement, Salva Kiir lapsed into Arabic and said, Pilate-like, "There, I've done what the chiefs want; take it away." The announcement quickly became the talk of Juba. The newspapers were crammed with paid advertisements congratulating the president (many likely from persons hoping for jobs: the president would appoint all twenty-eight governors and all the members of the new state legislatures) and there was some modest celebration.

The articulate and likeable Lawrence Korbandy, former chair of the National Human Rights Commission serving as the president's chief legal advisor, was deployed to argue the government's case to diplomats and in public fora. I attended a dangerously packed session at Juba University where he placed the presidential initiative in the context of longstanding popular demands for decentralization, describing it as "a problem-solving document." Contrary to indications from elsewhere in government (e.g. from the minister of information), he said that the order would be presented to the council of ministers (cabinet) and to parliament, and that it could be struck down in either place; "Until that point it is not unconstitutional." He also said that because the ARC gave the opposition only two states, Upper Nile and Unity, and this order would give them substantially more, "It's a positive adjustment to the peace agreement."

This argument did not go down well with the mainly student audience. Yes, the IO would get maybe four of the new states (if the president so chose), but that would be four out of twenty-eight, vs. the two out of ten that the ARC provided. Seeking to counter the argument that the change would be costly, he said that decentralizing authority would mean less expenditure at the centre "so you won't have to spend forty-eight million SSP on federal civil servants like Lawrence Korbandy." Although this self-deprecating remark saved Korbandy from being booed off the stage, it did not convince many people.

The Jieng Council of Elders was led by former Chief Justice of the Supreme Court Ambrose Riny Thiik, and he spoke next. He defended the initiative with an unashamedly nationalistic appeal, verging on the paranoid. His remarks were also a tacit rebuke to the EU and the troika. "If you believe in the sovereignty of South Sudan, if you reject UN trusteeship and those who would seek regime change, you must support this initiative," he declared. Tellingly, he cast the order as a riposte to the ARC. "Between you and me, that agreement was imposed upon us. It was not a result of negotiations. It has sown the seeds of discord. This order will bring relief to millions."

Civil society in South Sudan barely existed, with many former activists having been co-opted into government at the time of independence. But there were some brave and articulate souls, and prominent among them was Edmund Yakani of the Community Empowerment for Progress Organization (CEPO). He spoke next. "The fact that the president will appoint every single governor and every legislator in the new states," he began, "takes the country a significant distance along the path to authoritarianism, even dictatorship." Yakani thought the order was essentially a "testing of the waters" by the Jieng Council and influential power-brokers close to the president.

After he had spoken, Justice Ambrose, rattled by the groundswell of hostile murmuring in the hall, walked out and refused to face any questions. Dr Luka Biong, the university moderator who had introduced the panelists, bravely and fairly summed up by saying that there was a divergence of views but debate was healthy. Within a week, he had been dismissed from his job. Later he suffered an even greater insult when the government said that he was not South Sudanese, having been born in the disputed territory of Abyei.

The matter of the twenty-eight states rumbled on. Parliament balked; a large number of Equatorian lawmakers walked out when the order came up for ratification. It looked as though the government might be getting cold feet because nothing was done to implement the new state boundaries. It had become clear was that there was a group of very influential Dinkas who were not in the least interested in seeing the ARC prosper and the president seemed to be in their thrall.

In November 2015, with conflict sputtering on and implementation of the peace process in slow motion, I made two visits to the heart of IO-controlled territory. The first was to Motot, Uror County (Jonglei State), hosted by the international NGO Tearfund, whose sanitation and hygiene activities we were funding. From Motot ("Small Pond"), Tearfund helped populations up to fifty kilometres in all directions. With the exception of the International Committee of the Red Cross, which maintained a surgical field hospital twenty-five kilometres away at Waat, Tearfund was the only service provider in this entire area.

The terrain was utterly flat: grassland dotted with low acacia trees. It was counterintuitively difficult to traverse. Tearfund director Florence told me that for much of the year, ponds and swamps prevented anything but "footing." Even though it had been the dry season for the past month, we needed to traverse sections of track so inundated that water came through the floor of the Land Cruiser. Tearfund had the only two motor vehicles in the region, its other five having been seized, then wrecked, by the White Army when they attacked and ransacked Bor in December 2013 to January 2014. "No, the insurance did not cover this," Florence said with a smile.

Cows were more numerous than people, spending their nights in enormous *luaks* (conical, straw-roofed huts) that were much more commodious than the homes of the humans. Outside the odd hut, flags flew. Depending on the colour, they indicated that there was either a prize bull or a girl (twelve to fourteen years old, typically) for sale. So prevalent was early marriage that girls of eighteen were social outcasts.

For two years now, the only road linking this region to civilization – the state capital of Bor – had been closed by the SPLA vs IO conflict. This meant there was almost no trade anymore, in spite of a 15 per cent rise in the population as IDPs fled here from more violent areas. The market in Pieri, fifteen kilometres south of Motot, would have been laughable were it not so sad: one old lady sitting before two boxes of tea bags, three bars of soap, and a few twists of chewing tobacco, spread out on a white WFP sack left over from an air drop. Nobody had any money and the only commerce took place when, very occasionally, a family sold a single goat to Tearfund for cash. The big news during my three days in Motot was an Ethiopian man arriving with a donkey and a single sack of grain, having walked three days from Akobo on the Ethiopian border.

Its control of central Jonglei largely unchallenged, the IO divided the area into new administrative units; generally, as in Yau Yau's Pibor, counties had become states and *payams* (sub-counties) had become counties. And so on. It was all very confusing, as the Juba government was now doing the same thing with the twenty-eight-states order but using different boundaries. There existed three parallel sets of nomenclature.

In 10 parlance, old Uror County was now Bieh state, divided into Pieri, Yol (Motot), and Pulchuol Counties. Each of the three counties had its own commissioner complete with executive secretary and sundry support staff. All these people were working on a volunteer basis, which in a way was inspiring, but it was also worrying: even if peace arrived tomorrow and the nation's finances were somehow restored to health, there would be no resources to support such extensive administrative overheads.

By chance it was World Toilet Day (yes, there really is one) as I embarked on an all-day tour of Tearfund's community-led total sanitation projects, trudging through the low bush in thirty-five degrees from one latrine to another, each in a different stage of development. South Sudan had the lowest ratio of toilets per capita in the world so this organization trained communities to do away with open defecation, taught them how and where they should build three-metre-deep latrines, then gave a small number of tools to each community to get them started. The emphasis was on self-help, and the plastic or concrete platforms typically handed out by other agencies were eschewed in favour of log platforms pasted over with mud.

It was funny and touching as mothers and children asked to have their photos taken in front of their newly finished privies, and it was impressive to see the degree of engagement. In one community of 255 households, 250 had started their latrines. The other five? "Oh, we'll see to them!" said the chiefs with a laugh.

Tearfund also had a program rehabilitating and maintaining boreholes. This was cost-intensive as all materials, including cement and iron pipes, had to be flown in. But the alternative to a non-functioning borehole was competing with cows to drink from shallow ponds that started to go dry from February or March until the rains came in May.

In only one of the three county towns had there been educational activity during the past two years: in Pieri, six hundred primary-school children were taught by volunteers. But there were no textbooks and no other supplies of any sort.

As protocol required in such situations, I met formally with the three commissioners. One, dressed in the khaki quasi-military uniform of commissioners from the days of Sudanese rule, had just finished meeting with a senior 10 commander and was protected by a uniformed squad with a light machine gun; another had been meeting with his red-sashed chiefs. "We've been talking about the compensation that will come to us as part of the peace agreement," he said (optimistically, I thought). I remember the third for his silk kipper tie in the colours of the South Sudanese flag, and his bright yellow socks. All three were sanguine about the peace process, but Pieri commissioner John Tut insisted it would only hold if the international community exerted and maintained enormous pressure. The commissioners referred routinely to Riek Machar as "our president."

Everywhere there were men and boys with guns, so much so that until you got used to it and as you drove past them on the road, ignoring their pleas to be picked up, you had an uneasy feeling in your back. Uror County was the prime recruiting ground for the White Army, and it was here that in 2012 and 2013 they massed in columns of as many as 10,000 to march on the homeland of their traditional rivals, the Murle. In 2013 and in 2014 they deployed again as shock troops when the 10 stormed into Bor and Malakal. Currently they were quiescent, and the Murle were keeping themselves to themselves. "We just hope that Juba does not manipulate them," said one of the commissioners.

The regular SPLA was at a safe distance in Bor. "We're not going to march again on Bor or any other government stronghold," said the most outspoken of the trio, "until there is an accounting from the top leadership for all the young men who never came back in December 2013 and January 2014." But this did not mean that there was peace. At the ICRC hospital in Waat, I inadvertently interrupted Dr Kurt, a Canadian surgeon who was extracting a bullet from the abdomen of an unconscious young man. He was delighted to meet me, ask me my opinion about the recent Canadian elections, and reminisce about life on Vancouver Island. But I attached myself instead to the Finnish matron and hastily sent him back to his operating tent, where he had more pressing business.

The ICRC maintained thirty-eight beds here. All were occupied, almost exclusively by men with gunshot wounds in the lower limbs. The sole patient who spoke English sat up cheerfully as we looked at his shattered ankle. He'd "walked" fifteen kilometres to get here. "There is a lucky one," said the nurse, pointing to an unhappy-looking patient with an abdominal injury. She echoed what Apollo, the surgeon in Kodok, had told me: those with chest or abdominal wounds were usually considered hopeless and left to die.

All these men were the victims of intra-Nuer clan fighting. Such fights might involve cattle, but often as not they were about marriages gone wrong or represented a new stage in feuds that had been going on for years. One of the Tearfund staff explained that "one clan will sometimes wait ten or twenty years before a high-value target in the other clan emerges. Then they take him out." Returning and well-educated diaspora members were often considered good targets. A few months back, the employee had saved a Canadian of Nuer origin back in Uror for the first time in years, who had immediately gone on the rival clan's hit list. He had to be flown out by subterfuge. However, these killings were confined to men, and in normal times it was quite safe for a woman to walk around Uror alone.

Back in Motot, there was great excitement at the Tearfund compound. Mary, the cook, had somehow obtained a kob, a kind of antelope that roams the plains of central Jonglei. She'd cut it in half with a hatchet; its furry rump now protruded from one bloody bucket, its head from another. The evening staff volleyball game was cut short so this delicacy could be fully enjoyed. I cannot report that kob tastes good. Mary's butchering skills were inferior; every mouthful had to be filtered for splintered bone fragments.

Flying back to Juba, I reflected that every possible aid dilemma existed in Uror. Tearfund was unquestionably doing a great job but the dependence of the local population on the agency was total, the absence of government services correspondingly absolute. It was very difficult to see an exit strategy for Tearfund, or to contemplate the consequences should they fail to secure funding donors. More subtly, the manner in which they insisted on community involvement was undercut by other agencies, who might be very distant but about whom word spread. For example, that Oxfam, two hundred kilometres away, provided concrete slabs for latrines while Tearfund did not was reported in a complaining way by one chief. Issues of this kind cropped up wherever there were international NGOs at work in South Sudan, which was pretty much everywhere. And then, however many boreholes you fitted up, it seemed there were never enough. It was not easy to say "I'm sorry, you're going to have to walk for three hours for water – or re-locate," but sometimes this needed stating.

The prevalence of guns in Uror and the lethal buzz of inter-clan fighting reminded me that whatever peace emerged from the efforts of the IGAD mediators would be relative. South Sudan was a long-term project in terms of both development and stabilization.

My second foray around this time was with two colleagues: a return to Akobo, hard on the South Sudanese border with Ethiopia and also under the control of the armed opposition. It was quiet. On the main street, lined by trees planted in the colonial era, young men of military age strolled casually in their colourful Chelsea or Arsenal soccer shirts and graffiti on the walls praised Wayne Rooney. Women smiled and sought to sell us repulsive-looking owner-tested chewing tobacco from their stalls. The market area of town was emptier than usual, partly because a climate-caused humanitarian crisis across the river in Ethiopia meant that Ethiopian traders had been forbidden to take certain staples out of their country. But on the first day we were in town, shops were closed for a different reason. Traders were having a meeting to discuss the currency exchange regime in Akobo. The county commissioner had decreed that the going rate should be ten SSP to one USD versus the rate of twenty then prevalent in Juba, an interesting example of proactive "governmental" fiscal policy in action.

In a pair of breeze-block buildings in the middle of the town's main open space, baking in the thirty-five-degree sunshine, a number of male prisoners thrust their hands through the bars, pleading with us. Unfortunately, this kind of scene was common throughout South Sudan.

Commissioner Jut Chot Rian, locally the senior authority, received us at the airstrip and in his office, proud of his ceremonial stick and white-trimmed beige suit. In 10 parlance, this was Akobo East County. The commissioner seemed genuinely relaxed regarding the war. He was more concerned at the possibility of traditional Murle/Lou Nuer conflict re-emerging: "One of our commanders was recently killed in a Murle raid. This was organized by the SPLA, I am sure." Commissioner Jut said that the townspeople were very happy with the peace agreement and had held a large party to celebrate. "But I don't really know any of the details of the agreement. And tell me about this order of Kiir and the twenty-eight states, please."

On a day-to-day basis, his main preoccupation was inter-clan rivalries and the large number of armed youth who were not under anyone's control. I asked him whether the Nuer prophet, Dak Kueth, was currently active; the answer was negative. I was left with the distinct impression that there was little contact between the authorities in Akobo and the rebel leadership, whether military or political.

Next morning, travelling downriver to Gakdong, Payam, with Save the Children, we had another of those welcome glimpses of bucolic South Sudan. Small children swam and waved at us gleefully, fish eagles watched from high up in the trees, Marabou storks and Ugandan cranes waded in the shallows, young men fished from dugouts. The Nuer of Ethiopia and South Sudan came and went freely across this border and were, to all intents and purposes, indistinguishable.

At Gakdong, the Payam administrator received us formally in his bare office; like the commissioner, he received no stipend. He expressed appreciation for the food security and maternal health programs Canada had been supporting through Save the Children, and for the activities of others such as Oxfam and the national NGO, Nile Hope. He told us that in the last couple of weeks, 300 refugees had returned through Payam from Ethiopia; clearly, they believed peace was imminent but most, for now, remained in Akobo rather than travelling back to their remote farmsteads.

Having learned that this village was the home of Dr Riek Gai, the minister of health, I asked whether he would be welcome home despite being regarded as a traitor by senior Nuer. There were bemused smiles, then, "We educated people would welcome him, yes; but some would not understand ..." Amplifying, he went on, "We can forgive but we cannot and shall not forget. We want justice." But Riek Machar was not necessarily The Man in these parts. He was the Nuer leader by default. "You know the African saying 'When elephants fight, the grass is crushed'? Well, we are all grass. All of us."

As always, meeting with ordinary people was a humbling and fascinating experience, a welcome escape from the Juba circuit of politicians and officials. Nuer names alone gave a glimpse into a very foreign world. One girl at a small farm told us proudly that her name meant "Dust of Dry Cow Dung." A woman told me that her two infants were, respectively, "Court" and "Abuse"; the first because he had been born when she was taking his father to court for failing in his matrimonial responsibilities; the second because by the time he was born, the dispute with her husband's family had descended into open physical abuse. A monosyllabic name meant "Born the day after grandmother died," and Rambang, we learned, meant "Born sickly, likely to die."

Save the Children had been working with the Red Cross and UNICEF to help reunify children separated from their parents by the conflict. We met with Gatwech ("Son of the Land") who had been with his wife and five children in Bor when it was overrun by combined Ugandan and SPLA forces in December 2013. He had packed the family off to the UN's Protection of Civilians site and fled to the north (perhaps to fight – it was not appropriate to ask). His wife and children survived the April 2014 attack on the POC which saw more than fifty civilians killed when a Dinka mob had breached the perimeter. "But soon after this, my wife died. From TB."

Just last week, Save the Children had brought Gatwech's children home to him. They sat in a tight circle around him, the three little girls in bright, clean clothes, as he positively beamed with pride – although it could not have been easy to be a single dad in South Sudan. He had the prominent facial markings of most Nuer men. I asked him if he would have his sons undergo the same ritual when they grew older: "No, never. I do not want ever again to see men killed because of the facial markings."

Akobo was not entirely devoid of hazards. A memorable warning I retained from our security briefing was "Snakes are available." And late one stygian Jonglei night, feeling my way back from the latrine, there was a very loud rustling in the dry leaves. A nervous brandishing of my flashlight revealed a one-metre-long Nile monitor, a smaller version of the Komodo dragon, grinning at me in a less-than-friendly way, his eyes bright green and slit like a cat's.

Since the crisis broke out, we had not been kayaking on the Nile. It wasn't that the river was any more dangerous, but the SPLA and police we'd occasionally see on the riverbank had become a lot more nervous and it seemed best not to look for trouble. So, we jumped at the opportunity to take a pleasure cruise. Some months earlier, a businessman had imported a thirty-metre-long white boat called the *Nile Queen*; it had a cabin with aircraft-type seats and you could also stand on the roof in an enclosed area.

Unfortunately, a large number of other people also decided to make an escape from Juba when we did. Jenny, the office staff, and I were among the first to arrive, but our hearts sank as dozens more trooped down to the dock over the next hour. There must have been eighty or ninety people on board by the time we pulled out. Non-stop reggae and hip-hop music was blaring at a headache-inducing volume, and large quantities of beer and cheap red wine were consumed before we got under way.

It was not the usual NGO, diplomatic, or UN crowd. Most people seemed to be involved in oil, in the Coca-Cola concession, or in "import-export," plus there were a few non-uniformed Western UNMISS soldiers. I found myself wedged next to a garrulous Westerner called Ben associated with various business enterprises, who'd been in and out of South Sudan for years.

"Fuckin' kleptocracy, mate," he remarked to a man called Finn, who sold giant electrical pumps to the oil industry. "Those soft-headed NGOs, the UN, they're all being taken for a ride and they don't even fuckin' know it." Finn wandered off to find another cold can of Tusker. Ben leered at Finn's girlfriend, who was about forty years old but trying to look like twenty in a tight red mini-skirt, and put his arm round her waist. "Pleasure to meet you. What a lovely lady ... he shouldn't have left you alone."

We were cruising downstream along a narrow channel that ran parallel to the main river. Half-naked children waved from the bank or mimicked the men who were jiving on the top deck to the reggae. The adults eyed us silently as we passed by in our bubble of noise. "Fuckin' great isn't it!" Ben beamed. "And hardly any of those tossers in Juba ever get out and see this. It's the real South Sudan, this is."

We passed the location of an air crash a couple of weeks earlier. An Antonov crammed with unlisted passengers had failed to gain altitude and had fallen half in the river, half on land, killing forty people. "Yeah, I was out jogging that morning. Heard it go down. And what do you do for exercise, m'dear?" I couldn't make out her answer, but had the feeling she was becoming impatient with the still-absent Finn. "We know what the best exercise is, don't we? Sex, of course ... Hey look at those kids! Fuckin' great, aren't they? Yeah, man, this is real. Best thing in Juba."

On my other side, a muscular African-American man in a tight singlet was discussing with his Ethiopian friend the best route into American politics. "See, the thing is, I got ambition, man. I'm gonna change things by the time I'm thirty, at the latest. After that, nobody does shit." I couldn't hear what the Ethiopian said, but the American continued, "Well, yeah, joinin' State would be one way into politics.

But I'm figurin' on getting onto the Hill, wanna be a congressional staffer, know what I mean? Those guys really get to change things, to influence things, know what I mean?"

We were leaving a trail of beer cans and plastic cups in our wake. A white twenty-five-year-old, wearing only a pair of shorts, shinned up the angled plexiglass behind which the captain sat at his wheel. The glass cracked and a shouting match began. I caught the eye of Véronique, a young captain serving with the Canadian Forces who today was dressed in a skimpy red skirt complemented by a Santa hat. She shrugged apologetically.

We stopped for half an hour on an island in the middle of the river where there was a restaurant with different, competing, and even louder music. There were a few people here who'd taken a speedboat direct from Juba and grimaced sympathetically at us as we streamed off the grossly overloaded *Nile Queen*.

———————

It was December 2015 and the second anniversary of the crisis was approaching. The 10 couldn't decide whether to come back to Juba – as the peace agreement required – or not. Every time they seemed about to take the plunge, the government put new obstacles in their way.

One evening Stefano, the ambassador of the European Union, organized a musical performance in honour of International Human Rights Day. The artists were an American pianist and an Italian singer who could manage in four or five languages. The audience consisted of diplomats, a few UN officials, and NGO types. As always, there were disappointingly few South Sudanese; they seemed to come to such events rarely, or so late as to miss everything. Lam Akol and the Honourable Onote, the two leaders of the legitimate political opposition, attended the concert, but Stefano was disappointed that none of the government people that he'd invited had come.

Working the crowd was George, the white Greek / South Sudanese who owned the restaurant and who had once been Canada's consul here. He was the kind of person who knew everybody, and he was well informed about the history of Juba. He would tell you proudly that Theodore Roosevelt once stayed at Notos, and he took us on a vain mission one day to find a Victorian-era Belgian cemetery near Rajaf, fifteen kilometres outside Juba. George had even purchased a piano specially for this event, although we understood from the banter coming from the stage that it had arrived in-country only hours before.

The evening went unexpectedly well. There was John Lennon's "Imagine," which only a week or two earlier had made the headlines when an anonymous pianist performed it after the ISIL attack on the Bataclan concert hall in Paris. There was "Where Have All the Flowers Gone?" and "Blowing in the Wind," and the more rousing European anthem, Beethoven's "Ode to Joy." With the peace process faltering and the prospect of another year of war looming, it was the right time for such melodies. And it was the right crowd, of course. Idealistic, a little naïve, maybe deluded. The kind of people Ben of the *Nile Queen* despised, I thought.

I found myself drying a tear when we all stood for the final song of the evening, Pete Seeger's "We Shall Overcome." The last verse goes like this:

We shall live in peace, we shall live in peace;
We shall live in peace some day;
Oh, deep in my heart, I do believe,
We shall live in peace some day.

How Long Must We Suffer?

Juba and Malakal, January–March 2016

The common wisdom was that the Christmas and New Year period in Juba was very quiet, the crisis of December 2013 being the obvious exception. But before Christmas 2015, around the second anniversary of that crisis, the action picked up again.

On 15 December, after more nearly three years of prevarication, the government did what donors had long been calling for and allowed the South Sudan pound (SSP) to float against the US dollar. Predictably, it leapt to the black-market rate of around eighteen SSP to the dollar, versus three SSP the day before. The shorthand for this was "devaluation" but the term was misleading, because for months most of the economy had been operating at the black-market rate. More properly, this was an adjustment that allowed the pound to trade at its correct value. A day or two later, the government took an important accompanying measure and removed its subsidy of petroleum and diesel, meaning that the price rose overnight from six SSP per litre to twenty-two SSP.

Put together, these two steps meant, theoretically, that the dollars the government earned from oil would be injected into the economy at the proper rate, which would allow much of the government's enormous deficit to be addressed while outgoings were also reduced, there being no further need to subsidize fuel. So far so good. But the international price of oil was fathoming new depths. Indeed, once you subtracted both the oil companies' take and the twenty-four American dollars that Juba needed to pay Sudan for each barrel shipped (transit/refining fees and repayments of the oil debt incurred at independence in 2011), it was, in fact, costing South Sudan to produce oil.

So where were importers (who needed hard currency to bring in everything from vegetables to fuel) to obtain their American dollars, with the Central Bank having no hard currency to give commercial banks and the country's reserves long ago exhausted? The short-term answer was the last-resort tranche that all countries have the right to draw from the IMF. South Sudan's special drawing rights constituted a one-time allocation of US$140 million. As per the recommendations of the IMF, the Bank of South Sudan began a series of regular auctions at each of which banks made bids for portions of US$20 million. The highest bidders (in SSP terms) would win, and the banks would then resell at that rate, or marginally above.

In theory, this should have eliminated the black market, but the black market did not disappear. While the banks made their bids at around eighteen or nineteen SSP, the parallel-price market kept creeping up in fits and starts, and by late January 2016 was at thirty SSP (this as general customers found that, notwithstanding the banks' better rate, they never actually seemed to have any dollars). It looked as though something fishy was going on, but exactly what had happened would not emerge until US$80 million of the US$140 million had been expended.

Down at the end of our road, Haile – the Ethiopian shopkeeper who for some months had been our prime source of pounds – fretted over what rate to offer us. One day the rate was twenty-five but next morning it was twenty, only to go to twenty-eight by the afternoon. Some days it was too stressful and he would politely decline to sell at all, urging us instead to take away gratis a small box of teabags (the selling of tea and sugar was the flimsy cover for his line of business, whose legality was doubtful).

Inflation gathered speed, with many employers and vendors deciding that, since the SSP had been massively "devalued" against the US dollar and fuel prices had tripled, it was now appropriate to multiply salaries and prices by similarly large factors. The government announced a 300 per cent pay increase for civil servants; the price of newspapers – which had been one SSP in 2012 – hit ten pounds; the shortest ride on the back of a motorbike, previously three pounds, rose to fifteen. The IMF gloomily briefed us that South Sudan looked to be in a "death spiral" from which the only escape was a massive international bailout.

———

The governing SPLM had only held two national conventions; the nearest approximation to a third was the disastrously still-born meeting of the National Liberation Council in December 2013. So there was trepidation when the SPLM announced, late in 2015, that it intended to launch its First Extraordinary National Convention, the more so because the general secretariat was determined to go ahead with or without the IO and before the conclusion of negotiations over the proposed transitional government of national unity (TGNU). The event had to take place in the first fortnight of the year, because 15 January was the deadline for political parties to register their constitutions if they wished to compete in the next round of elections thirty months away.

Things went right to the wire. It seemed that the convention would be a complete bust or – at worst – there could be a repetition of December 2013. First the IO announced that, although it had delegates in town, it was boycotting the convention because the president had unilaterally created twenty-eight states out of ten. And on Wednesday, 6 January, just hours before the opening, negotiations over the allocation of ministerial portfolios – seen as a necessary precondition to a good event – were reported as having reached a deadlock. On the big day itself, in the vast white beer tent of Freedom Hall, the temperature and the tension mounted, with 1,500 delegates and a handful of diplomats milling around gossiping. Our row was sandwiched between one labelled "Governors," the other "Generals." The podium remained vacant and contradictory rumours spread. An increasingly desperate and sweating MC summoned various musical performers, one after the other, to fill the time. A highlight was the SPLM choir (imagine Kim Jong-Un's all-girl Morangang Band with an African flavour), while a hip-hopper sang,

> I remember John Garang
> Did he fight for nothing?
> Fallen heroes of Africa,
> How long must we suffer?

At 4:15, eight hours after the scheduled start, the president's sirens were heard. Ten minutes of faded colour footage of Salva Kiir and John Garang in the early days of the war was hurriedly screened as the band moved into place. There had been agreement over the ministerial allocations, it was whispered. Most notably, the government would hold Finance, Defence, and National Security; the 10 Petroleum, the Interior, and Federal Affairs; the former detainees Foreign Affairs and Transport; the other (non-armed) political parties Cabinet Affairs and Agriculture. Although no names had been announced, the betting was that ex-minister Deng Alor would receive Foreign Affairs. In tandem with this negotiation, the government had accepted the list of fifty nominees of the 10 to sit as members of the National Legislative Assembly for the duration of the transitional government of national unity.

As the president arrived, a further ripple of excitement ran through the hall when Taban Deng, the chief negotiator of the 10, was spotted huddling with SPLA generals; also circulating was Deng Alor of the FDS. It had been feared that neither group would attend – thus invalidating the whole concept of a reunifying convention – and/or that their mere presence could provoke violence. Things were off to a surprisingly good start.

The first possible flashpoint was Deng Alor's address to the convention. His was a generally statesmanlike intervention, acknowledging that the ongoing crisis had been produced by a failure of SPLM leadership. He did not lay out any red lines for the future cooperation of the former detainees – huge sigh of relief – but stole a little of Taban Deng's thunder by stating that the latter had told him that "the 10 is not going back to war."

Taban Deng started his own speech bizarrely with a complicated and obscure anecdote involving Emperor Jean-Bedel Bokassa that was apparently meant as a compliment to the mediation efforts of Tanzania's CCM party. But then he moved into clearer, more ringing language. "This is a great day ... we have achieved peace ... we are committed." Like Deng Alor, he insisted on the importance of Arusha being incorporated within the new SPLM Constitution, and like Deng Alor he expressed reservations about the twenty-eight-states order: "The problem is not so much the number as their boundaries; these can create permanent conflict."

Taban Deng took no direct swipes at the Juba administration, but concluded his remarks by emphasizing the need for the older generation to make way for younger blood. "People must leave office!" he declared. From the flutter that went through the audience there was little doubt how this was interpreted. He also commented that Riek

Machar would return to Juba very soon. Most agreed that he needed to get down here quickly ... lest Taban move into the de facto IO leadership vacuum.

Salva Kiir was the closing act of a very long day. The introduction was not auspicious. The punchy and rousing Tiger Battalion marching song was meant to evoke the glory days of the SPLA, but clearly reminded some of those present that infighting in this supposedly elite battalion had sparked the last two years of war. The president's speech was long (one hour) and very competently written – suspiciously so – but he did not deliver it well, and appeared to lose his way in sections regarding the economy. Even so, everyone understood his apparently sincere, emphatic *mea culpas*:

> I sincerely apologize for the unnecessary and unbearable sufferings you have gone through in the past twenty-four months, which have been the longest and most difficult of my life.
>
> As a Christian, I have tried to reconcile with myself ... now we must all do the same.
>
> There were two principal causes of this conflict: the dysfunctionality of the SPLM at all levels of government, and tribalism.
>
> The war has cost us not only lives but our dignity ... we have squandered the good will of the international community.
>
> Corruption has become rampant and entrenched. None of us is above the law, we must accept full responsibility.

These honest remarks were well received, and provided an effective counterpoint to the sycophantic interventions of speakers that preceded the three heavyweights. But Salva Kiir put down his prepared remarks three times to ad-lib. First, he could not resist stating again, as if for the record, that he signed the ARC under duress. Then he paused to bitterly excoriate those who had been waging war in the Equatorias. "As long as these people are attacking civilians, I will not stop my forces from hunting them down like rats," he said. The president did not directly accuse the IO of being behind the fighting in this region but he did challenge Taban Deng to either disown the fighters or accept responsibility and enforce a ceasefire. And finally, in defence of the twenty-eight-states order, he declared that it was the result of demands from those who felt the government had become too distant from the people. He described the order as a "Christmas gift" to the people, and challenged naysayers to go into the streets and take it back.

Perhaps the most inspiring speaker was not South Sudanese at all. Cyril Ramaphosa, deputy president of South Africa and deputy chairman of the ANC, spoke on behalf of the ANC and the CCM (Tanzania), which had played a key role in mediating the Arusha agreement. He described the day as "truly historic: a great movement is today reuniting itself." He drew a host of parallels between the ANC and the SPLM (perhaps flattering to the latter), insisting on the need to eradicate tribalism, to promote women and youth within the party, and to "obliterate" corruption. Consciously echoing the language of Mandela, he said, "We will walk this long road with you, at your side, not behind you."

Battling my way out through the crowds as the convention broke up, I found a massive traffic jam outside the tent. Mandrea was stuck far away in the embassy car, unable to advance. A big black Toyota V-8 – one of those vehicles that had come to be synonymous with excessive power and entitlement – was parked, driverless, in the middle of the road, blocking everything; a couple of bodyguards in shiny suits and shades lounged nearby. I craned my neck around and made out the number plate. It read "SS Tonj 01." This was evidently the car of the governor of one of those twenty-eight new states that were causing so much trouble. Somebody standing by me caught my eye, smiled, and said, "You know what? There's not even a single road in Tonj. That car will never leave Juba."

Taban Deng was at the convention because a few days after the float of the South Sudan pound, on 21 December, the IO had finally sent a modest delegation back to Juba to negotiate security conditions for Riek Machar's return. A few days later a second wave arrived.

These arrivals occurred very quietly, partly on account of extensive groundwork undertaken by the UN at the Juba Protection of Civilians site, where the IO was thought to have many semi-clandestine supporters. Among the returnees were several Canadians. I met with one on a sunny Saturday morning in February, at Rainbow, the Ethiopian restaurant around the corner from our apartment.

Like many in the diaspora, Ding had one family in Canada – he mentioned a fourteen-year-old daughter at school in Calgary – and another here. Although his South Sudanese family was currently in Kakuma refugee camp, Kenya, Ding's home was Ulang, Upper Nile, which I'd visited a couple of years earlier. He had been in South

Sudan on and off since 2004. He stayed in touch with the diaspora in Canada, and took a call from Calgary (where it must have been past midnight) as we sat over our coffee.

"Yes, our community is very worried about the slow progress of peace implementation and all the problems since August," he said, as he fished out a tatty old letter that identified him formally as a legal advisor within the 10's Foreign Affairs secretariat. He dismissed the significance of the SPLM convention, which supposedly finalized the reunification of the SPLM. "Neither Taban nor anyone in the 10 has even received a copy of the Constitution to comment on, so how can we say it is reunified?" He also said that a lot of his companions no longer saw the SPLM as the necessary vehicle for government; there was a need for totally new parties.

When we went further into what the 10 was thinking, Ding shook his head and said that none of the broader 10 delegation in Juba met with Chief Negotiator Taban Deng and his sidekick Dhieu Mathok. "We just see him on television, like you do." He commented bitterly that on arrival, each delegation member had been given one hundred South Sudanese pounds in cash (about five US dollars) and basically left to their own devices, "but Taban has his own V-8, his body-guards." Ding didn't discount the idea that Taban could have his own agenda (including the VP job currently on offer to Riek), saying that he had had a forty-minute meeting alone with President Kiir and had refused to divulge what they talked about.

Meanwhile, Ding had been round to the Ministry of Justice to see his old boss, my old friend Undersecretary Jeremiah Swaka, only to be given a formal letter of dismissal, accompanied by the comment, "You'd better see what job Riek has for you." Like many, he'd had a house in Juba at the time he fled; this was now occupied by an SPLA officer. He said he had spoken by phone to the officer, who admitted he was squatting, but that he was afraid to pursue the case aggressively. He assumed that matters such as this would be followed up once the new government was formed.

We talked a lot about the twenty-eight-states order. Ding said that the new borders represented a blatant attempt to impose Dinka hegemony, and that they were sure to lead to further conflict. He identified in particular the new Ruweng State, which annexed the Bul Nuer County of Abiemnon to Dinka-dominated Pharyang and put it under Dinka leadership. "The Nuer simply will not accept this." We had a mutual friend in fellow Canadian Peter Lam Both, who had been named governor of the new state of Latjor. "He's a fool if he goes up there; the government controls the town, but we are close enough to shell it if we wanted," Ding said. He conceded, however, that even the 10's counter-proposal of twenty-one states – based on colonial-era county boundaries – was ethnically based and almost equally unaffordable at this moment when the government's coffers were bare.

Was Riek Machar concerned for his security? "Well, yes."

But Ding admitted that none of the 10 delegation had been bothered in any way, and that the demilitarization plan for Juba – by which the SPLA were to pull out twenty-five kilometres from the city limits – actually placed the SPLA in full command of routes in and out, which was not necessarily advantageous to the 10. He blithely confirmed that solidarity behind Riek was far less than 100 per cent and that there was a school of opinion that favoured simply going back to war to achieve a more decisive result. He was under no illusion that, insofar as politicians conspired to loot and mismanage South Sudan upon independence in 2011, Riek was partly to blame.

Johnson Olony, Riek Machar's most powerful general, was not interested in Juba politics at all, Ding confirmed. He was incensed at the way Shillook territory in Upper Nile was being carved up under the twenty-eight-states proposal, and was ready to start fighting at any time. "We could walk into Malakal if we wanted"; only pressure from Riek and a bout of malaria was holding Olony back. En passant, Ding acknowledged the 10 had received some in-kind support from Khartoum. "They do not want to see Salva Kiir succeed." But he nodded with a smile when I added that maybe they didn't want to see Riek succeed either.

When I saw Ding later, he'd made another attempt to get his old job back. Jeremiah Swaka had greeted him with a few sarcastic remarks but reluctantly put him back on the payroll. "The trouble is," he said morosely, "with devaluation and everything else, that's now worth about two hundred dollars a month."

In the last quarter of 2015, in accordance with the peace agreement, the Joint Monitoring and Evaluation Commission (JMEC) was established.[1] This was meant to be the body responsible for overseeing peace implementation. It comprised two representatives each from the government and the 10, one each from the former detainees, two from religious denominations, one each from youth, business, the women's bloc, and a range from the international community. The JMEC was chaired by a former president of Botswana, Festus Mogae. After a short bout of unseemly inter-donor squabbling, I was elected to represent – in rotation with my Dutch colleague – a large group of Western and other interested countries known as the IGAD Partners' Forum, or IPF. The big players – UK, US, Norway, EU, China – all had their own seats.

We met every two to four weeks, initially in the cramped and hot premises of an NGO across the dusty dirt road from the American Embassy. Mogae was a quiet but dogged chair with a personal commitment to the ordinary people of South Sudan – whom he increasingly came to see as having been shamefully betrayed by their leaders – that was quite moving. He would often talk of his own childhood in Botswana. Although Mogae had not gone to school until he was eleven, he was grateful for all the chances given to him, which included a place at Oxford followed by a successful career in politics, and appealed to both the government and the rebels not to forget the children of South Sudan.

These appeals were studiously ignored.

The meetings were invariably long, and progress frustratingly slow. Taban Deng for the IO and Michael Makuei and Nhial Deng for the government would spend most of each meeting either engaged in mutual recrimination or blaming the donor countries on the other side of the table for not financing the peace process generously enough. But they would also find time to josh with each other, usually when the representatives of youth or the women's bloc were remonstrating at their manifest cynicism.

As had become my role, I pushed the cause of the humanitarians. By this stage of the crisis, forty-nine humanitarian workers had been killed; food convoys travelling from Juba to Bentiu had to pass through fifty to sixty checkpoints at which each truck had to pay an average of $1,500 to $2,000 USD (in total) to police or SPLA. Several civilian contractors had also been killed. Makuei's response to this was, "Tell the humanitarians they should not pay. They are actually bribing people." When I pressed him, pointing out that the money was being demanded at gunpoint by uniformed men in the employ of the government, he shrugged angrily and said, "Well, alright, tell them to pay, and then they should complain to the relevant authorities. But don't bring it up here; it's not my responsibility."

I also found opportunities to discuss my other obsession: accountability. The authorized version of the African Union's Commission of

Inquiry (CoI) was now out; although it eschewed some of the more emphatic recommendations of the leaked Mamdani excerpt (notably the call to prevent Riek Machar and Salva Kiir from seeking office again), it was still a hard-hitting document. It recommended the establishment of a hybrid court for South Sudan, and this provision had gone on to be incorporated into the peace agreement itself. Accordingly, I had diplomatic "cover."

I was – as I had been on the Juba diplomatic circuit – politely listened to in the JMEC, but not much more. The African Union, two and a half years from the onset of the atrocities in Juba, had developed a short matrix, on paper, of the main steps to set up the court. And there things stood.

More concretely, by late February 2016, the JMEC had a deal for the return of Riek Machar's advance guard to Juba, following which he would form the long-awaited transitional government of national unity. But the deadlines kept being deferred as new conditions were imposed. Had the SPLA truly withdrawn from Juba as it had promised? Why were the UN and the donors not prepared to fly in the IO's heavy weapons along with their troops?

The major donors had agreed to finance the IO's return, although many of the smaller Western countries, including Canada, had balked on ethical as much as financial grounds. Some of the opposition's requirements were outrageous, including US$500,000 for gymnastics equipment for their portion of the new joint presidential guard, and the latest model iPads. I was getting the feeling that we were forcing the peace process too hard. Had not the IO financed two years of war without any external support? Why couldn't they walk back, as they had walked out, if they really wanted peace? But the big players (i.e. the troika), insisted that we should do everything possible so that we could never be accused of having been cheap when it came to peace. A fine line was drawn by which they would bring in AK-47s and pistols, but not machine guns and RPGs.

A looming new issue was the presence of armed elements of the IO in Greater Equatoria and Greater Bahr-al-Ghazal. The peace agreement referred to post-peace "cantonment" sites for the IO only in the three states of Greater Upper Nile. But there had been outbreaks of organized violence in the two other regions, so that it was no longer appropriate to speak of only three "conflict states."

It was a moot point whether all these militias or armed groups were under the command or even the influence of the IO. Some were certainly sympathetic; many were more anti-Dinka than pro-IO and owed their existence as much to heavy-handed SPLA repression as to political grievance; and some were just bandits. It seemed that the closer we edged to peace, the more these groups gained strength, and there was a sense that some had gone into the bush largely because, when peace came, they wanted to be in a position to negotiate some kind of benefit.

It was politically advantageous for the IO to give the impression that they were a national movement while for the government the converse was true: they insisted that these groups were "criminals" to whom ceasefire agreements did not apply. There was a large dose of hypocrisy at play on both sides. While the government professed not to recognize any IO presence in the two regions, it was quick to lodge ceasefire-infringement allegations with JMEC's monitoring mechanism. As for the IO, we started to think that one reason Riek was delaying his return to Juba was that once he was back, he would have to bring these armed groups into line. This he manifestly could not do.

The longer this series of JMEC meetings went on, the more inevitable it seemed to me that everything we did would be in vain. Nobody had won the war, and all the peace process would do would be to put things back the way they had been in mid-2013. It was increasingly likely that the transitional government would see the same venal and self-serving politicians who had wrecked the country back in office. We would have one slate of ministers loyal to the president, another to the vice-president, huge distrust between them, and an economy in ruins. Surely it would only be a matter of time before full-scale violence broke out again?

By now I was the longest-serving Western diplomat on Juba, something of a Cassandra, the foreteller of doom. There were, no doubt, a few grimaces and rolling eyes behind my back when I spoke out. "So, what do you suggest?" they would retort, tiredly. I had little to put forward that had not been tried. The chances of lasting peace looked slimmer by the day, but what moral choice was there other than to persevere?

———————

Out in the POCs, 200,000 people waited, distrustful of all talk of peace. And on 17 February 2016, fighting broke out within the Malakal POC.

It started as a dispute between Shillook and Dinka youth but escalated, and uniformed members of the SPLA poured through a breach in the perimeter fence in defence of their fellow Dinka. Fighting intensified, and fires broke out in Sectors 1, 2, and 3, destroying shelters and humanitarian infrastructure, including a medical centre and health outpost. Twenty-four thousand IDPs – exclusively Shillook – fled into the adjoining UNMISS logistics base and old POC sites, while the six thousand Dinka IDPs left the camp and sought refuge in the ruins of Malakal, three kilometres away.[2]

So many of us had given up criticizing the state, and so many people liked to make the UN the scapegoat that, against all logic, the blame for this atrocity was directed at the hapless peacekeepers. In reality, everything seemed to point to the existence of a sinister plan by the authorities – at what level, it was not clear – to "cleanse" the east bank of the Nile of Shillooks. This fitted with the infamous twenty-eight-states scheme, and in fact the newly named governor of the (newly created) East Nile state, with its capital as Malakal, had recently said he would not employ any Shillooks in his government even though Malakal was traditionally multi-ethnic (Shillook, Dinka, and Nuer).

As humanitarians glumly picked through the wreckage, a further issue emerged. All river travel was banned by the SPLA, ostensibly to stop the flow of weapons into the camp from across the Nile. The principal effect, however, was to keep humanitarian assistance from the roadhead and airport at Malakal from the huge IDP settlement of Shillooks on the west bank, Wau Shillook. Under the auspices of UNICEF, and accompanied by fellow ambassadors from Norway, the UK, and France, I flew up to Malakal to see if we could free up access to Wau Shillook.

The morning we landed was oddly dark and grey; for some days, the shadow of an enormous *haboub* – a dust storm generated in the Sahara – had been blocking the sun across the north of the country. The feeling was eerie, like the hours before a tornado strikes. The scene within the POC was bleak in the extreme. An area the size of two or three football fields had been completely destroyed, leaving only charred debris and ashes; piles of still-smoking metal could be found on every corner. What had been the best medical clinic in all Upper Nile state, run by the NGO IMC, was reduced to a single table from its operating theatre that was too heavy to carry away. I watched small boys scavenging for scraps of metal while women tried to beat fire-blackened sheets of corrugated iron flat, for reuse.

Almost as shocking as the destruction was the neat delineation between the flattened Shillook areas and the intact Dinka zones. The

Shillook whose homes had been burned down were now living higgledy-piggledy in open spaces and wet ditches among the containers and bulldozers belonging to the UNMISS soldiers in the adjoining UN logistics base. Harassed UNICEF staff were attempting to marshal hundreds of children separated from their parents by flight or death into lines. Most humanitarian agencies – including War Child Canada, whose lonely flag I saw snapping in the hot breeze – had suspended routine operations to deal with this totally bereft population before the rains foretold by that hanging *haboub*.

I inspected the hole cut in the cyclone fence where, at 2:00 a.m. on the night in question, trucks had allegedly arrived to evacuate Dinka citizens, and through which SPLA soldiers subsequently poured, firing their weapons. There was a guard post directly opposite it. I hesitated to speculate about what had happened that night, but a key question to be answered by the UN board of inquiry was why the Rwandan peacekeeping troops did not prevent the entry of hostile militia.

Perhaps in reaction to what occurred (although UNMISS did not say as much), the UN's state coordinator had been replaced with an old friend, the eminently competent and indefatigable Hazel de Wet, who had the sad but salutary experience of fixing the Bor Protection of Civilians Site after its perimeter was similarly breached, in April 2014, with even more disastrous results. Hazel admitted frankly that her entire team was demoralized, not least by the avalanche of criticism that her peacekeepers were directly responsible for what had happened. Her top priority was to increase perimeter security. "But you know," she said in her South African twang, "the Indian engineering battalion, I don't want to be negative, but their gear belongs in a World War II museum."

After that, she needed to figure out what to do with the 25,000 people crowding the logistics base, and then she needed to develop a contingency plan for an attack on Malakal by Johnson Olony (recently back in the vicinity) that would likely drive 6,000 Dinka back into the POC. This in turn could generate another explosion. "You know," she mused, "while I insist that this is a site for the protection of all civilians, the fact is – and I hate to say this – but we're going to have to make arrangements to separate the Dinka from the other two ethnicities. I find myself thinking of those homelands back in the last days of apartheid."

I couldn't but be impressed by the enormity of these challenges and Hazel's quiet equanimity in taking them on. It put my job and those of my fellow diplomats into perspective.

We talked about the issue of access across the Nile, and Hazel despatched us to the port within the POC compound. Here several large UN barges and a dozen or fifteen smaller INGO craft were tied up; a couple of SPLA soldiers were lounging around, letting themselves be seen. The commander of the UN/Bangladeshi riverine unit came to greet us and proudly showed us his high-powered RIBs, hauled out on trailers. I was tempted to ask him how it was that humanitarians had trouble crossing the river when, unlike the SPLA, he had patrol boats and like the SPLA, his men were well-armed. Why couldn't he simply enforce the access? But this was a problem all across the country: the UN had caved in so many times that there was no longer any appetite to be proactive and forceful.

In town, we sought out Chol Thon, the governor. He was based in the only intact building in this post-apocalyptic city, which had changed hands eleven times. On this occasion, he was not wearing his lieutenant-general's uniform but rather a flowing cream and embroidered robe. He kept us waiting half an hour.

I led, by agreement with the other ambassadors. There was prevarication from the governor, repeated assurances were delivered, the SPLA blamed for not having followed the orders of the civilian authority. There was some economy with the truth, I suspected; Hazel had assured us that there was no daylight between the governor and the commanding general, whom Chol Thon outranked. The governor was also at great pains to address the persistent allegations that, as a Dinka, he was bent on ethnically cleansing Malakal of all Shillook. "I am here to serve regardless of the ethnicity of my people," he insisted. But he did suggest that the mayhem in the camp was due to Shillook loyal to Olony, who had smuggled weapons in. This explanation failed to take into account the fact that the only areas of the camp destroyed were the Shillook areas and that all the dead were Shillook.

Malakal itself was an eerie ruin, a tropical version of a *Mad Max* set. Driving repeatedly up and down, I did not observe a single building not severely damaged in some way, not one intact glass pane. The wrecks of burned-out cars and trucks cluttered the dirt roads; hunchbacked Marabou storks picked through vast piles of debris and garbage. Heavily armed soldiers loitered on every corner and under every balcony. When the governor drove past after our meeting (and we edged to the very side of the road), it was in his armoured V-8 with an escort of eleven other vehicles; at the head and tail of the convoy were camouflage technicals with heavy machine guns, their crew impassive in reflective shades.

On the edge of town were more expanses of wrecked cars; men and boys picked over them, presumably for spare parts. But who would need any?

The hapless Dinka IDPs were scattered in several locations, including the courtyards of abandoned schools and the large yard in front of the main mosque where a few enterprising Sudanese traders had set up their stalls. They were angry and fearful, conscious that they were seen as the villains of this piece. But they were victims as well: most of them had trekked here two years earlier when Pigi County in Unity State, 200 kilometres away, was overrun by the IO (armed opposition). Now they pleaded with the UN not to abandon them.

Humanitarians had taken up the gauntlet. With the city's water system long destroyed, World Vision installed two SWAT systems of a kind I'd seen them employing with Canadian support in Melut a few weeks earlier: huge bladders fed by river water that was then purified. I was pleased to find, lovingly tending the installation, Jackson: the ultra-keen and knowledgeable South Sudanese engineer who'd explained everything to me in Melut.

As we flew back to Juba, I remembered happier days eating curried goat bones as I'd waited to take the barge north from Malakal, another visit when the pilot had to start his engine with a baseball bat, and the time when I'd spent a couple of days here trying to get to Ulang. It had been vibrant, busy, multicultural; the streets and the waterfront crowded with people of every race and in every kind of dress. Now Malakal was a haunting vision of what all of South Sudan might become if its leaders did not pull back from the abyss: a lawless wasteland where all that mattered was your ethnicity and the calibre of your weapon.

Down at the waterfront that day I'd seen a single, sad donkey in the dusk, water being loaded into the blue barrel he was pulling. The spectacle of the destruction in the POC had left me simply mute. What hope remained was to be found in the spirit and courage of members of the humanitarian community. By no means were they all well-meaning but equally well-paid white people from outside.

Ninety per cent of the humanitarian effort was delivered by South Sudanese nationals.

But next morning, back at the office, I had an unexpected high. I heard from the team in Malakal that we had managed to break the logjam and that the first humanitarians in weeks were crossing to Wau Shillook. Contrary to our expectations, Governor Chol Thon had kept his word.

———————

In March 2016, with only a few months left in my posting, I made what I was sure would be my last visit back to headquarters to rattle a few chains and remind the powers that be that South Sudan existed. It was typical March weather in Ottawa: slushy snow on the streets, the temperature oscillating between minus twenty and plus five. I was ill-equipped for the weather with only rubber boots and a thin fleece sweater; friends remarked that I was more poorly clothed than the Syrian refugees who had been pouring into Canada for the past few weeks.

As I did my rounds at Foreign Affairs everyone listened politely, attentively even. But they inadvertently confirmed my impression that I was seen as slightly eccentric, oddly attached to a place that seemed to generate only horror. My shortcomings on the adminis-trative front – and these were legion – were kindly discounted in this regard, perhaps with the secret thought, "He'll be leaving soon anyway."

On the final night of a hectic week of meetings – I would need to be up at 5:00 the next morning to start a forty-eight-hour journey back to Juba via Cairo – I was feeling a little maudlin, knowing I had likely met many of my colleagues for the last time and that I would never have a reason to come back to Ottawa. My last event was a meeting with the South Sudanese diaspora at Ottawa University. I had asked for it, even though I feared the community could only be angry and grief-stricken.

The upstairs hall was full, the audience seventy or so expectant South Sudanese–Canadians. We were late, which made me nervous. Standing at the podium, feeling awkward in my dark suit and rubber boots, I riffled through my handwritten notes and outlined what I would talk about. It went well. I told anecdotes here and there, and there was laughter at the right moments, silence at the grimmer places. I dwelt at length on my experiences those two terrible days in

December 2013. I spoke for maybe forty minutes before Professor Baranyi, the moderator, opened the floor for questions.

In the second row to my left, a well-dressed and bespectacled man slowly stood up, pulling his shy seven-year-old to stand beside him. I looked over. As he started to speak, a rush of recognition surged through me.

"I am Peter Pal," he said. "I was there that day at the airport. This is my daughter. Maybe you remember her. We are here. We are safe ..."

I scarcely heard the rest.

Before I knew it Peter Pal, whom I'd last waved goodbye to as he boarded the Royal Air Force C-17 to Entebbe, was embracing me. I am not often speechless, but that night I was. It was the proudest moment of my career in the foreign service of Canada.

16

Riek Returns

Juba, April 2016

It was April, the start of the rainy season in South Sudan. Eight months had elapsed since the peace agreement had been signed, twenty-eight since civil war broke out. Still, Riek Machar procrastinated over coming back to launch the transitional government. Across the country and inside the grim Protection of Civilians sites, millions fretted that they were going to miss yet another planting season.

First a return date was set for Tuesday, 12 April. Then it slipped to the following Monday. As Monday morning crept closer and there were no further postponements, we started to believe it could actually happen. Large billboards welcoming Riek back – financed by his supporters – appeared around the city.

That day, from the early hours, diplomats began phoning, texting, and e-mailing each other. Would we be invited to the arrival ceremony? When would it be? What would happen then? Having learned that some colleagues had received official invitations, I spent much of the morning haggling and arguing with the Ministry of Foreign Affairs and State House protocol: how come some ambassadors were invited to participate and others not? A plasticized VIP pass with a red ribbon finally made it by messenger to the embassy.

Meanwhile, the city went into lockdown. The gates of the Juba POC were closed and by 7:00 in the morning, all the main streets were blocked by SPLA and police, with only diplomatic-plated vehicles allowed to move. The shops on Airport Road were all shuttered, the street lined with soldiers every fifty metres or so. It was the quietest I had ever seen the place.

Journalists tweeting from Gambella, Ethiopia, Riek Machar's point of departure just across the border from his HQ at Pagak,

informed us excitedly that two Ethiopian Airlines turboprops chartered by the US to bring him back were on the tarmac.

Nothing happened.

Until 4:00 in the afternoon everything in Juba was held in readi-
ness. US ambassador Molly Phee and the genial Ethiopian ambassador – "Fish," we called him, rather than attempt his real name
– worked the phones and their rolodexes all day. But Riek didn't
show. Now there was no way he could arrive before dark.

Next morning, 19 April and another sunny day, it was lockdown
again. Time for another try. The aircraft were back in Gambella and
this time, Riek was there. With our little Canadian flag flying,
Mandrea and I drove down in the mission's armoured vehicle to the
VVIP arrivals area, near the UN base at one end of the airport.

In a gloomy, heavily curtained room with very deep but impracti-
cal armchairs, we waited. The Dutch ambassador was here; so was
the Somali, the Arab League ambassador who barely spoke English,
the large and placid Egyptian. A tea lady brought us scalding glasses
of over-sweetened chai. A few representatives of the IO, oddly dressed
in suits but with commemorative white tee-shirts and white baseball
caps, wandered in and out. They didn't seem to know anything.
Outside, thirty or forty members of the media gossiped in a shady
area; every so often I walked out to see if the red carpet had been
rolled out. A group of colourfully dressed ladies arrived with a
wooden crate containing half a dozen white pigeons. They sat at one
end of the VVIP lounge under a flashing set of fairy lights left over
from Christmas, and we smiled at each other.

Rumours came and went; eventually Simona, from the *Guardian*,
told me that she had heard that IO chief of staff General Simon
Gatwech would be arriving first at 2:00 p.m., followed by Riek
Machar on a second plane at 3:00, followed by a third plane. The
Dutch ambassador and I sloped off, leaving all the others to wait in
silence. We returned in the early afternoon to find that military buses
had been arranged and a larger welcome contingent was now in
place. Even the pigeons seemed to be excited and were cooing loudly.
Things were looking up.

Then there was a commotion outside. Ezekiel Lol, the IO spokesperson and ex–South Sudanese ambassador in Washington, called a
brief press conference: "I am sorry; you must go home now. Dr
Machar will not be coming today. The government has refused to
clear the aircraft of our chief of staff, General Gatwech."

A small-scale propaganda war began. The government explained that it had refused to clear Gatwech's aircraft because he wanted to bring heavy weapons along with him: "laser-guided missiles, anti-tank weapons and heavy machine guns." They also said that he was insisting on a larger escort than that agreed to.

Diplomats huddled, and an emergency meeting was called of the JMEC for Thursday, 21 April. With the US ambassador in the lead but regional partners all in strong support, we agreed that we should have Chairman Mogae table a "take-it-or-leave-it" proposal:

- That the parties agree that the current security conditions in Juba are adequate and sufficient for the return of Dr Riek;
- That Dr Riek and his accompanying forces are allowed to return to Juba with 20 PKMs (light machine guns) and 20 RPG-7s, which are consistent with the SPLA practice of associating specified weapons organic to a specified military unit, and that CTSAMM (ceasefire monitoring mechanism; the successor to the MVM) should verify these weapons;
- That the SPLA-IO Chief of the General Staff be accompanied by a maximum of 195 security forces, which will be deducted from the remaining authorized Phase Two numbers;
- That Dr Riek is able to travel with his previously agreed delegation of 75, to include both his security detail and civilian staff, with the number of the security detail deducted from the remaining authorized Phase Two numbers.

If the parties did not respond affirmatively, either by reaching a different resolution between themselves or by accepting the compromise, then we proposed that Mogae take the following steps:

1 Request IGAD Heads of State to hold an emergency summit;
2 Report the failure of the parties to abide by the peace agreement to the AU Peace and Security Council and request consideration of an appropriate response;
3 Report the failure of the parties to abide by the peace agreement to the UN Security Council and request consideration of an appropriate response.

The JMEC gathered promptly at 10:00 a.m. in a half-completed office building owned by the UAP insurance company. Things started very badly.

Mogae, always urbane but sometimes lacking firmness, allowed the first hour to be consumed by a matter that was important but not germane to the crisis at hand: the representation in parliament and in the JMEC itself of "the political parties" comprising the non-armed parliamentary opposition to the SPLM. In an effort to resolve this matter, he had taken the liberty of inviting along the principal rival to Dr Lam Akol, who actually held the JMEC seat. This rival happened to be a cabinet minister (non-cognoscenti asked how it was that he could thus call himself "opposition," but that was a complicated question). It was an ill-advised move that led to acrimonious exchanges of barely veiled insults, with the interloper – Martin Elia Lomuro – forcing his way to the table and then ostentatiously either sleeping or interrupting at inopportune moments. There was some suspicion that he may have been intoxicated.

Once this distraction had faded, Mogae tabled the detailed proposal we had drawn up the previous day. Taban Deng, the IO's chief negotiator, immediately accepted it but the government did not. Its chief negotiator, Nhial Deng, argued vehemently that it was Riek Machar who had been moving the goalposts (true), and that the ratio of weapons should be based on the numbers brought in so far, which would have meant an allocation of seven of each class, not twenty. The discussion went back and forth, shifting steadily against the government. Sitting opposite Nhial Deng, American ambassador Phee argued, "The basis for the numbers is your own law and, in any case, it does not significantly alter the balance of military power in Juba, which is overwhelmingly in the government's favour."

The meeting ended with the threat that the three-step diplomatic offensive (referral to IGAD heads of state, then the AUPSC, finally the UNSC) would be deployed unless agreement was reached between the parties on their own, to allow a return by Saturday, 23 April. This was a quiet showing of the sanctions card. As we filed out, John Luk, of the former detainees' bloc, shook his head and said to me, "It's impossible. They will allow South Sudan to be taken to the United Nations Security Council … over thirteen machine guns? I just cannot believe it!"

That evening, the government almost caved. Later we learned that Nhial Deng reported the international proposal to President Salva Kiir, who immediately upbraided him for not having accepted it at the outset with much the same reproach that John Luk had expressed to me. But Nhial Deng and Makuei were determined not to lose face.

Under the pretext that the airport needed to close for repairs over the weekend, they said Riek's aircraft would not be permitted to fly until Monday. The US, which had kept that pair of aircraft waiting in Gambella for three days to no avail, lost patience. The planes were sent back to Addis and would not come back. A firm message was communicated to both parties that the US was now contemplating withdrawing all further support for the peace process. The gesture worked.

Around 2:00 p.m. on Tuesday, 26 April, eight months to the day after the signing of the Agreement on Resolution of the Conflict, Riek Machar – wearing a colourful Mandela-style African shirt and a pork-pie trilby – boarded the UN aircraft that SRSG Ellen Loej had stepped in to supply. They took off for Juba.

The combination of realistic threats, regional and broader international solidarity, and the US making good on its threat to withdraw financial support for one element of the peace process had a salutary effect. We had never achieved such solidarity before: both the government and the IO were nonplussed and reacted the way we hoped. But this modest success, I feared, would be hard to repeat.

Even at the very last moment, Ellen Loej later told me, there had been a heart-stopping glitch. The most suitable aircraft on hand was a white Bombardier CRJ jet on semi-permanent charter to UNMISS, which normally shuttled back and forth between Juba and Entebbe.

"Those Canadian crews, you know," she said with a rueful smile. "They are very safety-conscious. I like that, but I didn't that day."

"What do you mean?"

"Well, they were already in the air, flying direct from Entebbe to Gambella. Then, Lord and behold, the flight attendant protested that this service was outside the company's terms of reference, and that she did not feel safe flying with such a controversial personage as Riek Machar. She asked to be put off in Juba. Now you can imagine with all the issues we had had about landing permits ... The captain was sensible enough to say to the ground that he needed to land in Juba because of bad weather in Gambella – which was not so – and we were able very quietly to switch the attendant for a substitute."

Riek touched down in Juba at 15:45. He was greeted on the tarmac by those white pigeons (now tired-looking) and a chaotic line, one hundred metres long, of dignitaries. We diplomats were asked to arrange ourselves in order of seniority, which is the correct diplomatic protocol but which requires much exchanging of notes over who arrived first in South Sudan. There was some undignified scrimmaging and, by chance, I was able to jostle myself into a good spot by the time Riek reached me. He paused for a moment and his eye wandered to the small Canada/South Sudan flag pin I was wearing.

"Ah, the Canadian, haven't we met before?"

"Yes indeed. Welcome back ..."

The swearing in was held an hour later at the main auditorium of J-1, a hall I'd last visited on the first morning of the December 2013 crisis, when the then foreign minister – as machine guns crackled in the background, and having to pause as tanks clanked past – had assured us, "There has been a minor misunderstanding; it will all blow over." That minor misunderstanding had cost at least 50,000 lives over the past twenty-eight months. Two million people had fled their homes, and the country was now on the edge of economic collapse.

There was a palpable mood of optimism as Riek took his oath. Fair enough, I thought; we'd waited a long time for this moment. But what had we – the diplomats – really achieved? Salva Kiir was still president. Riek Machar was back as vice-president and – as we would discover in a few days' time – the new cabinet would be very much like that in mid-2013, when the conflict had started. The omens for South Sudan were not good.

Epilogue

For several weeks following Riek's return to Juba not much happened. Citing fears for his safety, he declined to occupy the office of the vice-presidency and operated from a suite of containers at one of the three sites designated to be occupied by the 1,370 armed soldiers who had been authorized to accompany him. IO troops could occasionally be seen on the city streets wearing non-standard olive-green fatigues that conspiracy theorists alleged to have been supplied by Khartoum, but with the regular SPLA shoulder flash. Paul Malong, chief of the mainstream SPLA, met with his IO counterpart, Simon Gatwech, and the two were photographed embracing and feasting on a sacrificial cow. Those such as myself who had wondered at the wisdom of the international community paying Riek Machar and his armed rebels to return to a city that was (contrary to the terms of the peace agreement) as highly militarized as ever started to look unduly pessimistic.

But Riek did not meet even once for face-to-face talks with Salva Kiir. Oddly, he did not meet either with his own de facto deputy and the IO's chief negotiator, Taban Deng. Bickering in parliament over the election of a speaker delayed the formation of the transitional legislature mandated by the ARC. A much-vaunted multi-party commission with a mandate to·review the matter of the twenty-eight states also failed to meet. The economic crisis deepened, with the South Sudan pound reaching new lows against the US dollar; by late 2016 the dollar could buy you about one hundred pounds (versus three on my arrival in 2012).

On Friday, 1 July, after nearly four years in South Sudan, Jenny and I flew out to retirement, with my successor due to arrive in September.

On Thursday, 7 July, a skirmish between 10 and regular SPLA soldiers in the Gudele neighbourhood of Juba left five dead. The next
day Salva Kiir, Riek Machar, and Second Vice-President Wani Igga
met at J-1 to discuss this incident and – as Salva later put it – discuss
implementation of the peace agreement. But even as they were meeting, fighting between the rival factions escalated. By the afternoon of
Saturday, 9 July – the fifth anniversary of the independence of South
Sudan – at least 146 people had been killed. Riek fled to his container
compound on the edge of the city.

Another twenty-four hours and the government confirmed
271 dead as combat continued.[1] Helicopter gunships were seen
launching rockets and machine-gunning over the areas assigned for
the cantonment of 10 troops. The UN would later blame the government for widespread violations of human rights, including killing
Nuer civilians,[2] and a separate UN panel concluded – in a confiden-
tial report whose findings were leaked – that much of the fighting was
directed from the highest levels of government and the SPLA.[3]
Canada evacuated its two diplomats and closed the embassy; most
other diplomatic missions, including the US, and many NGOs also
drew down their staff.

By 12 July 2016, the fighting was over and Riek Machar had disappeared. He resurfaced, accompanied by his wife Angelina and ten 10
soldiers, in the Democratic Republic of Congo, just across the border
from South Sudan, on 17 August. The UN arranged for him to continue to Kinshasa but did not facilitate travel within South Sudan.
On 23 July, Taban Deng moved into the vice-presidency, claiming
that he was the de facto leader of the 10 and that Riek had given up
his rights by fleeing. A number of other former 10 stalwarts shifted
– in fits and starts – to Taban's side; one of them was Hussein Mar.

On 24 August, American secretary of state John Kerry recognized
Taban Deng as the legitimate vice-president of South Sudan, and
added that Riek Machar should not seek to return. Other countries
were more hesitant: wasn't recognizing Taban tantamount to admitting that the Agreement on Resolution of the Conflict (ARC), which
had been signed by Riek, was now dead?

Apparently emboldened by the US's stance, Juba steadily hardened its language vis-à-vis Riek Machar, casting him as irrelevant
and discounting any future political role for him. In late September,
Riek called from Khartoum for a return to armed revolt. There was
no immediate or dramatic response but sporadic fighting began
occurring in places hitherto untouched by the conflict, notably Yei,

Kajo Keji, and other locations in the three Equatorias. Initially, this was a reaction to brutal, heavy-handed suppression by the SPLA of relatively minor expressions of discontent (or of criminality). No doubt seeking to capitalize on what was developing into a new front, Riek named Equatorian (and Canadian) Henry Odwar as his new number two in a reshuffle of deputies following the defection of several more IO officials to the government.

The government in Juba sought to declare that the civil war over, but ordinary people across the country felt otherwise. Following the resurgence of violence in July 2016, more had fled their homes. By February 2017, there were 1.85 million internally displaced persons, of whom 223,000 were housed at UN Protection of Civilians (POC) sites; 1.5 million more had sought refuge in neighbouring countries.[4] By October 2016, sixty-seven humanitarian workers[5] had been killed since the outbreak of the crisis in December 2013, making this the most dangerous location in the world for humanitarians.[6]

Is there light at the end of the tunnel? By early 2017, President Salva Kiir, seconded by top soldier Paul Malong, seemed to be relatively secure in his position. Although Riek Machar remained at large, his military capital was severely reduced, many of his allies having rejoined the government. The US was prepared to deal with a government led by Salva Kiir and Taban Deng rather than Salva Kiir and Riek Machar, even though this now rendered the ARC largely irrelevant.

Most of those on both sides who perpetrated the horrors of December 2013 and after remained in positions of influence. Impunity seemed to be the rule; the sense of injustice across the country was palpable. And those who knew Riek said that as long as he was alive, he would not renounce his ambition to govern South Sudan.

In late 2016, alarmed by reports that the government was once again training a special Dinka commando force at the president's estate at Luri, this time to finish off the IO, Ban Ki-Moon, outgoing secretary-general of the UN, raised the spectre of genocide. "I am afraid that process is about to begin unless immediate action is taken," he said. But it was Christmas time and there was no reaction from the broader international community. Even a modest proposal at the UN to impose an arms embargo on South Sudan failed when Japan, unwilling as ever to make waves, failed to vote in its favour.

Half a world away, I found myself recalling General Dallaire's comment, made more than a year earlier as he reflected on the similarities between pre-genocide Rwanda and South Sudan: "This place smells bad."

South Sudan: A Chronology

1955 – 18 August: The Southern corps of the Sudanese army mutinies in Torit, Eastern Equatoria. This is the beginning of the First Sudanese Civil War; the rebel movement becomes known as *Anyanya* (snake venom).

1956 – 1 January: Sudan becomes independent.

1972 – The Addis Ababa Peace Agreement ends the First Sudanese Civil War; a Southern Regional Government is established.

1975 – Low-intensity warfare starts as Anyanya veterans (Anyanya 2) rebel again.

1983 – May: The Sudan People's Liberation Movement/Army (SPLM/A) is founded in Ethiopia by Dr John Garang de Mabior; the Second Sudanese Civil War begins with a troop mutiny in Bor.

1988 – Anyanya 2 and the SPLA merge.

1991 – August: Shillook leader Dr Lam Akol and Nuer leader Dr Riek Machar head an internal revolt against the SPLM/A leadership of Dinka Dr John Garang and form the SPLM-Nasir (or SPLM United) faction.

1991 – 15 November: Riek Machar's troops attack Dinka civilians in Bor, killing up to 2,000. This becomes known as the Bor massacre.

1992 – The SPLM-Nasir faction announces its alliance with the central government in Khartoum.

1993 – SPLM-Nasir changes its name first to SPLM-United, then to South Sudan Independence Movement (SSIM); Dr Lam Akol quits the movement but retains the tag SPLM-United for his own faction.

1997 – 21 April: The central government signs a peace agreement (the Khartoum Agreement) with several Southern factions, including Riek Machar's SSIM. Riek becomes president of the Southern States Coordinating Council, and commander-in-chief of the South Sudan Defence Force, which retains autonomy from the main army of Sudan. However, the peace agreement does not gain international legitimacy as it does not take in the mainstream SPLM/A.

1997–2003: Bul Nuer General Paulino Matiep splits from Riek Machar; his forces clash periodically with Riek's, but primarily he opposes the mainstream SPLA. His becomes the largest Nuer faction aligned with Khartoum.

1989 – The UN-orchestrated Operation Lifeline Sudan (OLS) begins relief operations to the South, out of Lokichokkio (Kenya); factions loyal to Riek Machar have their own humanitarian wing, the Relief Association of Southern Sudan (RASS), while the mainstream SPLA's equivalent is the Sudan Relief and Rehabilitation Association (SRRA).

1998 – Canada's Talisman acquires Arakis Energy and full-scale development of the oil fields in Unity State begins.

2000 – Riek Machar withdraws from the Khartoum Agreement.

2002 – Riek Machar rejoins John Garang and the mainstream SPLM/A through the Nairobi Declaration on Unity and Integration.

2002 – July: Peace talks begin between Khartoum and the mainstream SPLM/A in Machakos, Kenya.

2003 – RASS and the SRRA (the relief arms of the two main factions) unite to become the Sudan Relief and Rehabilitation Commission (SRRC).

2003 – After intense shareholder pressure, Talisman divests and sells its share in the oil fields to ONGC of India.

2005 – January: The Comprehensive Peace Agreement (CPA), also known as the Naivasha Agreement, is signed in Kenya; it provides for a six-year interim period, to be followed by a referendum on independence for the South.

2005 – 30 July: Dr John Garang, founder of the SPLM, dies in a helicopter crash.

2006 – The Juba Declaration reintegrates Southern militias, including Matiep's, into the SPLA, which thus becomes numerically dominated by Nuers.

2011 – January: In a referendum, South Sudan votes by an overwhelming majority to secede.

2011 – June: Khartoum suspends plans for popular consultations in the disputed areas of South Kordofan (Nuba Mountains) and Blue Nile; SPLA units in those areas continue to fight against Khartoum, and become known as the SPLM/A-North (N).

2011 – 9 July: South Sudan becomes an independent state.

2013 – April: President Salva Kiir fires Vice-President Riek Machar.

2013 – July: The entire cabinet is reshuffled.

2013 – 4–5 December: The South Sudan Investment Conference is held.

2013 – Saturday, 14 December: The SPLM holds a meeting of its National Liberation Council (NLC) in Juba. On the evening of Sunday, 15 December, following the close of the meeting, heavy fighting erupts. Many Nuers are reported killed and the South Sudan Civil War begins.

2013 – Wednesday, 18 December: Reacting to news of the killings in Juba, rebel forces take Bor. It will change hands several times over the next few months.

2013 – Thursday, 19 December: Nuer militias attack the UN base at Akobo, killing two Indian peacekeepers and numerous civilians.

2013 – Friday, 27 December: The office of the Canadian Embassy closes; it re-opens in February 2014.

2014 – January through April: There is heavy fighting in the states of Unity, Jonglei, and Upper Nile, with the key towns of Bor, Malakal, and Bentiu changing hands several times. In April, in reaction to news of a rebel victory at Bentiu, Dinkas attack the UN's Protection of Civilians (POC) site at Bor.

2014 – January: The first Cessation of Hostilities Agreement is signed in Addis Ababa.

2014 – May: A second Cessation of Hostilities Agreement is signed.

2015 – February: A third Cessation of Hostilities Agreement is signed.

2015 – August: Following intense mediation on the part of IGAD, the Agreement on the Resolution of the Conflict in South Sudan (ARCISS) is signed, first in Addis Ababa by the rebels (IO), the former detainees, and the political parties, then on 26 August by President Salva Kiir in Juba, who appends a number of "reservations."

2015 – 2 October: President Salva Kiir unilaterally decrees the creation of twenty-eight states (out of the existing ten), in contradiction to the ARCISS (which is based on ten).

2015 – 27 October: The African Union's Commission of Inquiry report on South Sudan is released.

2015 – 24 December: President Salva Kiir names governors for each of the twenty-eight new states.

2016 – January: The First Extraordinary National Convention of the SPLM is held in Juba.

2016 – 17 February: Uniformed forces attack the UN's Malakal POC site.

2016 – 26 April: Riek Machar returns to Juba, and a few days later the transitional government of national unity (TGNU) is formed.

2016 – 8 July: Fighting breaks out in Juba between the IO and the SPLA; Riek Machar flees, to resurface in DRC on 18 August. The Canadian Embassy is evacuated for a second time.

2016 – 23 July: Taban Deng steps in to take over Riek Machar's job as first vice-president; the US acknowledges this and advises Riek not to return.

Acronyms

AMDISS – Association for Media Development in South Sudan (non-governmental)

ANC – African National Congress, the governing party of South Africa

ARC (ISS) – Agreement on Resolution of the Conflict (in South Sudan), signed in August 2015

AU – African Union

AUPSC – African Union Peace and Security Council (the African counterpart to the UN Security Council)

BBC – British Broadcasting Corporation

BP – British Petroleum

CARE – an international humanitarian relief agency founded in 1945

CCC – Confident Children out of Conflict; a non-governmental organization based in Juba

CCM – Chama Cha Mapinduzi; the governing party in Tanzania

CEPO – Community Empowerment for Progress Organization; an advocacy organization based in Juba

CIDA – Canadian International Development Agency; governmental (now merged with Global Affairs Canada)

CMI – Crisis Management Initiative, a Finnish non-governmental organization

CNN – Cable News Network

CNPC – China National Petroleum Company (state-owned)

CoI – Commission of Inquiry; an inquiry, mandated by the African Union, into the events of December 2013 in South Sudan

CPA – Comprehensive Peace Agreement; the agreement that brought the second Sudan civil war to an end in 2005

CRJ – Canadair Regional Jet; a family of aircraft made by Bombardier

CSI – Christian Solidarity International, a non-governmental organization focusing on human rights

CSR – corporate social responsibility

C-17 – a military transport aircraft made by Boeing

C-130 – a military transport aircraft made by Lockheed; also known as a Hercules

DDG – Danish De-mining Group; a non-governmental organization

DDR – disarmament, demobilization, and reintegration

ECHO – The humanitarian aid and civil protection agency of the European Union

EU – European Union

GDP – gross domestic product; a measure of a country's wealth

GFD – general food distribution; an exercise by which the World Food Program (inter alia) distributes free food to the population

GHQ – general headquarters; the headquarters of – in this instance – the SPLA

GOAL – An Irish development and humanitarian non-governmental organization

GPAA – The Greater Pibor Administrative Area; a semi-autonomous area within Jonglei State, South Sudan, coinciding with the former Pibor County, created in 2014; it was dissolved with the creation of twenty-eight states in 2015, becoming Boma State

GPS – global positioning system

G-8 – The Group of Eight (highly industrialized) nations: US, France, Italy, UK, Canada, Japan, Germany (plus Russia – suspended by the other seven in 2014)

ICC – International Criminal Court

ICRC – International Committee of the Red Cross

IDP – internally displaced person (as distinct from a refugee)

IGAD – The Intergovernmental Authority on Development, formerly IGADD, the Intergovernmental Authority on Drought and Desertification. A group of countries in East Africa (Djibouti, Ethiopia, Somalia, Sudan, South Sudan, Kenya, Uganda, Eritrea); mandated, in this instance, by the African Union to negotiate an end to the conflict in South Sudan

IHL – international humanitarian law

IMC – International Medical Corps; a non-governmental organization working in South Sudan and other countries

IMF – International Monetary Fund

INDBATT – Indian Battalion; when participating in UN peacekeeping operations, individual contingents are identified by such acronyms, cf CHINBATT (China), MONGBATT (Mongolia), etc.

INGO – international non-governmental organization

IO – See SPLM/A IO

IPF – The IGAD Partners' Forum; a large group of (mainly Western) countries and agencies acting in support of the development aims of IGAD

JDO – Joint Donor Office; a joint development partnership operational in Southern/South Sudan, originally including the UK, Canada, Netherlands, Sweden, Denmark, and Norway. Now wound down, but the acronym is still used to identify the old compound, on which the Dutch, Canadian and Norwegian Embassies now operate

JEM – Justice and Equality Movement; an armed rebel movement based in Darfur (Sudan)

JIA – Juba International Airport

JMEC – Joint Monitoring and Evaluation Commission; a body set up in the framework of the Agreement on Resolution of the Conflict in South Sudan to oversee implementation of the agreement; chaired by ex-president Festus Mogae (Botswana), its membership includes representatives of the international community, plus signatories to the Agreement

KCB – Kenya Commercial Bank

LES – locally engaged staff; a term used within the Canadian Foreign Ministry to describe national (i.e. non-Canadian) staff at missions

MNCH – maternal and neo-natal child health

MONUSCO – the UN's stabilization mission in the Democratic Republic of Congo

MSF – Médecins Sans Frontières; an international non-governmental organization, with a number of sub-groups (MSF/Spain, MSF/France etc.)

MVM – Monitoring and Verification Mission; an IGAD-sponsored monitoring mechanism initially set up to oversee ceasefire arrangements in South Sudan in early 2014; superseded by the Ceasefire and Transitional Security Arrangements Monitoring Mechanism (CTSAMM) following signature of the Agreement on the Resolution of the Conflict in August 2015

M-23 – A rebel movement in the Democratic Republic of Congo

NCA – Norwegian Church Aid; a non-governmental organization

NGO – non-governmental organization

NLC – National Liberation Council; group of approximately 200 senior members of South Sudan's SPLM; members are elected at national conventions (of which two have been held thus far); this is the party's main decision-making body

OCHA – (or UNOCHA); Office for the Coordination of Humanitarian Affairs, an agency of the UN

OLS – Operation Lifeline Sudan; a consortium of UN relief agencies and approximately thirty-six NGOs, established in 1989, based at Lokichokkio (northern Kenya); no longer operating

OXFAM – a large international development and humanitarian non-governmental organization

POC – Protection of Civilians; a concept central to the mandate of UNMISS, but an acronym now also applied to the several UN-protected enclaves of internally displaced persons within South Sudan, the largest of which is near Bentiu

RAF – (a) Royal Air Force (UK); (b) Rwandan Air Force (c) Red Army Foundation, a socially-oriented association of former child soldiers in South Sudan

RASS – Relief Association of Southern Sudan; during the civil war (1983–2005), this was the humanitarian agency of forces loyal to Dr Riek Machar

RIB – rigid inflatable boat

RPG – rocket-propelled grenade

R&R – rest and recreation; a term used to refer to special packages of benefits (extra leave, free air tickets) accruing to expatriates in South Sudan (and elsewhere)

SCC – Sudan Council of Churches; founded 1965; an ecumenical association of Christian churches based in Khartoum, Sudan. Following the independence of South Sudan, this was succeeded in the South by the South Sudan Council of Churches

SIGNET – The internal communications system of Global Affairs Canada

SPLA – Sudan People's Liberation Army; the army of the Republic of South Sudan. Founded as a guerrilla army in 1983, led by Dr John Garang, it was the dominant (but not sole) rebel movement in the civil war (note that the single S is retained)

SPLM – Sudan People's Liberation Movement; founded in 1983 as the political wing of the SPLA, this is the dominant political party in South Sudan (note that the single S is retained, notwithstanding the separation of South Sudan from Sudan)

SPLM/A – In light of the difficulty of distinguishing the SPLM from the SPLA, especially during the civil war years, the two acronyms are often combined thus

SPLM-N and SPLA-N – The political and military wings, respectively, of rebels in South Kordofan (Nuba Mountains; Sudan) and Blue Nile (Sudan), formerly integrated with the mainstream SPLM and SPLA, but separate entities since the independence of the South

SPLM-DC – SPLM-Democratic Change; an (unarmed) opposition party led by Dr Lam Akol; it subsequently changed its name to Democratic Change

SPLM/A-IO – SPLM/A In Opposition; the name taken by forces and politicians loyal to Dr Riek Machar following the incidents of December 2013 in Juba

SRRA – Sudan Relief and Rehabilitation Agency. During the war years, this was the humanitarian arm of the SPLM/A; it survives with the same acronym in South Kordofan and Blue Nile, but in South Sudan it merged in 2003 with RASS to form the South Sudan Relief and Rehabilitation Commission (SSRRC)

SRSG – Special representative of the secretary-general (of the United Nations); the top UN official in South Sudan; the first incumbent was the Norwegian Hilde Johnson, the second the Dane Ellen Loej

SSDF – (a) South Sudan Defence Forces, a pro-Khartoum militia that joined the mainstream SPLA after the Comprehensive Peace Agreement, in 2006; (b) South Sudan Democratic Forum, an unrelated political party that is currently in de facto coalition with the SPLM; its chairman, Dr Martin Elia Lomuro, serves as a cabinet minister

SSHARE – South Sudan Healthcare Accessibility, Rehabilitation and Education project, a program of CIDA that trained South Sudanese diaspora members as doctors and reinserted them into South Sudan

SSLM/A – South Sudan Liberation Movement/Army; an armed Nuer faction that resisted integration into the mainstream SPLA until 2013, remaining loosely aligned with Khartoum

SSNPS – South Sudan National Police Service

SSTV – The state broadcaster in South Sudan

SSUM – South Sudan Unity (or United) Movement. A pro-Khartoum, primarily Nuer Southern militia in the Sudan civil war (1983–2005), commanded by General Paulino Matiep; it was subsumed by the

South Sudan Defence Forces (SSDF), which in turn integrated with the SPLA under the Juba Declaration of 2006

START – Stabilization and Reconstruction Taskforce, a program of Global Affairs Canada

SWAT – Surface Water Treatment plant system; a technology used by development NGOs to produce clean drinking water

TGNU – transitional government of national unity; an interim administration mandated by the Agreement on Resolution of the Conflict in South Sudan in August 2015

TNT – trinitrotoluene; a form of explosive

UAP – An African financial services company that owns several buildings in Juba

UNAMID – United Nations/African Union (peacekeeping) Mission in Darfur (Sudan)

UNDP – United Nations Development Program

UNESCO – United Nations Educational, Scientific and Cultural Organization

UNFPA – United Nations Population Fund

UNHAS – United Nations Humanitarian Air Service; an air service for humanitarian agencies, with its own aircraft, operated by the UN's World Food Program

UNHCR – United Nations High Commission for Refugees

UNICEF – United Nations Children's Fund

UNMISS – United Nations (peacekeeping) Mission in South Sudan

UNPOL – United Nations Police

UNSC – United Nations Security Council

UPDF – Uganda People's Defence Force, the army of Uganda

USAID – United States Agency for International Development (governmental)

UXO – unexploded ordnance

VOIP – voice over internet protocol; a means of making telephone calls over the internet

WFP – World Food Program, an agency of the United Nations

WHO – World Health Organization, an agency of the United Nations

Notes

PROLOGUE

1 A note regarding capitalization. South Sudan, as the name of a new country, is capitalized throughout this narrative. As Southern Sudan was the
immediate predecessor of the same geographical and political entity, this
is also capitalized. The North and the South, when used as shorthand for
Sudan and South Sudan respectively, are capitalized, but when these terms
are used to indicate direction, they are rendered in lower case. The inhab-
itants of Sudan and South Sudan are described as Sudanese or South
Sudanese, northerners or southerners respectively. The West, when used
to describe that large bloc of countries that takes in, inter alia, the US,
Canada, and most European countries, is capitalized.

CHAPTER ONE

1 Karl Vick, "Ripping Off Slave 'Redeemers,'" *Washington Post*, 26 February
2002, https://www.washingtonpost.com/archive/politics/2002/02/26/
ripping-off-slave-redeemers/75b4d32e-e7da-417f-a293-87768c0294f4/.
2 In Sudan and South Sudan, people often refer to each other, and even to
public figures they don't know personally, by their first names.
3 For the full text of this 260-page document, see UNMISS, "The Comprehensive Peace Agreement between the Government of the Republic of the
Sudan and the Sudan People's Liberation Movement/Sudan People's Liberation Army," http://unmis.unmissions.org/Portals/UNMIS/Documents/
General/cpa-en.pdf.

CHAPTER TWO

1 Statistics Canada, Census of 2011, has 16,595 Canadians identifying themselves as of Sudanese origin. The vast majority of these are thought to originate from what is now South Sudan; some natural demographic growth will have occurred since 2011. See http://www12.statcan.gc.ca/nhs-enm/2011/dp-pd/prof/details/page.

CHAPTER FOUR

1 See Refugees International, "Jonglei 101," 10 September 2013, http://m.reliefweb.int/report/601328, among many other items discussing this allegation: "The Murle group has been widely stigmatized throughout South Sudan because of rumors that they suffer from congenital syphilis, and that sterility has driven them to abduct children from nearby ethnic groups. While reports indicate that there were indeed high levels of syphilis present in the early 1950s and 60s, a World Health Organization treatment campaign has brought the disease down to normal levels. The stigma, however, remains strong and, alongside the assumed affiliation with David Yau Yau, has increased the Murle's isolation."

2 See the report by anthropologist/missionary Jon Arensen, "The History of Murle Migrations," Chr. Michelsen Institute, https://www.cmi.no/file/1964-Murle.pdf

3 See Øystein H. Rolandsen and Ingrid Marie Breidlid, "What Is Youth Violence in Jonglei?," Oslo Peace Research Institute, 7–8, http://file.prio.no/publication_files/Prio/Rolandsen%20&%20Breidlid%20(2013)%20What%20is%20Youth%20Violence%20in%20Jonglei.%20PRIO%20Paper.pdf.

4 Arensen, "History of Murle Migrations."

5 Amnesty International, "South Sudan: Lethal Disarmament: Abuses Linked to Civilian Disarmament in Pibor County, Jonglei State," 3 October 2012, https://www.amnesty.org/en/documents/AFR65/005/2012/en/.

6 Human Rights Watch, "South Sudan: Army Unlawfully Killed Civilians," 12 September 2013, https://www.hrw.org/news/2013/09/12/south-sudan-army-unlawfully-killed-civilians.

7 "South Sudan: As Civilian Disarmament Takes Place, UN Urges Respect for Human Rights," UN News Centre, 6 April 2012, http://www.un.org/apps/news/story.asp?NewsID=41726#.WAqBY8ne9iY.

8 "The White Army continues the traditional mobilization structures of Nuer communities described by Evans Pritchard in the 1930s." Ingrid Marie

Breidlid and Michael J. Arensen, "Anyone Who Can Carry a Gun Can Go," Peace Research Institute Oslo, 2014, https://www.files.ethz.ch/isn/181312/Breidlid%20and%20Arensen%20(2014)%20-%20Anyone%20who%20can%20carry%20a%20gun%20can%20go,%20PRIO%20Paper.pdf.

9 *Shake Hands with the Devil: The Failure of Humanity in Rwanda* (Toronto: Random House, 2003), Dallaire's best-selling account of the Rwandan genocide.

CHAPTER FIVE

1 For background to the Muskoka Initiative, see Canada, "Canada's Leadership in Maternal, Newborn and Child Health – The Muskoka Initiative (2010–2015)," last modified 18 November 2016, http://www.international.gc.ca/world-monde/development-developpement/health_women-sante_femmes/canada_leadership_2010-2015.aspx?lang=eng.
2 Maternal mortality rate: 2,054 per 100,000 (est.); mortality rates for infants and under 5s was 75 and 104 per 1,000 live births, respectively, in 2012; UNFPA data can be found by searching for South Sudan data at World Health Organization, "WHO Country Cooperation Strategies and Briefs," http://www.who.int/countryfocus/cooperation_strategy/ccsbrief_ssd_en.pdf.

CHAPTER SEVEN

1 For the report by the UN on its investigation into this raid, see UNMISS, "Report on the 8 February 2013 Attack on Lou Nuer Pastoralists in Akobo West Sub-County, Jonglei State," April 2013, https://unmiss.unmissions.org/sites/default/files/april_2013_akobo_report.pdf.
2 Deborah Scroggins, *Emma's War: Love, Betrayal and Death in the Sudan* (New York: Pantheon Books, 2002).
3 For the text of this report, see "Report of the Committee for Investigation of Cde Pagan Amum, the SPLM SG," *PaanLuel Wël* (blog), 26 September 2015, https://paanluelwel.com/2015/09/26/report-of-the-committee-for-investigation-of-cde-pagan-amum-the-splm-secretary-general/.

CHAPTER EIGHT

1 For a discussion of the link between the New Deal Compact for South Sudan and currency harmonization, see Hafeez Wani's paper, "Why Did the New Deal Compact in South Sudan Fail to Get Signed?," GREAT

INSIGHTS magazine, 27 November 2014, http://ecdpm.org/great-insights/
peacebuilding-statebuilding/new-deal-compact-south-sudan-fail-get-signed/.

2 See "Machar and Canadian Diplomats Confer on Future of Democracy in
   South Sudan," Sudan Tribune, 6 November 2013, http://sudantribune.
   com/spip.php?iframe&page=imprimable&id_article=48715.

CHAPTER NINE

1 For the leaked and partial draft of the AU report from which this and
   accompanying quotations are taken, see "Draft Version of the Long-
   Awaited AU Report on South Sudan," *PaanLuel Wël* (blog), 7 March
   2015, https://paanluelwel.com/2015/03/07/long-awaited-au-report-on-
   south-sudan/. For the fully authorized, final, and longer version, see
   African Union, Peace and Security Department, "Final Report of the
   African Union Commission of Inquiry on South Sudan," last modified
   27 October 2015, http://www.peaceau.org/en/article/final-report-of
   -the-african-union-commission-of-inquiry-on-south-sudan.

2 For the UN's initial report on this attack, see "UNMISS Issues Preliminary
   Account of Akobo Base Attack," ReliefWeb, 20 December 2013, http://
   reliefweb.int/report/south-sudan-republic/unmiss-issues-preliminary-
   account-akobo-base-attack.

CHAPTER TEN

1 One of the earliest of many reports on human rights abuses committed by
   both sides during the conflict that began in Juba in December 2013 was
   that of the UN, in May 2014. See "Gross Rights Abuses Committed by
   Both Sides in South Sudan Conflict, UN Report Finds," UN News Centre,
   8 May 2014, http://www.un.org/apps/news/story.asp?NewsID=47752#.
   WArGTcne9iY.

CHAPTER ELEVEN

1 For an account of the attacks in Bentiu and Bor, see the report by
   UNMISS's Human Rights Division, "Attacks on Civilians in Bentiu and
   Bor, April 2014," 9 January 2015, at http://www.ohchr.org/Documents/
   Countries/SS/UNMISS_HRDJanuary2015.pdf.

2 See Reporters sans frontières, https://rsf.org/, for the latest press freedom
   rankings.

CHAPTER TWELVE

1 See Dr Young's paper on the Nuer White Army, *Popular Struggles and Elite Co-optation: The Nuer White Army in South Sudan's Civil War* (Geneva: Small Arms Survey, 2016), http://www.smallarmssurveysudan. org/fileadmin/docs/working-papers/HSBA-WP41-White-Army.pdf.

2 See "Leading Voices at Pagak Meeting Call for Dissolving SPLM," Radio Tamazuj, 13 December 2014, https://radiotamazuj.org/en/article/leading-voices-pagak-meeting-call-dissolving-splm.

3 See International Monetary Fund, "Republic of South Sudan 2014 Article IV Consultation – Staff Report; Staff Statement; and Press Release," December 2014, https://www.imf.org/external/pubs/ft/scr/2014/cr14345.pdf.

4 One of many accounts of the Fashoda Incident can be found in Jan Morris's *Heaven's Command: An Imperial Progress* (London: Faber and Faber, 1973), the first of her Pax Britannica trilogy.

5 Sharon E. Hutchinson and Naomi R. Pendle, "Violence, Legitimacy and Prophecy: Nuer Struggles with Uncertainty in South Sudan," *American Ethnologist* 42, no. 3 (August 2015), 415–30, doi:10.1111/amet.12138.

CHAPTER THIRTEEN

1 For the leaked and partial draft of the AU report, see "Draft Version of the Long-Awaited AU Report on South Sudan," *PaanLuel Wël* (blog), 7 March 2015, https://paanluelwel.com/2015/03/07/long-awaited-au-report-on-south-sudan/. For the fully authorized, final, and longer version, see African Union, Peace and Security Department, "Final Report of the African Union Commission of Inquiry on South Sudan," last modified 27 October 2015, http://www.peaceau.org/en/article/final-report-of-the-african-union-commission-of-inquiry-on-south-sudan.

2 The Toronto *Globe and Mail* would later catch up with this story: see Geoffrey York, "Canadian Company Sold Armoured Vehicles to South Sudan: Report," 28 July 2016, http://www.theglobeandmail.com/news/world/canadian-company-sold-armoured-vehicles-to-south-sudan-report/article31191713/.

3 See, inter alia, "'They Burned It All': Destruction of Villages, Killings, and Sexual Violence in Unity State South Sudan," Human Rights Watch, 22 July 2015, https://www.hrw.org/report/2015/07/22/they-burned-it-all/destruction-villages-killings-and-sexual-violence-unity-state.

CHAPTER FOURTEEN

1 Intergovernmental Authority on Development, "Agreement on the Resolution of the Conflict in the Republic of South Sudan," 17 August 2015, https://unmiss.unmissions.org/sites/default/files/final_proposed_compromise_agreement_for_south_sudan_conflict.pdf.

CHAPTER FIFTEEN

1 For updates on the work of JMEC, see http://www.jmecsouthsudan.com/.
2 For UNMISS's account of the episode, see "South Sudan: Special Investigation into Malakal Violence Completed, Says UN," UN News Centre, 21 June 2016, http://www.un.org/apps/news/story.asp?NewsID=54289#.WAreEMne9iY.

EPILOGUE

1 "War in South Sudan's Juba Resumes," Radio Tamazuj, 10 July 2016, https://radiotamazuj.org/en/article/war-south-sudans-juba-resumes.
2 Report of the UN's High Commissioner for Human Rights, "South Sudan's Government Forces Committed Widespread Violations in July Fighting – UN," UN News Centre, 4 August 2016, http://www.un.org/apps/news/story.asp?NewsID=54623#.WAwGocne9iY.
3 For references to a leaked report by the UN panel of experts originally nominated to consider possible targets for sanctions, see "UN Panel: South Sudan's July Fighting Was Well Planned by the Chief of Army and President Kiir," Nyamilepedia, 9 September 2016, http://www.nyamile.com/2016/09/09/un-panel-south-sudans-july-fighting-was-well-planned-by-the-chief-of-army-and-president-kiir/, and Justin Lynch, "South Sudan's Fighting Directed at Highest Levels: UN Report," AP News, 9 September 2016, http://bigstory.ap.org/article/653b1366885f4a5ea9cd733329602098/south-sudans-fighting-directed-highest-levels-un-report.
4 WFP situation report: UNMISS, "UNMISS POC Update No. 151," 6 February 2017, http://reliefweb.int/report/south-sudan/unmiss-poc-update-no-151.
5 UN OCHA: "South Sudan Humanitarian Bulletin Issue 16," ReliefWeb, 20 October 2016, http://reliefweb.int/report/south-sudan/south-sudan-humanitarian-bulletin-issue-16-20-october-2016.

6 In 2016, for the first time, South Sudan overtook Afghanistan as the
   most dangerous place for aid workers. "Aid Worker Security Report:
   Figures at a Glance, 2016," Humanitarian Outcomes, https://
   aidworkersecurity.org/sites/default/files/HO_AidWorkerSecPreview_
   1015_G.PDF_.pdf.

Index

Abraham, Ajak, 34, 136, 170

Abu John, Samuel, 17–18, 78

Abyei, 20, 24, 113; and Luka Biong, 211

Addis Ababa agreement (1972), 43, 249; failure explained by Kiir, 195; halted, 192; IGAD talks in, 173, 190; and sticking points for 10, 177

Adwok Nyaba, Peter, 114, 127

African National Congress (ANC), 227

African Union (AU); and Commission of Inquiry, 122, 190–1, 201, 230–1, 252, 264n1 (ch. 9), 265n1 (ch. 13); High Implementation Panel, 193

Agreement on Resolution of the Conflict in South Sudan (ARCISS, or ARC), 245–6; Kiir says signed under duress, 226; signed, 207, 208, 252; and twenty-eight-states order, 210–11; relevance in 2017, 247

Aguer, Philip, xviii, 119, 192

aid coordination, 29

aid diversion, 14, 16, 19, 147, 199; discussed at JMEC, 230

Ajuong Thok, 91, 93–4

Akel, 58, 60, 63, 72

Akobo, 32–3, 64–7, 216–18; attack at UN base by 10, 135, 251, 264n2 (ch. 9); and General Lul, 187–8

Akol, Lam. See Lam Akol

Al Jazeera, 54, 116; in Bentiu, 158–9, 162

al-Bashir, President Omar, 5, 11, 94, 150, 202, 209

Aleu, Akec Tong, 8

Aleu, Ayieny Aleu, 79, 145; at German National Day, 173; and slavery, 8

Alor, Deng, 103, 114, 127, 148; touted as minister of foreign affairs, 224

al-Turabi, Hassan, 5

Amnesty International, 58, 262n5

Amum, Pagan, 50, 103, 112, 114–17, 125, 127, 263n3; dismissed as SPLM secretary general, 105; and trial, 148–9

anti-personnel mines (APMS), 85

Arakis (oil company), 8; acquired by Talisman, 250

Arensen, Jon, 55, 262n2, 262n4

Arensen, Mike, 55

Arusha process, 193, 225, 227; discussed at Pagak, 176–7

Association for Media Development in South Sudan (AMDISS), 171

Atak, Wol, 171

Athor, George, 56

Australia, 145, 166; and South Sudanese diaspora, 31, 62

Ayii, Ayii Duong, 61

Azande (tribe/language), 4, 78, 208

Baird, John, 128, 164

Bakasoro, Joseph, 78

Bangladesh, 235

Bashir, President Omar al-. See al-Bashir, President Omar

Bashir, Peter, 124–5

Bentiu, 83, 92, 137, 144, 146, 149, 161–2; and allegations of 10 atrocities, 158, 264n1 (ch. 11); and 10 attack of April 2014, 157–8; PoC, 154, 160–1, 199; in second civil war, 8–9

Biar, Madut, 114, 127

Biar, Peter, 31

Biel, Tito, 9

Biliu, Johnson, 58, 60

Bilpam, xvii, 119–20, 207; meeting of general staff, March 2015, 192

Blue Nile State (Sudan), 20, 24, 88–9, 92, 209, 251, 258

Bol, Deng Bol Aruai, 31

Bol, Nhial: in Khartoum, 5; in Juba, 45–7, 50

Boma, 58, 60, 63, 70, 254

Bor, 31, 54, 57, 60–1, 73, 141–2, 149–50, 162–3, 170, 188; capture by 10, 130, 134–7, 212, 214, 251; IDPs flee to Minkamman, 166, 168; massacre of 1991, 249; opening of Canadian-financed maternity ward in, 77; PoC, 135, 146, 157–8, 168–9, 218, 234, 251, 264n1 (ch. 11); recapture by government, 138, 218; sacking of hospital, 144, 149–50, 170; and second civil war, 34, 62, 249

Buay, Gordon, 86–8

Bul Nuer, 8, 10, 87, 189, 228, 250

Canada: and aircraft for Machar's return, 243; and alleged arms sales, 203, 265n2 (ch. 13); financing 10 return, 231; government interest in South Sudan, 197; investment in South Sudan, 108; mediation suggested by Riek Gai, 201; as member of JMEC, 230; policy on social media, 203; reaction to July 2013, 105; role in CPA, 19; role in Darfur, 23; stance on relations with Sudan, 23; in UNMISS, 40, 141, 151–2. See also Canadian aid; Canadian embassy; diaspora

Canadian aid (development/ humanitarian): and Canadian volunteers, 161; and demining, 83–6; extent in South Sudan, 25; to ICRC, 180–5; in Jonglei, 211–17; in Melut, 236; to MNCH, 76–80, 144, 166, 170, 263n1 (ch. 5); oversight, 28–9;

SSHARE program, 33–4; to
War Child Canada, 234; to WFP,
68–9, 199. *See also* Canadian
International Development
Agency
Canadian embassy
– office, Juba, 24–7; accommodation, 114; and evacuation flights,
128–9; first closure, 138–9, 251;
made "unaccompanied," 196–7;
one-day visits authorized, 141;
second closure, 246, 252; staff-
ing, 196–8; upgrade to embassy,
163–5; warns citizens, 121
– office, Khartoum, 3, 23–4
Canadian International
Development Agency (CIDA),
17, 24, 170
CARE, 92
cattle, 47, 56, 66–7; as dowry, 4,
9, 33, 63, 97, 154–5; and intra-
Nuer fighting in Jonglei, 215;
Kuol Manyang's views about,
63; in Motot, 212; and Mundari,
37; and Murle, 55, 59, 65; and
problems near Minkamman,
167; and prophet Nyachol, 187;
in Ulang, 9
Ceasefire and Transitional Security
Arrangements Monitoring
Mechanism (CTSAMM), 241,
256
Central African Republic (CAR), 21
Central Bank, 110–11, 179, 223;
printing money, 178
Chad, 21
Chama Cha Mapinduzi (CCM),
225, 227; and Arusha process,
176
Chanda, Cosmas, 93–4

Chanuong, Marial, 123
Cheng Chan, 85
Chevron (oil company), 8
child soldiers, 56, 70–5, 158; and
Johnson Olony, 198; in second
civil war, 9, 31–2, 62
China, 40, 45, 194; arms sales, 179;
and failure to coordinate, 193;
and investment, 109; and JMEC,
230
China National Petroleum
Company (CNPC), 42, 109
Chol Thon, 235, 237
Christian Solidarity International
(CSI), 7–8, 14, 254
Chuong, Gier, 114, 126
Cirilo, Thomas, 87
Citizen, The, 45–6, 49
civil war, first Sudanese (1955–72),
12, 43, 151, 249; second
Sudanese (1983–2005), 3, 12, 17,
20, 31, 34, 55, 102, 136, 166,
182, 185, 249
Cobra Faction, 69, 73–4. *See also*
Yau Yau, David
Comboni sisters, 13, 79
Community Empowerment for
Progress Organisation (CEPO),
211, 253
Comprehensive Peace Agreement
(CPA; 2005), 6, 23, 35, 40, 43,
45, 102, 191, 250, 254, 258,
261n3; analysis of by AU
Commission of Inquiry, 191
Confident Children out of Conflict
(CCC), 152–3, 253
Corporate Social Responsibility
(CSR), 10
corruption, 44, 46, 50, 99, 105,
109, 113, 116–17, 148;

acknowledged by Kiir, 226; condemned by Ramaphosa, 227; in exchange-rate manipulation, 179, 222; in SPLM, 106, 263n3

Crisis Management Initiative (CMI), 176, 253

Cuban Jubans, 30–5

Da Vinci restaurant, 37, 39, 172; and German National Day, 172–3

D'Agot, Majak, 114, 124, 126, 148; trial of, 148

Dak Kueth (prophet), 56, 216–17; at Pagak consultations, 174

Dallaire, Roméo, 152, 247; visit to South Sudan, 73–5

Danish Demining Group (DDG), 83–6

Darfur, 20–1, 23, 43, 89, 144, 158, 160, 170

demining, 84–6

Deng Ajak, Oyai 114, 126; trial of, 148

Deng Ayei, William, 94

Deng Dau, 154

Deng, Chol, 4

Deng, David, 178

Deng, Nhial, 104, 115, 124; at JMEC, 230, 242

Deng, Taban, 104, 114, 127–8, 148; and ambition, 228; attends SPLM convention, 225–7; claims 10 leadership, 246–7, 252; and 10 membership, 228; at JMEC, 230, 242; tension with Machar, 245

Denmark, 164, 255

Dhieu Mathok, 228

diaspora, Canadian (from South Sudan), 24–5, 43, 62, 154–5, 166, 215, 237; via Cuba, 32–5; and December 2013 crisis, 127, 131–3, 136–7, 140–3, 238; numbers of, 262n1 (ch. 2); typical background of, 29–30

diplomatic community in Juba, 39–40, 118, 128, 172–3; and financing of 10 return to Juba, 231; and humanitarian affairs, 198, 202–3; and 10, 174, 177, 227–9, 247; and return of Machar, 239–40, 244

disarmament, demobilization, and reintegration (DDR), 70–1, 254; likely costs of, 179

Djibouti, 135, 163, 202, 255

Dorein, 69

early, forced marriage, 79, 212, 215

East Timor, 110

economy of South Sudan, 110–11, 216, 226, 232, 245, 265n3 (ch. 12); deterioration in 2014, 177–80; and devaluation of SSP, 222–3; discussed by 10, 175; effect of twenty-eight-states order on, 210. See also IMF

Egypt, 12, 36, 133; ambassador of, 240

Ekvall, Thomas, 15

elections, 78, 99, 117, 207, 224; postponed, 195–6

Emin Pasha, 39

Eritrea, 41, 47, 163, 255

Ethiopia, 32, 56, 97, 108, 163, 170, 185, 217, 255; effect of drought on South Sudan, 216; as federal model, 209; participation in

UNMISS, 201; and refugees, 30–2, 62, 217; role in Machar's return, 239, 240

European Union (EU), 65, 111, 118, 120, 128, 130, 135, 138, 151, 192, 211, 220, 254; lead on international statements, 203; member of JMEC, 230; rebuked by Ambrose Riny, 210; role in Machar's return, 240; support for IGAD, 173; and troika, 40, 43, 193

Exxon (oil company), 45

Fashoda incident (1898), 11–12, 96, 180–1, 265n4. *See also* Kodok

federalism, 112; discussed at Pagak, 174–6; and twenty-eight-states order, 209–10

flag of South Sudan, 31

former detainees, 137, 145, 149, 191, 225, 229, 242, 252

France, 233

G-8, 40, 76, 255

Gadet, Peter, 56, 58, 60, 130–1, 134, 136–7, 141, 183; assessed by Kuol Manyang, 208; attacks Bentiu, 157, 160; birthplace of, 217; in discussion with author, 200–2; in Nhialdu, 182; at Pagak consultations, 174; quits 10, 189; in second civil war, 8–10, 84

Gai, Riek, 4, 78–80

Gakdong, 217–18

Garang, John, 62, 114–17, 224, 250; death of, 62, 251; founds SPLM/A, 249, 257; and "lost

boys," 31–4; and the New Sudan, 18, 115; and slavery, 7; tomb of, 39, 47, 193; and "towns to the people," 176

Garang, Rebecca, 103, 114–17, 127, 145, 171

Gatwech, Simon: meets Malong, 245; return to Juba, 240–1

Germany, 128, 130, 133, 180, 255; ambassador of, 194; and National Day, 172–3

Ghana, 48, 146

Girard, Mireille, 45

Giri, Colonel, 59

GOAL, 97–8, 254

Gondokoro, 12

Gordon, Charles, 39

Grant, James, 12

Greater Pibor Administrative Area (GPAA), 69, 72, 188, 254; as model for General Lul, 188

Gumuruk, 69–71

Guzman, Diane de, 187

Harper, Prime Minister Stephen, 25, 76

Hassan, Rizik Zachariah, 51

Heglig, 8–10; attack by South Sudan, 42–3, 124

Higgins, Ettie, 74

Hiteng, Cirino, 115, 127

Hoth Mai, James, 51, 87–8, 103, 122–4, 144–5, 200; dismissed, 159

Hothnyang, Gatkuoth, 176

Hughes, Ian, 124, 133–4, 142

human rights, 5, 7, 48, 147, 159, 203, 210, 220, 262n1 (ch. 10); abuses of in Unity, 204, 265n3 (ch. 13); and accountability,

200–2, 230–1; allegations of AU, 190–1; and alleged arms sales by Canada, 203; attacks by SPLA on civilians, 206; and diplomatic community, 198; and impunity, 247; and international human rights day, 220; in Jonglei, 56, 58, 262nn5–7; and prisoners, 216; and responsibility of Kiir, 191; and UN reports on violations of July 2016, 246, 266nn2–3 (epilogue). *See also* child soldiers; hybrid court; media freedoms; sexual violence; slavery

Human Rights Watch (HRW), 56, 58, 262n6; criticized by Makuei and Lomuro, 171

humanitarian country team (HCT), 198; mission to Leer, 204–6

Hutchinson, Sharon, 186–7, 265n5

hybrid court, 231

IGAD Partners' Forum (IPF), 230, 255

India, 23, 250–1, 255; and participation in UNMISS, 56, 59–61, 64–5, 169, 234; peacekeepers killed at Akobo, 135, 51, 264n2 (ch. 9)

Intergovernmental Authority on Development (IGAD), 163, 241–2, 252, 255–6; and Addis talks, 173, 177, 189, 192–3, 202–3, 216; and Arusha process, 176; and CPA, 191; criticized by Lomuro, 194; mandates Pagak consultations, 171; methodology of, 201

internally displaced persons (IDPs), 255; in Bentiu, 160–1; at Bor PoC, 146, 169; in Jonglei, 64–5, 212; in Khartoum, 4; in Malakal, 144, 233, 236; at Minkamman, 166–7; at Thaker, 186; in Wau Shillook, 233. *See also* PoC (Protection of Civilians) sites

International Committee of the Red Cross (ICRC), 13, 128, 255; air drop, 182–5; and coordination with NGOs, 198; at Kodok, 180–2; in Waat, 212, 214

International Medical Corps (IMC), 233, 255

International Monetary Fund (IMF), 255; diagnosis of economy, 178–9, 265n3 (ch. 12); and the New Deal Compact, 111; predicts "death spiral," 223; special drawing rights for South Sudan, 223

International Organization for Migration (IOM), 161

International Rescue Committee (IRC), 94, 158

investment conference (2013), 108–10, 251

Italy, 128, 255

Itto, Anne, 115

Jaffer, Mobina, 19, 200

Japan, 40, 127, 247, 255

Jau, 90, 93

Jieng Council of Elders, 203, 210–11

Jikany Nuer, 87

Johnson, Hilde (SRSG), 40–2, 61, 75, 104, 127, 145–7, 162, 258

Joint Donor Office (JDO), 24, 127, 129–30, 134, 138, 148, 255; proposed new sharing arrangement, 164

Joint Monitoring and Evaluation Commission (JMEC), 256, 232; established, 229–31, 266n1 (ch. 15); meeting in April 2016, 241–2

Jonglei State, 4, 31, 33, 109, 113, 130, 135, 149, 157, 166, 175, 188, 209, 211–18, 251, 254; administrative reorganization by 10, 212–3; and oil, 45; and Yau Yau rebellion, 52–74, 103–4, 108

Juba: airport, 52–4, 109, 120, 127, 143; in July 2013, 105; on/after 15 December 2013, xvii–xviii, 116–18, 120–39; description of, 38–9; and expat life, 28, 35, 37; PoC site, 144, 227, 239; and renewed fighting July 2016, 246, 252; and rising crime, 180; in second civil war, 4, 6, 12–13

Juba Declaration, 251, 259

Juba Monitor, 45, 49–50

Justice and Equality Movement (JEM), 89, 144, 160, 255; allegations of support to SPLA, 158–9

Jut Chot Rian, 216

Kaarstadt, Hanne-Marie, 42

Kadugli, 43

Kajo Keji, 80–1, 247

Kapila, Mukesh, 20–1

Kenya, 44, 48, 133, 148–9, 163, 202, 250, 255; civilians killed in South Sudan, 61; and CPA, 19–20; failure to exert leverage, 193; investment in South Sudan, 44, 62, 108; and refugees, 30–2, 43, 62, 227

Kenyatta, President Uhuru, 145

Khartoum, 3–6; seat of government (see Sudan)

Khartoum Monitor, 5, 46, 49

Kiir, President Salva: accepts author's credentials, 165–6; Addis agreement signed by, 207; and Addis talks walkout, 192; AU Commission of Inquiry, Kiir blamed in, 190–1; dismisses cabinet, 105; drops charges against Juba, 4, 149; in first year of mandate, 43–4, 50–1; fitness for office, 202–3, 231; IDPs' views on, 161, 168; at investment conference, 110; JMEC proposal, reaction to, 242; Khartoum's views on, 229; Kuol Manyang, relationship with, 62; Machar challenges Kiir, 103, 113; Machar, comparison with, 102, 202; Machar, meeting with, Wani Igga, 8 July 2016, 246; Machar's powers removed by, 103; Machar, power-sharing with, 176, 192, 201, 207–8; Paul Malong, relations with, 51, 192; and NLC, 116–17; public address, March 2015, 193–5; SPLM convention attended by, 226; statement on 16 December 2013, 121, 145; and supporters, 115; and twenty-eight-states order, 209–10, 216, 252; at Wau hospital, 80, 166; and Yau Yau, amnesty offer to, 65; status in February 2017, 247

Koang (or Kong), Gordon, 87

Koang, James, 157, 159–60
Kodok (Fashoda), 12, 87, 96; and
 ICRC hospital, 180–2, 215
Kongor (Jonglei), 67–8
Konyi, Joshua, 58–60, 64–6, 69
Korbandy, Lawrence, 210
Korea, 169
Kosti (town in Sudan), 11
Kosti Manibe, 50, 115, 117, 127
Koul Tong Makai, 12
Kuajok, 166
Kuburin, James, 58
Kuol Manyang, 113, 115, 131;
 meets author as Jonglei governor,
 62–3; meets author as minister
 of defence, 207–9; meets Roméo
 Dallaire, 74–5
Kwaje, Joy, 6, 47–9

Labrap, 63, 69
Lado Gore, Alfred, 115, 127
Lam Akol, 46, 103, 106, 220; and
 AU Commission of Inquiry, 191;
 and JMEC, 242; role in second
 civil war, 4, 102, 249–50
Lam Both, Peter, 228–9
Lanzer, Toby, 147, 158–9, 161–2,
 166–8, 203
Leer, 144, 185; and HCT mission,
 204–6
Leithead, Alistair, 159, 162
Likuongole, 66–7, 69–72
Loej, Ellen (SRSG), 75, 243, 258
Lok, Peter, 123
Lokichokkio, Kenya, 14–15, 19,
 182, 185, 189, 250, 256
Lol, Ezekiel, 115, 127, 240; trial
 of, 148
Lomuro, Martin Elia, 80, 258; and
 HRW, 171; and humanitarian

agencies, 199; and JMEC, 242;
 public speech, March 2015, 194
Lou Nuer, 56, 64–6, 69, 103, 135,
 216; and General Lul, 188; par-
 ticipation in White Army, 64
Luka Biong, 211
Luk Jok, John, 114, 126, 145, 242
Lukudu Loro, Paulino, 117
Lul Ruai Koang, 187–9
Luri, 123, 247
Lutheran World Federation, 94

M-23, 44, 256
Maban refugee camp, 89, 92
Mabior, Moses, 108
Mac Paul, 122, 149
Machakos Protocol (2002), 19, 250
Machar, Riek: and alleged atrocities, 158–9, 191; AU testimony,
 124–6, 264n1 (ch. 9); author
 meets, 112–13, 244; calls press
 conference, 114–16; confirmed
 alive, 130; consolidates leadership, 177; and coup accusations,
 120, 125, 200; Taban Deng, tension with, 245; dismissed, 105,
 107, 251; and donor countries,
 relations with, 147; early career,
 4, 8, 14, 22, 102, 249–50; and
 federalism, 209–10; fitness for
 office, 191, 202–3, 231; flees
 Juba, 246, 252; flight, reported,
 120, 127–8; and Gadet's loyalty,
 137; Riek Gai, relationship with,
 201; Gakdong's views on, 217;
 IDPs' views on, 161, 168; Kiir,
 Machar's challenge to, 103; Kiir,
 Machar calls for overthrow of,
 135–6; Kiir, meeting with, Wani
 Igga, 8 July 2016, 246; Kiir,

power-sharing with, 176, 192–3, 201, 207–8; Lomuro's criticism of, 194; General Lul's views on, 188–90; in Nasir, 151; at NLC, 116–17; oil mediation, 104; on Pagak consultations, 175; and peace/reconciliation commission, 145; and prophets, 187; return to Juba delayed, 226–7, 232, 239; returns to Juba, 239–44, 252; Sudan, contacts with, 150, 188, 202, 208, 228; and twenty-eight-states order, 210; on Ugandan intervention, 150; vice-president, first year as, 44, 51; status in February 2017, 247

Makuei, Michael, 113, 120, 127, 137, 146, 158, 171; at JMEC, 230, 242

Malakal, 34, 95–6, 101, 142–4, 149, 162–3, 214, 229, 234–5, 237, 251–2; fighting in April 2015, 199–200; hospital destroyed, 181; PoC, 143, 200, 232–3, 266n2 (ch. 15); in second civil war, 6, 11–12, 236

Mali, 150

Malong, Paul, 51, 75, 247; becomes chief of general staff, 159; blamed by AU Commission of Inquiry, 124, 191; and Gatwech, 245; and Nation Mirror, 171; and red lines, 192; viewed by General Lul, 189

Mamdani, Mahmoud, 190–1, 202, 231

Mamur, Obuto, 145

Mandela, Nelson, 117, 227

Manyabol, 64

Manyading, 65–6

Manyang, Kuol. See Kuol Manyang

Mapel, 18, 166

Mar, Hussein, 130–1; aligns with Taban Deng, 246

Marial Benjamin, Barnaba, 124–5; at German National Day, 172–3

Mary, Commander, 17–18, 78

Matiep, Paulino, 8–9, 17, 84, 86–7, 103; early career, 250–1, 258

MatMedia, 95–6

Mayom, 10, 83–7, 157, 160; taken by 10, 15

Mayom, Paul, 115

Mbeki, Thabo, 104

McCune, Emma, 102, 151

McPhail, Alastair, 41–2, 44

Medair, 205

Médecins Sans Frontières (MSF), 16, 69, 79, 89, 92, 143–4, 161; and coordination with other NGOS, 198

media freedoms, 45–50, 116, 264n2 (ch. 11); and Nation Mirror, 170–1

Mengistu, Haile Mariam, 32

Mesfin, Seyoum, 176; critiqued by Riek Gai, 201–2

Milli Hussein, Michael, 77–8

Minkamman IDP settlement, 166–9

Mogae, Festus, 256; appointed JMEC chair, 230; at April 2016 JMEC meeting, 241–2

Mongolia, and participation in UNMISS, 157, 160, 162, 255

Monitoring and Verification Mission (MVM), 162–3, 256; succeeded by CTSAMM, 241

Monoja, Luka, 115

MONUSCO, 56, 256

Monytuil, Bapiny Wecjang, 88
Motot, 211–16
Mundari, and cattle, 37
Murle (tribe), 54–75, 98, 103–4, 154, 188, 209, 214, 216, 262nn2–4
Murrahaleen, 7
Museveni, President Yoweri, 150

Nasir, 96–7, 142, 151, 162; Nasir faction, 115, 117, 249–50
Nation Mirror, 170–1
National Liberation Council (NLC), 112, 116–18, 121–2, 125, 224, 251, 256
National Security Service, 171
Nepal, 64–5
Netherlands, 40, 128, 130, 133, 138; ambassador of, 44, 138, 230, 240; co-membership of JMEC, with Canada, 230; and JDO, 164, 255
New Deal Compact, 107–8, 110, 145; collapses, 111, 263n1 (ch. 8)
New York Times, 159, 162
Ngor, Mading, 120, 154–5
Nhialdu, 182–5
Nimeiri, 34, 83
Nimule, 109, 137, 188
Non-Violent Peace Force (NVPF), 69, 84, 161
Norway, 40–4, 138, 147, 191; and CPA, 19; and evacuations, 130; and JDO, 164, 255; and JMEC, 230; mission to Malakal, 233; and NGOs, 15, 42, 256; and Nuba Mountains, 20
Norwegian Church Aid (NCA), 42, 256

Norwegian People's Aid (NPA), 15, 42
Nuba Mountains, 15, 20, 24, 43, 45, 88–94, 159, 173, 209, 211, 258
Numeri. See Nimeiri
Nyachol (prophet), 187
Nyal, 204, 206
Nyandit, 64
Nyirol county, 56; and General Lul, 188
Nzara, 79

Odwar, Henry, 174, 247
oil industry, 42–3, 45, 94, 104; impact of crisis on production, 177–8; impact of low price, 222; at Pagak, 175; and Petroleum Revenue Management Act, 179; in second civil war, 8–9, 19; threatened by White Army, 177
Okello, Joseph, 194
Olony, Johnson, 87, 234–5; alleged involvement in WFP hijack, 198; assessed by Kuol Manyang, 208; attacks SPLA in Malakal, 199–200; and attempts to buy him off, 201; defection to 10, 182, 187, 200; perceived local agenda of, 229
Operation Lifeline Sudan (OLS), 13–15, 182, 185, 256; founded, 250
Oxfam, 215, 217, 257

Pagak, 239; 10 consultations, 171, 174–7; NGOs evicted, 199
Page, Susan, 44–5
Pal, Peter, 132, 238
Paridi Taban, Bishop, 69

Payamo, Ken, 146

Petronas (oil company), 104

Pharyang, 10, 91–2, 94; and twenty-eight-states order, 228

Pibor, 54–75, 169, 188, 209, 212, 254. *See also* GPAA

Pieri, 56, 212–14

PoC (Protection of Civilians) sites, 161, 232, 239, 247, 266n4; in Bentiu, 157, 159–62, 199; in Bor, 146, 157–8, 168–9, 218, 234, 251, 264n1 (ch. 11); in Juba, 144, 227, 239; in Malakal, 143, 200, 232–3, 252, 266n2 (ch. 15)

Pochalla, 70

politburo (of SPLM), 103–4, 115–16, 118

polygamy, 100

prophets, 56, 174, 216–17; role in Unity State, 186–7, 265n5. *See also* Dak Kueth; Nyachol

Radio Mille Collines (Rwanda), 158

Radio Miraya, xvii, 119, 121, 130–1; criticized by Makuei, 171

Radio Tamazuj, 29; and General Lul, 188

Rajaf, 12, 35–7, 220

Ramaphosa, Cyril, 227

Ranawat, Lt. Col, 65

Red Army, 31–2, 62, 194, 257

refugees (Sudanese in South Sudan). *See* Ajuong Thok; Maban; Yida

Relief Association of Southern Sudan (RASS), 14, 250, 257–8

Renk, 11, 170

Reporters Without Borders, 170

Rice, Susan, 101

Riny, Ambrose Thiik, 210–11

Roosevelt, Theodore, 220

Royal Air Force (UK), 133–4, 238

Rubkona, 8, 83, 144, 157, 159

Rumbek, 146, 204

Rwanda, 59, 73, 75, 137, 247; and parallels with Bentiu massacre, 158; and troops' inaction at Malakal PoC, 232–4

Sackett, Mike, 20

Samaritan's Purse, 33, 45, 90, 92, 137, 185

Save the Children (SCF), 69; in Akobo, 217–18; and slave retrieval in Sudan, 7

scarification, 3, 100, 125–6, 218

security sector reform, 175, 192

sexual violence, 152, 182, 204, 265n3 (ch. 13)

Shillook (language, tribe/kingdom), 4, 12, 46, 62, 87–8, 102–3, 105, 115, 160, 175, 187, 198; and twenty-eight-states order, 229; and fighting in Malakal PoC, 232–7

slavery (modern), 7, 14

Sobat River, 11, 96–8, 101–2

Solidarités, 92

Somalia, 163, 240, 255

South Africa, 102, 104, 145, 201; engagement with Arusha process, 193, 227

South Sudan Defence Force (SSDF), 84, 87

South Sudan Democratic Movement/Army (SSDM/A; aka Cobra Faction), 69

South Sudan Human Rights Commission (SSHRC), 48, 210

South Sudan Independence Movement (SSIM), 250

South Sudan Liberation Army (SSLA), 87, 258

South Sudan National Police Service (SSNPS), 92, 258

South Sudan Unity Movement (SSUM), 8, 84, 258

Southern States Coordinating Council (SSCC), 4, 78, 250

special representative of the secretary-general (SRSG). See Johnson, Hilde; Loej, Ellen

Speke, John, 12

State (oil company), 8

Sudan, 249; contacts with/support for Machar, 150, 163, 202, 208, 229, 245–6; fees for transit of South Sudanese oil, 104, 178, 222; as key to peace, 202; relations with South Sudan, 42–3, 104, 113, 124, 193, 229; and support for Yau Yau, 58, 61; views of Kuol Manyang about, 208–9

Sudan Armed Forces (SAF), 16, 89, 173

Sudan Council of Churches (SCC), 6, 47, 48–9, 257

Sudan People's Liberation Army (SPLA), xvii; and aid diversion, 16, 199, 230; and alleged support by Juba, 209; and APMS, 85; attacked by Olony, 199–200; and child soldiers, 31, 73; and dependence on Uganda, 150; failure to support UNMISS in Bor, 158; founded, 249; and human rights abuses, 32, 56–8, 63, 71, 147, 171, 232–4, 246–7;

internal divisions, 21, 43, 51, 67, 87–8, 103, 117, 182, 189; and JEM, 158–9; in Jonglei, 55–8, 60, 63–4, 66–7, 71; in Juba, December 2013, 119–29; July 2016 Juba clashes with IO, 246, 252; loses Bentiu, 157; in Malakal, 233–4; and mining, 110; motivation of, 150; and Nuba Mountains, 90; perceptions in Ulang, 99; red lines in peace talks, 192; in second civil war, 6–10, 12–14, 16–18, 20–4, 31, 37, 62, 117; shoots down UNMISS helicopter, 59; and slavery, 7–8; stance in Juba, July 2013, 105; standing orders 2015, 192; takes Leer, 144, 206; transformation of, 146, 175

Sudan People's Liberation Army-North (SPLA-N; Nuba Mountains and Blue Nile), 43, 45, 89–92, 158–9, 258; and start of war, 251

Sudan People's Liberation Movement (SPLM), 249; at Addis talks, 192; in Akobo, 216–18; and ARCISS, 207; attacks Bentiu, 157–9; and corruption/dysfunctionality, 106, 226; and Extraordinary National Convention, 103, 224–7; and internal divisions, 43, 78, 106, 112, 114–16, 226; and legacy effect, 196; and one-party state, 191; perceptions by IO, 176–7; perceptions in Ulang, 99–100; and presidential succession, 193; and reform, 112–13, 115, 146; in second civil war,

19–20, 23, 102. *See also* NLC;
politburo
Sudan People's Liberation
Movement/Army In Opposition
(SPLM/A-IO), 258; attacks Pigi,
Unity, 236; in control of Thaker,
185–6; delegates welcome
Machar, 240–1; exonerated for
White Army atrocities, 191;
and July 2016 Juba clashes with
SPLA, 246, 252; motivation,
150; and MVM, 163; nomencla-
ture, 149; at Pagak consultations,
171, 174–7, 199; and percep-
tions by membership of Taban
Deng, 228; reorganizes Jonglei,
212–13; returns to Juba, 227,
231, 245
Sudan People's Liberation
Movement-Direct Change
(SPLM-DC), 103, 258
Sudan Relief and Rehabilitation
Association (SRRA), 14, 250,
258
Sudan Tribune, 29, 112, 116, 120,
130
Swaka, Jeremiah, 6, 49, 228–9
Sweden, 164, 255
syphilis, alleged prevalence among
Murle, 55, 262n1 (ch. 4)

Taban, Alfred, 45, 48–51; in
Khartoum, 5
Talisman (oil company), 8–10, 19,
94; acquires Arakis, 250; depar-
ture from Sudan, 23, 250
Tanzania, 48, 201; and Arusha
process, 176, 193, 225, 227, 253
Tearfund: in Mapel, 18–19; in
Motot, 211–16

Teny, Angelina, 102, 117
Thaker, air drop, 185–7
Tissa Sabuni, Aggrey, 108, 110–11;
replaced as finance minister,
178
Tonj, 171, 227
Toposa (tribe), 55
Total (oil company), 45
Transitional Government of
National Unity (TGNU), 176–7,
179, 192, 207, 224–5, 231–2,
239, 245, 252, 259
Tribe Hotel (Nairobi), 14
troika (UK, US, Norway), 40–1, 43,
45, 107; and Addis talks, 176,
201, 208, 211, 231; and CPA,
191; and coordination with EU,
193, 203; internal differences,
203; and JMEC, 230; rebuked
by Ambrose Riny, 211
Turabi. *See* al-Turabi
Tut, John, 214
Tutu, Desmond, 102
twenty-eight states, 224–5, 227,
233, 245, 252; created by
order, 209–11, 252; defended
by Kiir, 226; effect in Jonglei,
213, 216, 218; IO views of,
228–9

Uganda, 18, 43–4, 108, 111,
132–3, 143, 255, 259; interests
in South Sudan, 193; sends
troops to South Sudan, 137,
144, 150, 163, 169, 218
Ulang, 87, 95–102, 227, 236
United Kingdom (UK), 20, 40–1,
171, 203, 233, 255; and CPA,
19, 191; and evacuation flights,
128, 130, 133; and JMEC, 230;

role in defining border, 20, 209; and SPLA reform, 146; views on US in South Sudan, 41

United Nations Children's Fund (UNICEF), in Akobo, 218; in Bentiu PoC, 161; and child soldiers, 70–4; on mission to Malakal, 233–4; and slave retrieval in Sudan, 7; at Thaker, 185; and Truth/Reconciliation, 102

United Nations Development Programme (UNDP), 21–2, 168

United Nations Educational, Scientific and Cultural Organisation (UNESCO), 48

United Nations High Commission for Refugees (UNHCR), 45, 89–93

United Nations Humanitarian Air Service (UNHAS), 73, 77, 81, 95–6, 259

United Nations Mission in South Sudan (UNMISS), 144, 243, 259; in Akobo, 135; in Bentiu, 157–8, 161; in Bor, 131, 146–7, 157–8, 169; and Canada, 141; and Ethiopia, 201; in Juba, 124, 128, 144; loses helicopter in Malakal PoC, 200, 233–4; at Nhialdu, 183; in Pibor, 56–9, 64–5. See also Johnson, Hilde; Loej, Ellen; PoC

United Nations Office for the Coordination of Humanitarian Affairs (UNOCHA, or OCHA), 147, 205, 256

United Nations Police (UNPOL), 153, 169

United Nations Population Fund (UNFPA), 29, 76

United Nations/African Union Mission in Darfur (UNAMID), 23, 259

United States: attempts Bor rescue, 135; and corruption list, 46; and CPA, 19–20, 22; draws down staff in July 2016, 246; and evacuation flights, 128–9, 131–3; and investment conference, 108; and JMEC, 230, 240–2; and Machar's return, 240–3; and Nation Mirror, 171; recognizes Taban Deng as vice-president, 246–7, 252; reported harbouring Machar, 120; and sanctions on Sudan, 21; and South Sudan diaspora, 62; and SPLA reform, 146; UK perspective on, 41; views of Ambassador Page, 44–5

Unity State, 8, 83–94, 104, 130, 137, 144, 149, 157, 175, 181–2, 185–8, 203–4, 210, 236, 251, 265n3 (ch. 13); oilfields, 137, 177, 179, 250. See also Leer

University of Calgary, 33

Upper Nile State, 4, 87–9, 95–102, 149, 151, 170, 181, 198, 200, 251; and twenty-eight-states order, 209–10, 229; oilfields, 177, 179. See also Fashoda; Kodok; Malakal; Pagak; Ulang

Uror county, 56; and General Lul, 188; and Tearfund, 211–16; and White Army, 214

US Agency for International Development (USAID), 44, 130, 259

Vertet, 70
von Burgsdorff, Sven Kuhn, 65,
    151, 173

Waat, 56, 212, 214
Walgak, 98, 263n1 (ch. 7)
Wanawilla, Paulino, 149
Wani Igga, James, 106, 115–16,
    125, 151; meets with Kiir and
    Machar, 8 July 2016, 246
Wani Konga, Clement, 194
War Child Canada, 234
Warrap State, 103, 147, 154, 160,
    171
Wau, 6–7, 11, 18, 51, 79, 166
Werkok, 136–7, 170
West Kordofan State, 7
White Army, 64–5, 138, 262n8;
    attacks on Bor, 2013–14, 136,
    212; attack on Werkok, 170;
    blamed for atrocities, 191; in
    Uror County, 214; viewed by
    Young, 177
Whitman, Shelly, 74
Wilson, Lois, 19
Wood, Levison, 109
World Food Programme (WFP),
    160; air drop at Thaker, 185–7;

and ICRC, 182; in Kongor, 67–9;
    in Minkamman, 167–8; in Pibor,
    66; and OLS, 15–16; trucks
    hijacked/looted, 147, 199;
    vehicles/staff hijacked in Akoka,
    198; in Yida, 93
World Health Organization
    (WHO), 76, 79–80
World Vision, 236

Yakani, Edmund, 211
Yambio, 16–18, 78–9
Yau Yau, David, 60, 63–5;
    blamed for peacekeepers'
    deaths, 61; and child soldiers,
    70–3; and General Lul, 188;
    government attempts to buy
    him off, 201–2; and Kuburin,
    58; meeting with author, 72–3;
    negotiates peace, 70; starts
    insurrections, 55–6; and sympa-
    thizers at Kongor, 67–9; and
    Walgak raid, 98
Yei, 199, 246
Yida refugee camp, 45, 89–94,
    159
Young, John, 174, 265n1 (ch. 12)
Yuai, 56